The
Biology Teacher's
Handbook 4th Edition

Key to Cover Illustration

The
Biology Teacher's
Handbook 4th Edition

National Science Teachers Association

BSCS

Arlington, Virginia

National Science Teachers Association

Claire Reinburg, Director
Jennifer Horak, Managing Editor
Judy Cusick, Senior Editor
Andrew Cocke, Associate Editor
Betty Smith, Associate Editor

ART AND DESIGN
Will Thomas, Jr., Director
Tim French, Senior Graphic Designer, Cover and Interior Design

PRINTING AND PRODUCTION
Catherine Lorrain, Director
Jack Parker, Electronic Prepress Technician

NATIONAL SCIENCE TEACHERS ASSOCIATION
Francis Q. Eberle, PhD, Executive Director
David Beacom, Publisher

Library of Congress Cataloging-in-Publication Data
The biology teacher's handbook / by BSCS.
     p. cm.
 Includes bibliographical references and index.
 ISBN 978-0-87355-244-8 (alk. paper)
 1. Biology--Study and teaching. I. Biological Sciences Curriculum Study
 QH315.B622 2009
 570.71--dc22
                         2008048243

Contents

Section I

Section II

Section III

Section IV

Section V

APPENDIXES

BSCS Contributors

BSCS Project Team

April L. Gardner, *Project Director*

Section I
Janet Carlson, *Executive Director*
Susan Kowalski, *Science Educator*
April L. Gardner, *Science Educator*
Brooke Bourdélat-Parks, *Science Educator*
Sarah Wise, *Science Educator*

Section II
Anne Westbrook, *Science Educator*

Section III
Mark Bloom, *Science Educator*
Paul Beardsley, *Science Educator*

Section IV
David Pinkerton, *Science Educator*
Betty Stennett, *Science Educator*
Anne Westbrook, *Science Educator*
Deb Jordan, *Science Educator*
April L. Gardner, *Science Educator*
Janet Carlson, *Executive Director*
Pam Van Scotter, *Director, Center for Curriculum Development*
Jody Bintz, *Science Educator*

Section V
Janet Carlson, *Executive Director*
Rodger Bybee, *Director Emeritus*
April L. Gardner, *Science Educator*

Appendixes
April L. Gardner, *Science Educator*

BSCS Production Services Team

Annette Plemmons, *Publications Manager*
Stacey Luce, *Production Coordinator*
Susan Hawkins, *Production Assistant*

BSCS Administrative Staff

Jerry Waldvogel, *Chair, Board of Directors*
Janet Carlson, *Executive Director*
Robert Foulk, *Chief Financial Officer*
Pam Van Scotter, *Director, Center for Curriculum Development*
Nancy Landes, *Director, Center for Professional Development*
Joseph A. Taylor, *Director, Center for Research and Evaluation*
Susan Rust, Director, *Communications*

Editor

Barbara Resch, *Colorado Springs, CO*

Acknowledgments

BSCS thanks the following teachers for providing their insights and experiences for Chapter 9:

- Cathy Box, Lubbock Christian University, former high school and middle school teacher, Tahoka High School, Texas
- Elizabeth Ann Hickey, Cocoa High School, Florida
- Jim Pardikes, retired from Smoky Hill High School, Colorado
- Hans Wigand, retired from Smoky Hill High School, Colorado

BSCS thanks Ed Drexler, consultant, for contributions to Section IV and Appendixes.

Preface

History of *The Biology Teacher's Handbook*

The Biological Sciences Curriculum Study (BSCS) was established in 1958 with the mission to improve the quality of biology education at all levels. Not long after the inception of the organization, our mission was expanded to include the improvement of *science education*, not just biology education. In 2000, we further articulated this mission to describe the work we would do in curriculum development, professional development, and research and evaluation.

In this book—a handbook for biology teachers—you will be exposed to some of our tradition and some of our future. The tradition comes from focusing on the quality of biology education. The future comes from approaching the quality of biology education from multiple perspectives—instructional materials, teacher development, student learning, controversial issues, classroom management, and inquiry teaching.

The Biology Teacher's Handbook was first released in 1960 as an experimental volume. The first through third editions were released between 1963 and 1978. In the mideighties, the book was taken out of print. We are grateful to the National Science Teachers Association (NSTA) for having the foresight to understand the value of a handbook for practicing teachers. Because of NSTA, we are able to launch the next generation of this publication.

The world of the classroom is more complex than in 1958, when BSCS began its work. More than ever before, teachers have to attend to a greater range of discipline challenges, multiple native languages, an exploding volume of new content, and high-stakes testing. In this handbook, we have done our best to acknowledge the challenging environment in which you work, while providing the scaffolding to help you be the kind of teacher who enables every student to learn as much as he or she is willing to.

BSCS is first and foremost a research and development organization. We do our best to translate research into practice. This handbook fully represents that philosophy; however, just because the pages are bound between a cover does not mean this is a finished product. At a curriculum study, we do our research, in part by listening to the practitioners in the field. As you use this handbook, do not hesitate to let us know what was useful, what was not useful, what you found missing, what you found redundant. Please go to *handbook.bscsonline.org* to make your comments and suggestions. We will address your suggestions in the next edition.

Jerry Waldvogel, PhD
Professor
Department of Biological Sciences
Clemson University

Janet Carlson, PhD
Executive Director
BSCS

Introduction

Planning Your Biology Course

When you embark on a year of teaching biology, you are faced with myriad issues, including the number of students you will have, the class periods you will be teaching, and the academic and social backgrounds of your students. You must make many decisions about the design of your course. *The Biology Teacher's Handbook* is intended to support you in making these decisions. We suggest five broad categories of questions to ask yourself, which correspond to the five sections of the handbook:

1. What are the goals of the program for my students and me? (Section I)
2. How can I help students understand the nature of science? (Section II)
3. How do I teach controversial topics? (Section III)
4. How can I create a culture of scientific inquiry in my classroom? (Section IV)
5. Where has biology teaching been, and where is it going? (Section V)

In the first section of the handbook, we set up a context for good teaching in biology. All decisions about teaching should be grounded in what we know about how students learn. The first chapter provides a brief summary of our current understanding about what people need to help them learn most effectively. Chapter 2 extends that understanding to consider how these understandings are applied and nuanced for students of diverse genders, ethnicities, and social experiences. The final two chapters in Section I focus more specifically on the biology course, identifying six fundamental principles that organize our understanding of biology and specific concepts that are often challenging and frequently misunderstood by students.

Section II of *The Biology Teacher's Handbook* continues an innovative feature first introduced in the original edition of the book, the Invitations to Inquiry. The section includes chapters that provide background about teaching for inquiry in the context of the *National Science Education Standards* (NRC 1996), the invitations themselves (which are "thought experiments" about biology content that highlight different aspects of scientific inquiry), and an invitation to a full inquiry experience.

Modern biology includes many topics that are controversial, and they are controversial for a variety of reasons. Section III describes three different types of controversy and makes the case for including controversial topics in your course syllabus. It also offers suggestions for handling these topics in a way that helps students apply their scientific understanding to ethical analyses. Students develop critical-thinking and inquiry skills as they wrestle with societal issues that are related to biological sciences. Finally, this section includes specific discussion of five topics that are currently controversial in biology.

The longest section of the book, Section IV, will help you create a culture of inquiry in your classroom. The nine chapters in this section provide detailed information and recommendations about instructional components and styles that encourage students to question, wrestle with ideas, and construct their understanding of biology concepts. For example, there are chapters on using science notebooks (chapter 11), encouraging scientific discussions (chapter 15), and selecting instructional materials that support inquiry teaching (chapter 17).

The final section of the book may be less relevant to your immediate needs in course planning, but it provides a context for examining your profession. The first chapter in this section provides a brief history of biology teaching, with a particular focus on the role of BSCS in this history. The final chapter of the book describes the dilemmas and opportunities that are before us.

Section I

Introduction

A Context for Good Teaching

In this first section of the handbook, we set up a context for good teaching in biology. We identify four general areas to consider as a common context in which good biology teaching takes place:

- Beliefs and understandings about how students learn effectively;
- Approaches for successful teaching for students from diverse backgrounds;
- Unifying principles of the science of biology; and
- Recognition of and strategies for addressing pervasive prior conceptions about biological topics that impede learning.

We begin by discussing the current status of our understanding about how people learn and how to teach to enhance this learning process (chapter 1). Currently, the idea of "science for all" appears in most goal statements for science teaching, but frequently information about specifically how one goes about teaching for equity is sparse. Chapter 2 fills in this gap for teachers. The last two chapters in section I focus specifically on the biology course. Chapter 3 introduces six unifying principles of biology that form the framework for a complete, though basic, understanding of biology. In addition, we suggest 20 major concepts that are linked to the six principles. Chapter 4 identifies, within each of the six principles, prior conceptions that research has consistently found to impede student learning. This chapter also includes strategies for identifying which prior conceptions students hold and for addressing them through instruction.

The four sections that follow this first section of *The Biology Teacher's Handbook* provide more specific advice and support for biology teaching. You should consider each of those sections, however, in light of the general context for good teaching offered in this initial section.

Chapter 1

The Relationship Between Teaching and Learning

"I taught it … why didn't they learn it?" Has this thought ever crossed your mind? When considering this question, you are pondering the relationship between teaching and learning. In chapter 1, we will introduce a summary of research about learning and discuss the implications for teaching. We will also describe characteristics of professional development that can help you and your colleagues transform your teaching beliefs and practices in ways that address current understanding about learning. Finally, we will close with a challenge that you can use in your classroom to help you more fully consider the relationship between teaching and learning.

Research on Learning

In recent years, science educators have focused on the theory of *constructivism* to help understand students' learning. There are two common theoretical bases for constructivist research, including Ausubelian theory (Ausubel, Novak, and Hanesian 1978), which states that a learner's prior knowledge is an important factor in determining what is learned in a given situation. L. S. Vygotsky (1968) is a second important source for constructivism. He wrote of student conceptions and teacher conceptions, and of how students and teachers might use similar words to describe concepts yet have different personal interpretations of those concepts. Vygotsky's work implies that science instruction should take into account the differences between teacher and student conceptions and should provide time for student-student interaction so learners can develop concepts from those whose understanding and interpretations are closer to their own.

In a constructivist model of learning, students construct knowledge by interpreting new experiences in the context of their current conceptions and experiences. Students' construction of knowledge begins at an early age so that by the time students encounter the formalized study of science, they have developed stable and highly personal conceptions for many natural phenomena. If we accept this model, which has a growing body of research supporting it, the challenge of classroom instruction is to facilitate change in students' understanding of scientific ideas when it does not align with currently accepted explanations. Some researchers (Posner et al. 1982; Smith et al. 1985) have likened this process of conceptual change to the process by which scientific theories undergo change and restructuring.

In the comprehensive review of the literature on learning, *How People Learn,* the authors summarize three key ideas about learning (Bransford et al. 2000, 14–19). The following statements capture the essence of these ideas:

1. *Students come to the classroom with preconceptions about how the world works.* These preconceptions shape how new learning is assimilated. This means

your students know something when they walk into your room. What they know may or may not be scientifically accurate, but it shapes how they connect the ideas you expose them to in your teaching.

2. *To develop competence in an area of inquiry, students must have a deep foundation of knowledge, they must have an understanding of how this knowledge relates to a framework, and they must be able to organize that knowledge so that it can be retrieved and applied.* This finding articulates the important connection between facts and concepts. We need not choose between teaching facts and concepts; rather, we need to understand the major organizing ideas (concepts) in biology well enough that we know how the small ideas and myriad facts connect to those concepts. In addition, we need to help our students develop systems for retrieving and applying facts and ideas within a framework for the discipline of biology. We cannot assume they walk into our classrooms with this skill.

3. *Students must be taught explicitly to take control of their own learning by defining goals and monitoring their progress toward meeting them.* This finding speaks to the role of metacognitive skills in successful learning. Students can take control of their learning if they are able to articulate learning goals and their progress in reaching those goals.

Implications for Teaching

The key findings about student learning from *How People Learn* have parallel implications for classroom instruction. As the authors of *How People Learn* note (Bransford et al. 2000, 19–21), these three findings imply that teachers must be able to do the following:

- Recommendation 1: Recognize and draw out preconceptions from their students and base instructional decisions on the information they get from their students. In other words, for students to learn effectively, we need to teach from a perspective that acknowledges the knowledge students walk into the classroom with and to use this knowledge and experience as the base for building new concepts.
- Recommendation 2: Teach the subject matter in depth so that facts are conveyed in a context with examples and a conceptual framework. We must help students build a rich foundation for science. This is accomplished by considering science content not as isolated pieces of information but rather as a set of larger concepts with associated facts that illustrate the concepts. Implicit in this recommendation is the idea that we must help students understand the framework of each scientific discipline they study.
- Recommendation 3: Integrate metacognitive skills into the cur-

riculum and teach those skills explicitly. We must be direct in our teaching about "how to learn." Students do not automatically know how to set reasonable goals for learning, to connect ideas together so that their learning is meaningful, or to be reflective about their own progress.

Competent teachers who know their subject matter well and who have a strong grasp of the pedagogical content knowledge needed to effectively teach that subject matter can accomplish the type of teaching advocated by *How People Learn*. (Pedagogical content knowledge is the information that enables a teacher to teach a particular subject area in an appropriate manner. This includes knowing which ideas build on each other and what prior conceptions students might bring to the classroom. (See Shulman 1986 for more detail.)

Table 1.1		Relating the Key Findings From *How People Learn* to Curriculum Materials
No.	**Key Findings: Students**	**Key Findings: Teachers**	**As a Result, Materials Need to**
1	Come to class with preconceptions.	• Recognize preconceptions and adjust instruction.	• Include structured strategies to elicit and challenge students' preconceptions. • Incorporate background for the teacher about common preconceptions.
2	Need to develop a deep factual understanding based in a conceptual framework.	• Understand the content and conceptual framework for a discipline. • Provide examples for context.	• Be organized around a conceptual framework. • Connect factual information to the framework. • Provide relevant examples to illustrate key ideas.
3	Set goals and analyze progress toward them.	• Provide class time for goal setting and analysis. • Teach metacognitive skills.	• Make learning goals explicit. • Integrate metacognitive skill development into content.

Source: Powell, J. C., J. B. Short, and N. M. Landes. 2002. Curriculum reform, professional development, and powerful learning. In *Learning science and the science of learning*, ed. R. W. Bybee, 124. Arlington, VA: NSTA Press.

The task of identifying prior concepts and building upon them can be simplified, however, if the curriculum materials available for teaching science incorporate these essential ideas. It is clear from the analysis of curriculum and instruction in the Trends in International Mathematics and Science Study (TIMSS project; Schmidt et al. 1999) and the work of the American Association for the Advancement of Science (AAAS 2005) that these ideas for instruction are not commonly practiced in U.S. classrooms or well supported in the most widely used instructional materials. Despite these findings, we believe that it is possible to make connections from the research about learning to specific means of instruction and science curriculum materials. Table 1.1 provides an overview of how the key findings from *How People Learn* might be explicitly addressed in instruction and curriculum materials.

Example of Curriculum Materials Designed to Increase Learning

BSCS Biology: A Human Approach (BSCS 2006) is an example of a curriculum program that exemplifies many of the ideas listed in table 1.1. The BSCS program was highly ranked in a recent review of biology textbooks (Morse and AIBS 2001). In particular, the reviewers noted that "this book is clearly linked to NSES, not only in the content, but also in the pedagogy, professional development and implementation suggestions" (16). Three key features of *A Human Approach* help highlight aspects of curriculum materials that could increase student learning, if implemented well. These three features also provide support for teachers who are committed to instruction that incorporates the key ideas of *How People Learn*:

- First, the materials are organized around an instructional model that helps teachers access students' prior knowledge.
- Second, the materials are organized around six unifying themes of biology, not around isolated facts and biological topics.
- Third, students are active participants in the assessment of their own learning.

Each of these features provides an opportunity for teachers to increase student learning. Because this approach is novel, however, the resulting materials look different from what teachers are used to seeing. The following descriptions of each feature will provide you with an idea of how the curriculum materials are different.

Feature 1: An Instructional Model

To help learners understand key concepts and meet the designated outcomes, BSCS develops curriculum materials and designs professional development around an instructional model based on a constructivist theory of learning, known throughout the educational community as the BSCS 5E Instructional Model. (See chapter 14 for a description of the 5Es.) In *BSCS Biology: A Human Approach* (BSCS 2006), each chapter is organized around the 5Es. Students begin their study of a biological concept by articulating what they know already (or think they know), and then they explore the concept further through experimentation. Next, the teacher introduces the currently accepted scientific explanation in the context of the student explorations. This sequence of exploring before explaining is the most difficult aspect of the 5Es for teachers because it feels like they are holding back information. But the 5E sequence pro-

Table 1.2	Units and Chapters in *BSCS Biology: A Human Approach*
Units	**Chapters**
1: Evolution: Patterns and Products of Change in Living Systems	1: The Human Animal 2: Evolution: Change Across Time 3: Products of Evolution: Unity and Diversity
2: Homeostasis: Maintaining Dynamic Equilibrium in Living Systems	4: The Internal Environment of Organisms 5: Maintaining Balance in Organisms 6: Human Homeostasis: Health and Disease
3: Energy, Matter, and Organization: Relationships in Living Systems	7: Performance and Fitness 8: The Cellular Basis of Activity 9: The Cycling of Matter and the Flow of Energy in Communities
4: Continuity: Reproduction and Inheritance in Living Systems	10: Reproduction in Humans and Other Organisms 11: Continuity of Information Through Inheritance 12: Gene Action
5: Development: Growth and Differentiation in Living Systems	13: Processes and Patterns of Development 14: The Human Life Span
6: Ecology: Interaction and Interdependence in Living Systems	15: Interdependence Among Organisms in the Biosphere 16: Decision Making in a Complex World

Source: BSCS. 2006. *BSCS biology: A human approach*. Dubuque, IA: Kendall/Hunt.

vides students with an opportunity to place new knowledge in the context of what they already know and therefore addresses recommendations 1 and 2 from *How People Learn*.

Feature 2: Conceptual Organization

The second feature of *BSCS Biology: A Human Approach* (BSCS 2006) that is different from most biology textbooks is the organization of the content. The six units of the program are organized around six unifying principles. These principles form the framework for each unit, and the content is connected back to the big idea within a context that makes sense to the learner. See table 1.2 for a list of the units and the chapter titles within each unit for an illustration of how a biology program can be organized conceptually. This feature is one way that curriculum materials can attend to the second recommendation from *How People Learn*, but it is not necessarily a familiar approach for teachers who may have learned biology from a topical or taxonomic approach.

Feature 3: Metacognitive Skills

One way in which students develop their metacognitive skills when using *BSCS Biology: A Human Approach* (BSCS 2006) is their involvement with their own assessment. The fifth *E* of the 5E sequence is for *Evaluate*. During this phase of the instructional model, both the teacher and the student are responsible for assessing the student's understanding. Students do this by identifying what they have learned and how they learned it. This level of reflection helps increase students' awareness and understanding of the learning process. This direct student involvement is not common in U.S. schools and requires using a set of strategies that may be unfamiliar to the teacher or not supported by the administration.

As indicated, implementing standards-based curriculum materials may be a significant change for how teachers approach learning and teaching science. Comprehensive professional development aimed at improving instruction and learning is important, because curricula such as *A Human Approach* require conceptual understanding of science content, knowledge of the research on how students learn, and pedagogical content knowledge to effectively use them. Highly structured, standards-based curriculum materials, when combined with effective, sustained professional development, can potentially change teaching practices in a way that leads to improved student achievement and attitudes about science. For this potential to emerge, professional development needs to incorporate multiple elements of instruction—the teachers, students, content, and environments—and the interactions among these elements (Cohen and Ball 2001). The following paragraphs describe the type of professional development that will be most helpful in your efforts to enhance your biology instruction and grow professionally.

The *National Science Education Standards* (NRC 1996) states that professional development for science teachers must provide opportunities

- to learn science content through the perspectives and methods of inquiry;
- to learn how to teach science in a way that integrates knowledge of science, learning, pedagogy, and students; and
- to build an understanding and ability for lifelong learning.

Also, the professional development programs must be coherent and integrated. The National Institute for Science Education (Loucks-Horsley et al. 1996) synthesized a variety of professional development standards to produce a list of principles of effective professional development experiences that includes the following:

1. They are driven by a clear, well-defined image of effective classroom learning and teaching.
2. They provide teachers with opportunities to develop knowledge and skills and broaden their teaching approaches, so that they can create better learning opportunities for students.
3. They use instructional methods to promote learning for adults that mirror the methods to be used with students.
4. They build or strengthen the learning community of science teachers.
5. They prepare and support teachers to serve in leadership roles that require them to step beyond their classrooms and play roles in the development of the whole school and beyond.
6. They consciously provide links to the other parts of the educational system.
7. They include continuous assessment.

Although professional development experiences designed to support the implementation of new curriculum materials need to incorporate all of these principles, we have chosen to focus on the third principle listed above. Curriculum materials designed to increase student learning, such as *BSCS Biology: A Human Approach*, convey a view of teaching largely as a process of provoking students to think and to conduct scientific inquiries. These materials support students in their efforts and guide them along productive paths to reach the intended learning outcomes. To educate those teachers who are unaccustomed to this approach to learning and teaching, we ask,

"How can they learn the strategies and pedagogical content knowledge necessary to effectively implement curriculum materials that have these goals?" We suggest that professional development experiences for teachers model the instructional approach intended for students by using the same strategy for how teachers learn to implement the new curriculum materials. In other words, professional development that is a powerful learning experience for teachers should be designed so that it incorporates the same elements that provide powerful learning for students.

Standards-based curriculum materials are designed to challenge teachers to think differently about learning and teaching science. Instead of a textbook that provides only what to teach, these curriculum materials also provide instructional support for how to teach. Because incorporating this type of support into curriculum materials makes the materials different, most teachers need a rich form of ongoing professional development to help them learn to use such materials effectively. When professional development models the instructional approaches used in the curriculum materials themselves, it is a powerful learning experience for teachers. Our contention is that professional development that supports standards-based curriculum materials must challenge teachers' current beliefs about learning and teaching science. In other words, the professional development needs to transform—change the nature of—teachers' beliefs and practices. Five features that characterize transformative professional development (Thompson and Zeuli 1999) do the following:

- Create a sufficiently high level of cognitive dissonance to disturb in some fundamental way the equilibrium between teachers' existing beliefs and practices on the one hand and their experience with subject matter, students' learning, and teaching on the other.
- Provide time, contexts, and support for teachers to think—to work at resolving the dissonance through discussion, reading, writing, and other activities that essentially amount to the crystallization, externalization, criticism, and revision of their thinking.
- Ensure that the dissonance-creating and dissonance-resolving activities are connected to the teacher's own students and context, or to something like them.
- Provide a way for teachers to develop a repertoire for practice that is consistent with the new understanding that teachers are building.
- Provide continuing help in the cycle of (1) surfacing the new issues and problems that will inevitably arise from actual classroom performance, (2) deriving new understanding from them, (3) translating this new understanding into performance, and (4) recycling.

Table 1.3	Relating the Key Findings From *How People Learn** to Professional Development

Key Findings: Students	Key Findings: Teachers	As a Result, Professional Development Needs to
Come to class with preconceptions.	• Recognize preconceptions and adjust instruction.	• Include strategies to elicit and challenge teachers' preconceptions about science, curriculum, and how people learn.
Need to develop a deep factual understanding based in a conceptual framework.	• Understand the content and conceptual framework for a discipline. • Provide examples for context.	• Be organized around a conceptual framework. • Connect factual information, research, and actual experiences to the framework. • Provide relevant examples to illustrate key ideas.
Set goals and analyze progress toward them.	• Provide class time for goal setting and analysis. • Teach metacognitive skills.	• Make learning goals explicit. • Integrate metacognitive skill development into content.

*The key findings are from National Research Council (NRC). 2000. *How people learn: Brain, mind, experience, and school.* Exp. ed. Washington, DC: National Academy Press.

These characteristics of transformative professional development are related to the constructivist philosophy of teaching and learning and are consistent with the key findings about learning and teaching from *How People Learn*. In other words, powerful learning for adults looks a lot like powerful learning for students (see table 1.3).

A Challenge for Practicing Teachers

Here is something you can do individually or with a group of your colleagues to begin reconsidering the relationship between teaching and learning:

1. Establish a reflective practitioner journal.
2. In your journal, respond to these questions:
   • What is real learning?
   • How do you recognize learning?
   • What does it take for real learning to occur?

3. Team up with a colleague and watch each other teach a lesson. (As an alternative, set up a video recorder and record a lesson when you are teaching.) During the lesson, focus on what the students are doing and saying.
4. After the lesson, reflect on these questions:
   - Did you see any "real learning" in the lesson you observed?
   - What is your evidence that real learning took place?
5. Create a table with three columns. Put these questions at the top of the columns:
   - What were the students doing physically in the lesson when you observed real learning?
   - What were the students doing mentally when you observed real learning?
   - What was the instructional leader (you, the teacher) doing?
6. Fill out the table created in step 5 in response to your examples of real learning from step 4.
7. Reflect on these questions in your journal:
   - What patterns do you see in the table?
   - How would you revise your response to the questions from step 2?
   - Based on the evidence, what, if anything, would you like to change about your practice to improve the relationship between teaching and learning?

If you repeat this exercise multiple times, you will continue to learn more about your teaching and increase the opportunities for students to learn in your classroom.

Chapter 2

Teaching
Science for Equity

The well-accepted notion of *equity* is defined as the absence of overt barriers to educational access. Lynch (2000, 13) refers to the absence of overt barriers to educational access as "equality of inputs." A wide variety of factors can prevent equality of inputs, such as unequal access to texts and lab equipment across school districts, a shortage of highly qualified teachers in some districts, and formal institutional barriers. (Institutional barriers include policies that prohibit the participation of women or minorities in various scientific institutions. Most of these policies have been eliminated over the past 35 years.) Lynch describes a second level of equity, "equality of outputs." Equality of outputs refers to the success of all students on tests of minimum standards and to an even distribution of students who excel in science throughout all gender and racial subgroups. Lynch concludes that equality of outputs on school tests would eventually manifest itself as equality of participation in scientific careers.

In a legal sense, *equity* refers to the process of making all parties "whole." In other words, when one party suffers a loss, what has been lost must be restored to achieve equity. Equity in science education takes the same fundamental meaning. Women and minorities have had a lack of meaningful access to science education and the science professions as well as a lack of influence on the specific research questions science should address (Clewell and Campbell 2002; NSF 1999; Rosser 2000). Although formal barriers have been removed in education and the professions, the lack of access remains, as evidenced by the unequal participation in the sciences (Rosser 2000). The unequal participation of various racial and ethnic groups and gender subgroups in the sciences is particularly troubling given that research has shown that minority students express greater interest in science at an early age than white students (Creswell and Exezidis 1982; Hanson and Johnson 2000; Hueftle et al. 1983; Mau et al. 1995). Thus, in a legal sense, equity in the sciences would restore what has been lost: All groups would be uniformly distributed throughout all academic and professional levels of science and would influence the production of scientific knowledge proportional to their overall representation in the population.

Finally, Lynch (2000, 13) describes a third level of equity as "equity as fairness: making tradeoffs." To Lynch, equity as fairness is the most realistic goal, balancing student needs with available resources. Indeed, limited resources will determine what services may be available to needy students. So, unless science educators maintain the higher goal of equality of outcomes, it may be too easy to dismiss that goal as being cost prohibitive.

The International Covenant on Economic, Social, and Cultural Rights (United Nations 1966) recognizes access to education and access to scientific information as a fundamental human right. Although we recognize that the full realization of human rights requires financial resources that some governing agencies lack (in this case, the states that fund school districts), the international community of human rights signatories expects governments to make changes that progressively realize those rights. Thus, "equity as fairness: making tradeoffs" cannot and should not be a permanent solution. Rather, teachers and communities should fight for the resources to provide full access to science education for all students. The science education community should acknowledge that the lack of such resources is a failure to provide for all students' fundamental human rights.

What Accounts for *Inequality* of Outputs? How Can a Teacher Combat Inequality?

Unequal participation of women and minority men in the sciences can be traced to several factors, including unequal district resources for all schools and students' socioeconomic status. Of the many factors related to inequality in the sciences, three are directly related to the climate of the classroom and the nature of the curriculum. These three factors are the focus of the rest of this chapter:

- Bias (both teacher-student and student-student),
- An overemphasis on content that interests white males only, and
- The failure of science teachers and textbooks to acknowledge that science is a fully human and culturally influenced discipline.

We will address each factor related to inequality in turn. Following each factor, we will propose actions teachers can take to mitigate the forces that breed inequality in the classroom.

Bias

We would all like to believe that we treat others as we would like to be treated. We have never met a teacher who thought that he or she treated boys differently from girls or white students differently from black, Latino, or Asian students. Nevertheless, study after study has documented teacher-student bias in the classroom (AAUW 1992; Kurth et al. 2002; Sadker and Sadker 1994; Spencer et al. 2003). Indeed, Spencer et al. found an "intriguing contradiction" between the self-reported lack of bias in classrooms by students and teachers alike and the data from classroom observations that students "continued to have disturbingly different experiences in the classroom" (1800). What does bias look like? Gender bias and race-and-ethnicity bias overlap in some respects and differ in others. We will address each separately.

Gender bias. Some forms of gender bias are blatant, others subtle. For example, Sadker and Sadker (1994) documented examples of a male teacher referring to female students as "dizzy," "ditzy," or "airhead," but not all bias is so easily detected. Indeed, the most pernicious forms of teacher-student bias can be those that are most difficult to detect. For example, teachers of both genders tend to call on male students more than female students; female students generally wait longer for teacher attention and, when attention is given, receive less of it. And teachers often set rules requiring students to raise hands before being called on but enforce rules primarily when girls speak out of turn (Houston 1985/1994; Sadker and Sadker 1994).

Finally, teachers and students may see different treatment of boys and girls, but an acceptance that boys are more boisterous than girls, need more help, and require more management directly leads them to justify the treatment. This results in boys receiving far more attention than girls: "Coincidental with the array of gender-fair practices perceived by students in the school, the same students did observe inequities between boys' and girls' experiences in the classroom. ... The girls had concluded that they were less in need of their teachers' time and attention and this belief seemed to be continuously reinforced" (Spencer et al. 2003, 1799–1800). The effect of this more subtle form of bias is to silence girls, preventing their full participation in the science classroom. To the extent that participation breeds confidence and promotes learning, girls are often effectively shut out of access to a full science education.

Race-and-ethnicity and language-difference bias. A difficult-to-detect, common form of teacher-student bias related to race-and-ethnicity and language differences is the bias of low expectations. Haberman (1991) detailed the characteristics of a "pedagogy of poverty," or the widespread use of directive teaching strategies in urban schools—strategies that require good behavior and cognitive acquiescence from students but never require students to think critically. Griffard and Wandersee (1999) identified a "cycle of cognitive disengagement" in which teachers attend to behavior rather than learning, students fail to engage in critical thinking even in the presence of a strong work ethic, and cognitive passivity predominates. By succumbing to the bias of low expectations of what a student can accomplish, teachers inadvertently deprive students of a science education.

Teaching science as inquiry demands that students participate in a sense-making process while exploring scientific ideas. It demands that students think critically about content, using evidence to build their understanding. Several studies have shown that teaching science as inquiry promotes equity as well as excellence in science education. In other words, students of all ability levels (both special education and mainstreamed students), socioeconomic backgrounds, race and ethnicities, English proficiency levels, and genders benefit from learning science through inquiry (Kahle et al. 2000; Lee and Avalos 2002; Marx et al. 2004; Palincsar et al. 2001). Teaching science as inquiry to all students ensures that you will avoid the pedagogy of poverty and the cycle of cognitive disengagement that indicate teachers had low expectations of students.

How can you know if you, like most teachers, disproportionately call on white males rather than girls, spend a greater proportion of your time attending to the demands of boisterous boys, or have lower expectations of your minority students or English language learners? The most effective way to see your own bias is to videotape your own classroom. Count how many times you call on each student, respond to each student's comments, and provide feedback to each student. Include not only the frequency of comments but also the length and nature of the comments. Is your feedback for girls as frequent, lengthy, and encouraging as it is for boys? Do you express the same high expectations for all students? Becoming aware of your own bias is the very first step in changing your practice. Without awareness of a problem, change is impossible.

To help provide all students with equal access to your attention, feedback, and assistance, you must diligently attend to the needs of all students—both boisterous and quiet:

1. *When students are engaged in group work, develop a system whereby each group has an equal opportunity to ask questions.* Asking the students to write their group name or number on the board when they have a question will prevent the most-demanding students from jumping ahead of those students who may be quietly and politely raising their hands in the back of the room. Never underestimate the ability of more-demanding students to monopolize your attention and prevent you from attending the needs of all students in the class.

2. *When students are working in groups, never answer the question of a student when she or he is away from group members.* Doing so deprives the less-assertive group members of your feedback and any subsequent discussion. If a student has stepped away from the group to ask you a question, return with the student to the group before answering.

3. *Keep a list of which students you have called on and which you have not.* Even if you are not requiring students to volunteer answers as part of

a grade, the list will help you see which students are getting more than their share of your attention.

4. *Allow students the opportunity to share their thinking with a table partner before you call on students to volunteer answers.* Students will have more time to formulate a response, and those students who prefer to think through a response before blurting out an answer will have greater opportunity to participate. For students identified for special-education services, allow them time to rehearse ideas with you or an aide before presenting ideas to the class. These students will gain confidence through the rehearsal.

5. *Rather than having single students answer questions, provide students with options and have students vote on which option they think may be correct.* Ask one student from each "camp" to justify why he or she chose that response.

6. *Use a voting and justification strategy in combination with student science notebooks to have students participate in and document a class discussion.* Students first write their own predictions and their justifications for those predictions. Next, students vote on which option they consider correct. When students from each camp provide their respective explanations, each student must document in the science notebook the reasons their peers give for the alternative views: "Mary chose 'c' because ..." Finally, students consider the explanations of other students and decide whether to revise or keep their initial response.

7. *Maintain high expectations of all students.* Research shows that all students of all levels of academic achievement and English language acquisition benefit from science teaching that emphasizes sense making and critical thinking rather than rote memorization. Use the inquiry process to build literacy skills: English language learners can use the opportunity of writing their own lab procedures to practice writing complete sentences. Students with reading difficulties will be able to make more sense of their own plans to test an idea than they would of someone else's instructions. If available, use classroom aides to transcribe ideas for students who have extreme difficulty writing.

Student-student bias. Although teacher-student bias can be difficult to detect, student-student bias is often almost invisible to a busy classroom teacher. Nevertheless, student-student bias is pervasive in schools in general and in math and science classrooms in particular. Student-student bias manifests itself along all varieties of difference: gender difference, racial-and-ethnicity and language differences, and differences related to the categorization of some students as having special needs.

Student-student bias often occurs when students work in groups. Yet research has shown that competitive classrooms hinder the learning of students in general and interfere with learning for girls and minority students in particular (Johnson et al. 1991; Rosser 1995). Furthermore, competitive classrooms value the individual over the group and thus fail to prepare students for team-based projects in the workforce (Johnson et al. 1991). Some research (Johnson et al. 1991; Slavin and Oickle 1981) has emphasized the importance of heterogeneous groups to allowing white students access to multicultural experiences. Others claim that random, heterogeneous groupings can be harmful to girls and minority students (Rosser 1997). The purported benefit of heterogeneous grouping is prejudice reduction according to Slavin and Oickle (1981). Although using collaborative learning groups can promote student interest and achievement, random assignment of students to heterogeneous groups formed without understanding the implications of group selection will generally exacerbate the effects of student-student bias (Rosser 1997). For example, Kurth et al. (2002) examined the difficulty Carla, an African American student, had in holding the floor with her group members. On the first day of an inquiry activity related to density, one group member was absent and Carla spent most of the time enthusiastically engaged with the materials on her own. Her attempts to interact with her group members (two boys) were rebuffed. On the second day, when the absent student returned, Carla again attempted to interact with her group members, wanting to show her teammate what she had learned the day before. Yet the two "high-status" white students prevented Carla from speaking. The students told Carla to wait her turn and then refused to give her a turn. A white boy, Zach, assumed that his turn involved sharing everything that he had learned. Furthermore, he took it upon himself to share what "somebody" had figured out; the "somebody" was Carla. Though her understanding and efforts to participate were strong, Carla could not overcome the student-student bias of her teammates. Carla's group members made assumptions about what she had to offer. They privileged particular ways of speaking about the ideas and planning the activity, rebuffing Carla's attempts at participation.

Likewise, Palincsar and colleagues (2001) documented the difficulty special education students (or "identified students") had in attaining access to group work. The authors describe video records that "capture group members removing materials from the hands of identified students and precluding their involvement" as "painful to watch" (23). Ultimately, Palincsar and colleagues identified advanced teaching practices as those that attend to issues of access, "not only the identified child's access to the instructional context," a context that includes interactions in small groups, "but also the teacher's and peers' access to the identified child's thinking and reasoning" (29). Clearly, a student's ability to fully participate in the classroom, whether in whole-group or small-group discussions and activities, hinges on the degree to which the student's teacher and peers allow participation to occur.

To combat the student-student bias that may deprive students of an education, the following actions may be useful:

1. *Never isolate students of a particular gender, race, or ethnicity in a group.* Isolation has the effect of putting the minority student or girl in the spotlight, particularly when the class is math or science related. Rosser (1997) found that students in elective science and math classes who were isolated as the only minority or female student in a group were more likely to drop the class than those students who were paired with at least one other person of the same race, ethnicity, or gender.

2. *Consider student personalities, levels of assertiveness, and speech patterns carefully before assigning students to groups.* Equal participation demands that a student's access to the floor in a science discussion not rely on her or his form of speech, aggressiveness, or degree of confidence in asserting claims. Such differences often manifest themselves along strict lines of male and female—but not always. Thus, anyone (male or female) who uses a linguistic style of speech involving "hesitations, false starts, a questioning intonation when making a statement, an extensive use of qualifiers that serve to weaken what is said, and extensive use of modals" may have difficulty "holding the floor" and achieving full participation in a group of assertive, confident speakers (Houston 1985/1994, 124).

3. *It is perfectly acceptable to have groups of students who are all male or all female, if such a grouping facilitates the participation of all students.* Several studies (Gillibrand et al. 1999; Haussler and Hoffmann 2002; Labudde et al. 2000) have shown that single-sex environments may help girls feel more comfortable in science class. Although students of one gender should never be prevented from working with students of the opposite gender, single-sex groups may be an effective way to combat student-student bias.

4. *Try to avoid placing students with the highest grades in a group with students who have the lowest grades.* Such groupings tend to frustrate both groups of students. To achieve some degree of academic heterogeneity, consider grouping high and middle students or middle and low students.

5. *Try to include at least one student per group who will be likely to attend to turn taking and the even distribution of resources and tasks.* Palincsar and colleagues (2001) found that having at least one student per group who attends to issues of fairness can combat student-student bias against special education students.

6. *Evaluate students on their student-student interactions in a group.* Students who ultimately join the science workforce will, without question, be required to work in large teams. Indeed, employers repeatedly cite the ability to work in teams as an essential skill in science and engineering (Shakespeare et al. 2007), thus making it perfectly reasonable to evaluate students on their ability to work with other students.

7. *Ask students to discuss with their group members how well they functioned in terms of fairness.* Make sure everyone speaks, fully listening to each other's ideas, and make sure everyone has a chance to use the equipment. See the discussion of working-relationship skills in chapter 10. Johnson and colleagues (1990) found that students who participated in teacher-led and student-led processing showed greater gains than students who did not. Although students may not be able to resolve every conflict immediately, group processing at least clears the air and allows students to voice concerns. Students can solve only the problems that have been brought out into the open.

Overemphasis on Content That Interests White Males Exclusively

Teacher-student bias and student-student bias play an important role in the exclusion from science of minority students, girls, special education students, and English language learners. Yet bias is only one aspect of the equation. A second reason for the disproportionate numbers of white males in the sciences is related to the content emphasis made in science classrooms. Gearing instruction to students' interests is, without question, an important pedagogical strategy. Science topics generally of interest to girls and minorities are often a subset of those that are of interest to boys: Specifically, what is interesting to girls is almost always interesting to boys, but the converse is not true (Haussler and Hoffmann 2002).

Girls and minority students tend to have greater interest in topics that more concretely relate to society and human experience (Rosser 1995). Thus, overemphasis on abstract principles without addressing how and why the science is important to human beings works to the detriment of girls and minority students. Including societal implications, however, does not interfere with boys' interests: Boys demonstrate an interest in the social implications of science equal to that of girls and minorities (Haussler and

Hoffmann 2002). By emphasizing social implications, teachers will be teaching to the interests of all students.

The following will help you maximize the likelihood that the science content you teach will appeal to all students:

- If you can choose which topics to teach, choose those topics with the most social relevance.
- Whenever possible, draw connections between abstract scientific concepts and their societal implications. For example, ask students to consider the complex scientific and social issues of global warming or other environmental issues.

Failure to Acknowledge Cultural Influences on Science and the Culture of Science

We have considered the role of bias and the role of content in the exclusion of certain students from the sciences. We now consider cultural influences on science, the culture of science itself, and the role both play in excluding students from the sciences. A popular misconception about science is that it is somehow removed from social and cultural influences—existing in a vacuum—enabling the gradual discovery and accumulation of "Truth." Although evidence for claims and objectivity are highly valued by the scientific community, scientific empiricism exists within the human cultures that create and practice it. Furthermore, scientific questions are those that can be proved false. Science seeks to falsify ideas and gradually accepts ideas as "true" only when extensive testing over many years fails to prove them false. Thus, science is fundamentally about falsification rather than verification.

Harding (2001) and Keller (1985) have described science as both empirically reliable and socially and culturally bound. The most common way in which social and cultural bias plays out in science is the selection of which scientific questions are worthy of study. The work of Ashok Gadgil (Gadgil 1998), a physicist born in India, stands out as an example. After conducting research in solar energy and heat transfer at Lawrence Berkeley National Laboratory, Gadgil turned his attention to a problem that scientists in the Western world have largely ignored: treating contaminated water in developing countries. Gadgil developed an inexpensive and portable water purification system that uses ultraviolet light to kill deadly bacteria and that runs on a car battery. The science behind Gadgil's device was not revolutionary, but its application was. Scientists in the United States and Europe did not have an immediate cultural need to address water contamination in India—so the question was simply not seriously addressed before Gadgil's work. His work exemplifies the best of socially situated, empirically valid science.

Not only is science embedded in social and cultural values, but science also has its own culture. Scientists have their own ways of speaking and writing, or science classrooms tend to have norms that may differ markedly from the norms of social studies or English classes (Lemke 1990). Aikenhead and Jegede (1999) held that science is a foreign culture to many minority students. Lee (1999) examined the relationship between race, gender, and students' scientific and nonscientific worldviews through student explanations of hurricane formation. She found that white male students tend to hold alternative views significantly less often than minority students. Further, she found that students who held nonscientific views (supernatural or religious views) pertaining to hurricane formation held scientific views (sometimes tenuously) alongside the nonscientific explanations. The implication of Lee's study is that minority students will be more likely to find a fundamental conflict between their prior understanding and the scientific worldviews they are learning. Consequently, minority students will have to find some way to resolve any cognitive conflict that results.

In the past 20 years, some research has been conducted identifying the cultural traits, based on race and ethnicity, of groups of students and identifying strategies for incorporating the differences in the science classroom. Yet the tendency to assume that students who belong to a particular group have particular cultural characteristics runs the risk of perpetuating stereotypes.

According to C. D. Lee (2003, 3), "culture is never static and ... the belief systems and practices associated with cultural groups are always under negotiation with new generations and new material as well as with social conditions." Furthermore, it is important to consider the many facets of life that shape every individual: No student can be completely described as black or white, male or female, wealthy or poor. Instead, a student's race, gender, socioeconomic status, sexual orientation, and religious beliefs weave together to construct an identity (Dill 1983/1994; Hanson and Johnson 2000). Examining one thread of the weave while ignoring the entire fabric of the individual is unlikely to provide a teacher with any useful insight to helping a student. Thus, although it is important to consider students' gender, race or ethnicity, values or ideology, and cultural understanding, assumptions about that understanding should never be imposed on students.

Allowing students the opportunity to write in their science notebooks about their prior understanding (whether it consists of typical misconceptions or nonscientific ideas that are culturally or ideologically based) will show students that you honor who they are as complete and complex individuals. Furthermore, maintaining awareness that students from a variety of backgrounds may not understand classroom cultural norms and expectations will ensure that you explicitly teach expectations to students. Never assume that students automatically understand unstated classroom expectations.

Although cultural differences between students exist, it is impossible to predict exactly how those differences will manifest themselves. Nevertheless, it is possible to help students successfully "cross the border" into the culture of science. According to Aikenhead and Jegede (1999), teachers must assist students with a cultural border crossing to provide them with access to science. To facilitate border crossing, Aikenhead and Jegede proposed that teachers foster "collateral learning" (276). *Collateral learning* refers to the coexistence of two or more different cognitive schemata for a given natural phenomenon. According to Aikenhead and Jegede, the goal of the science teacher is to assist students in developing scientific understanding without damaging their ideologically based worldviews. The teacher should assist students in their efforts to adjust their existing schemata—perhaps by promoting metacognitive awareness of schemata and encouraging playfulness and flexibility in the classroom. That said, science teachers are not and should not be in the business of teaching religion or philosophy. The best practice is to do the following:

1. Help students understand what constitutes a scientific question and what does not. Avoid belittling ideologically based ways of knowing.
2. Help students become aware that science is but one of many ways of understanding and interpreting natural events. Science is evidence based, while other forms of understanding are typically faith based. Because scientific and ideological understandings have different foundations, they need not be in conflict with one another.
3. Help students learn that it is possible to hold two or more different understandings at the same time. Students do not have to choose between science and ideology. If scientific and nonscientific ideas contradict one another, students should be encouraged to accept the contradiction as a mystery yet to be resolved. After all, science needs students with a variety of backgrounds and understanding to ensure that scientific advancements serve all of humanity. Ashok Gadgil is a testament to the importance of diversity to science's ability to truly serve all people.

A final way that the culture of science tends to alienate students is through its extensive use of technical language (Aikenhead and Jegede 1999; Lemke 1990). If students are to become competent in science, they must develop facility with scientific language. Yet that language use must be grounded in a fundamental understanding of ideas associated with the language. If students simply memorize technical terms and their definitions, scientific language will feel foreign to them. Rather, students must develop conceptual understanding using familiar language and gradually add the scientific terminology to the developing concepts. In a sense, students are making translations from their observations and understanding; to their everyday speech; to technical, scientific descriptions—part of the cultural border crossing into science. Each level of formality in speech is a difference in speech "register." Kowalski (2008) found evidence that minority students and girls may shift registers less frequently than white males. Thus, providing students with the opportunity to practice shifting registers when describing scientific ideas may help minority students and girls succeed in science. You can implement the following to help students develop facility with scientific language:

1. Require students to extensively use their science notebooks to document their learning and changes in thinking and language use.
2. Use "what I see, what it means" strategies (Sweller 1999) to help students concretely articulate and understand abstract ideas. When using this strategy, students consider an abstract representation of an idea (such as a graph), identify what they see on the graph (or abstract representation) in terms of its characteristics, and write short, simple sentences about what the abstraction means.
3. Require students to use multiple representations of abstract ideas. For example, Bunce and Gabel (2002) found that students who learned to balance chemical equations using chemical formulas and algorithms could successfully balance equations on a test; however, the students did not understand the fundamental rearrangement of atoms that was occurring in the chemical reaction. When students were asked to balance equations using pictures of each molecule to illustrate the rearrangement of atoms and then balance equations using chemical formulas and coefficients, test gaps between girls and boys disappeared. Students still learned the technical, abstract representations of chemical equations, but they learned them with an understanding grounded in another, more concrete representation.

Chapter 12 includes several strategies that help students make scientific terminology personally meaningful.

Conclusion

We have outlined three major areas that play a role in equity in the science classroom, each residing under the control of the classroom teacher. The three areas (addressing issues of bias, making connections between science and society explicit, and helping students cross the border into the culture of science) ultimately deal with one of two important strategies: building students' confidence and sense of belonging in science. The second important strategy is maintaining expectations that students will critically think about important scientific concepts and develop facility with technical scientific terminology.

We emphasize that both strategies are essential to achieving equity in science education. Attending only to students' sense of belonging without challenging students to think critically about content breeds confidence without competence. Perpetually challenging students to reevaluate their prior understanding in light of scientific evidence without providing them with a safe environment in which to explore ideas, make mistakes, ask questions, and take part in discussion can make students feel adrift. If students gain competence in science without feeling confident that they belong in the classroom, they will likely drop out of science at the earliest opportunity. Students require both confidence and competence in science to maximize the likelihood that they will consider pursuing a career in science. Teachers play an important role in ensuring that every student has full access to the human right of science education.

Chapter 3

Unifying Principles of Biology*

What should secondary students know, value, and be able to do after completing a contemporary biology course? A biologically literate individual should understand unifying principles and major concepts of biology, the impact of humans on the biosphere, the processes of scientific inquiry, and the historical development of biological concepts. A biologically literate individual also should develop personal values concerning scientific investigations, biodiversity and cultural diversity, the impact of biology and biotechnology on society, and the importance of biology to the individual. Finally, a biologically literate individual should be able to think creatively and formulate questions about nature, reason logically and critically and evaluate information, use technologies appropriately, make personal and ethical decisions related to biological issues, and apply knowledge to solve real-world problems. A contemporary secondary biology course, then, should provide students with a foundation in the unifying principles of biology that they can build on throughout their lives, in both further formal study and informal experiences.

The diversity of life on Earth is readily observed and fascinating to most people. Biologists seek to understand how the millions of different species differ from one another, but they also recognize that there are fundamental principles of life that apply to all organisms. An understanding of these unifying principles is the lens that helps us make sense of the diversity of life around us. Although BSCS supports using biological topics that are interesting and engaging to students, we encourage teachers to structure their courses around the fundamental principles rather than biological topics. When AIDS, global warming, and stem cell therapy are used as vehicles for teaching fundamental principles of life, rather than as unrelated biological topics, students emerge from their biology courses not only fascinated by current issues in biology but also firmly grounded in understandings that will help them engage in scientific discourse about biological issues that come up throughout their lives.

Six Unifying Principles

BSCS has identified six unifying principles of biology that can help organize the biological content of a course and the patterns and processes of natural phenomena in the living world:

- Principle 1: Evolution: Patterns and Products of Change
- Principle 2: Interactions and Interdependence
- Principle 3: Genetic Continuity and Reproduction

*Adapted from BSCS. 1993. *Developing biological literacy*. Colorado Springs, CO: BSCS.

- Principle 4: Growth, Development, and Differentiation
- Principle 5: Energy, Matter, and Organization
- Principle 6: Maintenance of a Dynamic Equilibrium

These principles should play a central role in the design of any biology course. For example, when evolution is used as a unifying principle of biology, cell parts, tissues, and hormones may be seen as adaptations that have contributed to an organism's successful reproduction and to a species' reproductive success through evolutionary history.

The unifying principles represent a comprehensive foundation for the biological sciences and thus are common to high school and two-year and four-year college programs. Individual programs may emphasize a molecular, organismic, or ecological level of organization, and they may give greater emphasis to inquiry or societal problems, but the unifying principles should provide the foundation for the biological knowledge in all contemporary biology programs. This chapter outlines six unifying principles educators can use to organize biological concepts, thus helping to unify the otherwise disparate facts of biology. The six principles are briefly described in the following sections.

Principle 1: Evolution: Patterns and Products of Change

Living systems change through time. This principle contains the major concepts of evolution as well as other causes and consequences of change. One aspect of this unifying principle is the change in the number and genetic constitution of individuals within a population through time. In the biological world, long-term success is related to the number of surviving offspring an organism produces: The more offspring that survive and reproduce, the more successful the organism is. To reproduce, organisms require resources such as energy, nutrients, and water, so reproductive success depends on the acquisition of resources that allow an organism first to grow and develop and then to reproduce. The physical characteristics used to acquire resources are determined by genetic information: Genes direct the development of structures that help an organism obtain and use the raw materials of life that are in limited supply. Because individuals within most populations produce more offspring than survive, the result is competition for the finite resources necessary for living. Within a population, however, organisms are not identical. Each member of a population may possess a unique complement of genes, which can lead to the expression of different phenotypes in the population. Those individuals that are better suited to acquire necessities are able to produce a greater number of offspring and thus pass their genes on to a greater proportion of the next generation. This genetic variation is the basis for evolution and is the major focus in the study of population genetics.

Organisms live within an environment that is constantly changing. Those individuals with little tolerance for environmental fluctuations may fail to reproduce. Thus, their unique combination of genes will not be passed on to any offspring. A species of organisms can become extinct with a resultant loss of its entire genetic complement, as has happened many times since the origin of life on Earth.

Natural selection is the process whereby individuals best adapted to their environment survive and reproduce successfully. Through time, the characteristics of individuals within a population will change as natural selection acts on the genetic variation within that population. This change in the frequency of alleles within a population through time is evolution. To appreciate the field of biology, we must comprehend the difference in scale when considering the size of the universe and the atoms composing it and to appreciate evolution as a process, we must comprehend the length of time Earth and the life on it have existed. A billion years is difficult to comprehend—and a challenge for teachers to present to students. Evolution can occur on a small scale, as in microevolutionary events, or on a large, macroevolutionary scale. Whereas mutations, gene flow, genetic drift, and nonrandom mating may affect the frequencies of alleles in a population, natural selection is the major driving force behind evolution.

Principle 2: Interactions and Interdependence

Living systems interact with their environment and are interdependent with other systems. Organisms must obtain the necessary resources of life from their environment, which consists of biotic and abiotic factors. Ecology is the study of the relationship between an organism and these factors—how the organism affects and is affected by the world in which it lives. The ecology of an organism includes the methods and mechanisms it uses to obtain nutrients and energy and the interactions with other organisms that compete with it, eat it, or break down its body after it has died. Both biotic and abiotic factors limit the ability of an organism to live and reproduce in a particular ecosystem. By its very existence, an organism exploits its environment and thus modifies it, often to the organisms disadvantage. An organism, however, also may thrive in a particular physical setting and may benefit from its interactions with other species.

Population ecologists study the growth or regulation of a group of organisms of the same species and the life history of that species. Community ecologists study the interactions among species. Because all species of a community are linked to others by their dependence on resources, community ecologists explore such interactions as predation, parasitism, or mutualism. The links established among organisms on the basis of their requirement for energy and nutrients describe the web of life. Another aspect of the community is the change, or succession, in species composition through time. Finally, the study of the biosphere and the physical environment includes large-scale patterns of plant associations within biomes, distinctive major communities found around the world.

Principle 3: Genetic Continuity and Reproduction

Life is a continuing stream of genetic information passed from generation to generation. Through reproduction, organisms produce other, similar organisms, maintaining the line of genetic continuity that links generations. Reproduction may involve one parent (usually asexual reproduction) or two parents (sexual reproduction). In eukaryotes, sexual reproduction begins with the production of special reproductive cells, or gametes, through a process called meiosis and, later, through the fusing of two gametes in fertilization to form a zygote. The type of reproduction depends on the species of organism, although some organisms may switch from one form to another depending on environmental factors.

Gametes contain the information for the development of characteristics passed from one generation to the next. Geneticists can determine the parents' genetic makeup by studying the patterns of inheritance revealed in the characteristics of the offspring. The biochemical basis of heredity is a set of genes made of the nucleic acid DNA and located on chromosomes. DNA is an information molecule. Each gene is a unique coded message formed by a combination of four types of subunits termed nucleotides. A gene directs the production of a specific polypeptide that regulates other genes, catalyzes a reaction leading to a distinct characteristic of an organism, or constitutes a needed structural component of the cell. Gene regulation involves the gene's expression and control, and this regulation is influenced by the environment of the cell in which the gene is located. Although different organisms have different individual coded messages, the basis for all genetic codes is virtually universal. That is, the same types of nucleotides make up DNA in all organisms, and the methods of transcription and translation from code to characteristic are similar in nearly all living organisms.

DNA is stable, generally replicating with great fidelity. The four bases of DNA, in their multiple combinations, harbor all of the genetic variation represented by life on Earth. Genetic control mechanisms provide for duplication of living forms, but they also may introduce variations through mutations and genetic recombinations that create new material for natural selection, leading to evolution. Modern genetic engineering technology has allowed humans to rearrange genetic material in an organism and to move genetic material from one organism to another, creating new combinations of genes. It also has allowed scientists to study the genetic material in minute detail.

Principle 4: Growth, Development, and Differentiation

Living systems grow, develop, and differentiate during their lifetimes based on a genetic plan that is influenced by the environment. Most multicellular organisms begin as a zygote, the single cell produced at fertilization that grows into a mature organism. The zygote first develops into a multicellular embryo through mitosis, the cell division that increases the number of body cells, followed by an increase in cell size. Thus, the zygote must contain all the genetic information necessary to form a complete organism, and this information must be passed from cell to cell in the developing body. In all multicellular organisms, cells begin to differentiate through time, taking on specialized roles. Division of labor at the cellular level begins during the early development of an organism and continues throughout its life. Eventually, morphogenesis—the growth and development of body parts—takes place so that the adult has many different structures with unique functions.

Growth conforms to a well-defined pattern of differentiation controlled by an organism's particular genetic makeup. Animal development proceeds through an orderly series of stages after fertilization, including the embryonic stages of the blastula and the gastrula. Plants have an open-ended, indeterminate growth pattern. That is, at least part of the plant's body continues to grow and develop throughout its life, and, although the development of the plant body is under genetic control, the environment can have a major influence on the final shape the plant takes. Because no organism lives isolated from the physical world, its genetic plan for growth and development and the rate at which this plan unfolds are affected also by the environment. Growth and development are powered by an intake of energy and are supported by the uptake of material resources. Thus, the body of an adult organism is characterized by structures that optimize the intake, transport, and use of necessary resources.

Organisms that obtain an ample share of resources have the potential to produce a greater number of offspring than their less successful competitors. One key to such a successful harvest of resources is efficiency. Division of labor at the level of cells can lead to such efficiency, a quality found in both unicellular and multicellular organisms. When an organ, a cell, or a molecule assumes a distinct role, the function of the structure may be greatly enhanced. The efficiency of a structure can be optimized by its form:

The broadness of leaves can contribute to more efficient capture of sunlight; the shape of molars helps grind food. Natural selection favors individuals with structures that are better suited to carrying out the demands of daily living, so the morphological characteristics of an organism contribute to its physiological needs. Not all organisms, however, have achieved the same resolution to environmental problems, so there are numerous adaptations for obtaining and using resources, many of them morphological. The environment may even directly affect the morphology of an organism, with limits to such changes in form imposed by the individual's genetic constitution. Although the form may help reveal function, it also is true that the function and habitat to which an organism has adapted can be inferred from the anatomy or morphology of a given structure. The enhancement of function due to the form of a structure is a phenomenon that is seen at the molecular, cellular, tissue, and organ level in the hierarchy of organization as well as in the overall morphology of the individual.

Principle 5: Energy, Matter, and Organization

Living systems are complex and highly organized, and they require matter and energy to maintain this organization. All living systems consist of organized matter composed of atoms. Their activities of life depend on the interactions between these atoms and their subatomic parts, so organisms and life processes conform to the principles of physics and chemistry regarding the conservation and transformation of energy and matter. Living organisms differ from their physical environment. They are different because they build a nonrandom selection of atoms from Earth's crust and atmosphere into small molecules held together by chemical bonds. Genes direct the building and maintenance of this organization.

From small molecules, larger, more complex molecules are built. The most important of these are the biological macromolecules—carbohydrates, lipids, proteins, and nucleic acids. These macromolecules have carbon skeletons, and all living systems are built of these macromolecules. Each type of organism may have macromolecules arranged in a unique way or have a few different elements added to the basic molecular structures. In some cells, macromolecules are organized into organelles, and organelles into cells. Cells are self-contained and are, at least partially, self-sufficient units that conduct the basic functions of life. Each cell has a membrane at its boundary that maintains cell integrity, provides structures for self-recognition, and aids in regulating the influx and outflow of materials. Each cell also contains genetic material that determines its functions.

The body of each organism is made of at least one cell, and all cells come from preexisting cells. Larger organisms may consist of trillions of cells arranged into a hierarchy of structures—tissues, organs, and organ systems—with each structure composed of units of the preceding level within the hierarchy. In turn, organ systems make up an individual, individuals make up populations, and populations are part of ecosystems. At each level within this hierarchy of biological organization, emergent properties appear that differentiate higher from lower levels. For instance, whereas cells exhibit characteristics of life, the macromolecules that make up the cell do not use energy, grow, or reproduce on their own. The many different types of cells reflect the myriad life forms on Earth, but, despite all the differences, organisms are unified by the processes within cells and the macromolecules that make up cells.

The complexity and organization of a living system are maintained by its metabolism, that is, the constant intake, conversion, and use of energy and matter. Matter provides the chemical building blocks for the structure of an organism, and energy is needed for these materials to be assembled and for the structure to be maintained. Without a constant supply of energy, the organization breaks down and the organism dies. In addition, the work done by organisms is powered by the energy taken in by individuals. For almost all organisms, the energy supporting the activities of life comes from the Sun—either directly or indirectly. Autotrophs obtain energy from the physical environment. The most important autotrophs are plants, which use the Sun's energy through photosynthesis to assimilate carbon into energy-rich macromolecules that they then use to grow and reproduce.

Heterotrophs rely on producers or other consumers for their resource needs, digesting food that supplies both energy and building materials. In more advanced animals, this process involves the interaction and coordination of the digestive, gas exchange, and circulatory systems. Living organisms, whether they are consumers or producers, undergo cellular respiration, during which the energy of macromolecules produced or taken in is transferred to readily usable high-energy molecules called ATP. This transfer may occur in the presence of oxygen or, in limited situations, without oxygen during anaerobic respiration. The complex chemical reactions of photosynthesis and respiration, as well as most other reactions, are controlled by specialized proteins called enzymes. Enzymes, which are organic catalysts, help process the energy and matter taken in and help maintain the organization of the cell.

Principle 6: Maintenance of a Dynamic Equilibrium

Living systems maintain a relatively stable internal environment through their regulatory mechanisms and behavior. An organism requires a relatively stable internal environment to obtain and use resources efficiently, to grow, and to reproduce. Organisms, however, are confronted by a constantly changing environment—one that varies on a daily, seasonal, and yearly basis. Many of these changes can be lethal, and living organisms therefore must have the capacity to adjust to or avoid these fluctuations. They must regulate the amount and type of materials they take in and the ways in which they use these materials. They also must avoid extreme fluctuations in internal temperature, maintain water balance, and eliminate waste products through excretion.

Homeostasis is the maintenance of a relatively stable internal environment within a varying external environment. To maintain that stability, an organism first must sense a change and then regulate its physiological activities to adjust. The ability to regulate is made possible by feedback mechanisms that sense changes inside and outside the organism and then respond to them. In response to environmental stimuli, organisms may, with different degrees of ability, regulate their body temperature and the chemical composition of their cells and defend themselves against foreign material and organisms. For example, the symptoms of disease are indicators that a host is regulating its internal environment after invasion by a disrupting pathogen. These highly specific defensive reactions are part of an animal's immune response. Some plants also produce chemicals that confer disease resistance on themselves because the chemicals are toxic to certain pathogens.

Organisms also may respond to the environment by switching chemical reactions on or off, transporting materials from one place to another, moving, or experiencing differential growth and reproduction under the influence of hormones, enzymes, or other chemicals. Hormones are organic molecules that regulate the function of specific tissues or organs. While growing and developing, a living system may adjust to changes in its environment—both inside and outside itself—through a combination of behavioral, physiological, and morphological changes.

All organisms respond to stimuli, or environmental cues. Plants, for example, may demonstrate tropisms in response to light and gravity. Animals respond to their environments through their behavior. Behavior is an individual's response to an environmental stimulus, a set of actions determined in part by the individual's genes and the physical manifestation of an internally orchestrated process. A behavioral response usually involves some action that must be coordinated among the activities of many cells. Such coordination depends on communication between the sensory receptor cells that receive stimuli from the environment and the motor response cells, such as muscles, that carry out the behavior. Communication may require hormones produced by the endocrine system. In organisms with well-developed nervous systems, communication involves neurons—highly modified cells that transmit information from sense receptors to a central nervous system and then to cells that respond. Such complex organisms also possess sophisticated means to sense the environment, bodily structures that allow quick reactions, and a brain to coordinate incoming stimuli and outgoing responses.

An organism's behavior encompasses a wide range of activities in response to particular stimuli important for its survival and reproduction. How an organism responds, where it goes, and what it does when it gets there all are aspects of its behavior. Such behavior may be innate, resulting in a complex, predictable response to a first-time encounter with a particular stimulus. As an animal matures, behavior related to reproduction may develop. More complex animals may learn and, therefore, modify their behavior based on some of the experiences they have accumulated. Because an animal does not live an isolated existence, it may exhibit territoriality against its rivals and altruism toward its gene-sharing relatives. It also may be part of a dominance hierarchy within the group it belongs to, another behavior of individuals within certain animal societies.

Twenty Major Biological Concepts

Table 3.1 lists 20 major biological concepts that can serve as a foundation for a core curriculum in biology. These concepts are linked to the associated unifying principles that all students at the high school level should understand at the end of their biology program.

We recommend that teachers use the six unifying principles described in this chapter to organize their biology program and consider the 20 major biological concepts for elaborating these principles to students. The six principles represent a comprehensive foundation for the biological sciences, based on the well-documented research of many biologists throughout the history of scientific investigation. The criteria in the following list were used to identify these principles:

- They reflect the most comprehensive, reliable information about living systems.
- They are well supported by scientific investigations.
- They incorporate fundamental knowledge for understanding living systems.
- They demonstrate the underlying unity of living systems.
- They are characteristic of all living systems.
- They are applicable to all levels of biological organization, from molecules to the biosphere.

Table 3.1 	Twenty Major Biological Concepts Related to the Six Unifying Principles

Unifying Principle	Major Biological Concepts
Evolution	• Patterns and products of evolution, including genetic variation and natural selection • Extinction • Conservation biology, including wise use of resources • Characteristics shared by all living systems • Overview of biodiversity, including specialization and adaptation demonstrated by living systems
Interactions and Interdependence	• Environmental factors and their effects on living systems • Carrying capacity and limiting factors • Community structure, including food webs and their constituents • Interactions among living systems • Ecosystems, nutrient cycles, and energy flow • The biosphere and how humans affect it
Genetic continuity and reproduction	• Genes and DNA, and the effect of interactions between genes and the environment on growth and development • Patterns of inheritance demonstrated in living systems • Patterns of sexual reproduction in living systems
Growth, development, and differentiation	• Patterns of development • Form and function
Energy, matter, and organization	• Hierarchy of organization in living systems • Metabolism, including enzymes and energy transformation
Maintenance of a dynamic equilibrium	• Homeostasis, the importance of feedback mechanisms, and certain behaviors • Human health and disease

Individual biology programs may emphasize a molecular, organismic, or ecological level of organization. They may give greater emphasis to inquiry or societal problems. The six unifying principles of biology, however, should provide the foundation for the biological knowledge in all of these contemporary biology programs.

Chapter 4

Attending to Conceptual Challenges*

Any teacher can relate to the experience of trying to respond to an off-the-wall question or answer from a student. Frequently, input from students will relate to the class material but appear to have little grounding in biologically accurate information. Where do students' strange questions and answers originate? Do they have any value for the teaching and learning process? How can teachers anticipate and work with them?

These questions are central to a large area of educational research about students' conceptual and reasoning difficulties in biology. The answers to these questions have important implications for how teachers view the role of student input and for the overall structure of the learning environment. In chapter 4, we examine some of the conceptual and reasoning difficulties commonly encountered within each unifying principle of biology, as well as those inherent to understanding the nature of science. We provide suggestions for teachers to uncover students who have these difficulties and strategies with which teachers can help students correct their own conceptions so they arrive at biologically accurate ideas about the world.

Student conceptions that are outside the scientific understanding of phenomena are known variably in the research as *misconceptions, naive conceptions, alternative conceptions,* and *preconceptions.* BSCS uses another term from the literature, *prior conceptions,* to reflect the idea that these are non-scientific conceptions that students frequently hold prior to instruction.

Where do conceptual and reasoning difficulties in biology originate? In part, they arise from the complexity of concepts and terminology that the study of biology presents. More than other sciences at the high school level, biology challenges students to construct integrated understanding over a wide range of microscopic and macroscopic scales. Students struggle to understand the language of biology as well—a large amount of new vocabulary is introduced in a biology course. Simply put, studying biology is challenging for the brain in several ways (Adams and Griffard 2001; Modell et al. 2005).

Conceptual and reasoning difficulties also emerge from students' mental models. Mental models are the sophisticated understandings of phenomena that people construct based on their personal experience and prior instruction. Although students' mental models are full of information, they are rarely entirely accurate. Inaccuracies may arise from the fact that students may not yet recognize that their personal experience is just a slice of the larger biological world. They may draw upon inaccurate mental models

---

*Adapted from BSCS. 2006. *BSCS biology: A human approach, teacher guide.* 3rd ed. Dubuque, IA: Kendall/Hunt.

of the chemical and physical world, or they may have misunderstood scientific language (Modell et al. 2005).

When students construct questions and answers in class, they are applying their mental models to a problem. When a mental model leads them to an inappropriate answer, they display a prior conception. These prior conceptions could stem from inaccurate information, the formation of an inappropriate connection between information, or a failure to integrate all relevant bits of information in a mental model (Modell et al. 2005). These may appear in the classroom as pseudoscientific or nonscientific beliefs, conceptual misunderstandings in which students fail to have a concrete understanding of a concept, vernacular misunderstandings in which a word has one meaning in everyday life and another in scientific terms, or factual misunderstandings in which a falsity is learned at an early age (Committee on Undergraduate Science Education 1997).

The presence of flaws in students' mental models and the prior conceptions that emerge from these flaws provide you with a tremendous opportunity for teaching and learning. As a teacher, your first inclination may be to correct those flaws for students by supplying accurate information. Research shows, however, that prior conceptions are extremely robust and persistent in the face of new information (Bransford et al. 2000). In fact, students can change their mental model only by confronting the flaw themselves (Modell et al. 2005). The best role a teacher can play is to give students opportunities to display prior conceptions, confront experiences that call those prior conceptions into question (also known as eliciting cognitive dissonance), and access information that helps them appropriately reconstruct their mental models.

You can prepare yourself to work with students' prior conceptions by becoming familiar with the most common prior conceptions in biology and by learning how to structure learning experiences to give students opportunities to become aware of and reconstruct their mental model. In general, students benefit from an opportunity to examine their mental models before beginning instruction for a particular topic. Strategies on how to prepare for handling specific prior conceptions are given throughout the remainder of this chapter.

Prior Conceptions About the Nature of Science

Students need a big-picture understanding of science to conduct and understand experiments. In an ideal sense, a student's nature-of-science mental model serves as the umbrella from which all other learning about science will hang. The nature of science is an area, however, in which students are likely to have weak mental models. Words like *model, theory,* and *law* have general meanings for students that differ from their scientific definitions. In fact, conflicting interpretations of these words provide fuel for several of the public controversies surrounding science in the United States (Bybee 2001).

It would seem that an inquiry-oriented curriculum would provide a way for students to build a robust mental model of the nature of science. Inquiry-oriented activities that do not draw students into an explicit discussion of the nature of science, however, may fail to affect students' mental models about the nature of science (Sandoval and Morrison 2003). Activities in which students are asked to explicitly use and reflect on the terminology of the nature of science will help you assess your students' current understanding of the nature of science. They will also facilitate common experiences that can help students recognize the roles that evidence, reasoning, and investigation play in scientific inquiry.

The Project 2061 *Atlas of Science Literacy* (AAAS 2001) notes that the principal middle school benchmark for understanding scientific investigations is central to nearly all aspects of students' understanding of the nature of science. That benchmark states, "Scientific investigations usually involve the collection of relevant evidence, the use of logical reasoning, and the application of imagination in devising hypotheses and explanations to make sense of the collected evidence." Many high school students hold the prior conception that the scientific method of investigation is a single, linear process, but in practice scientific investigations follow many models and are most frequently nonlinear in nature (Wivagg and Allchin 2002). Frequent use of a diagram similar to figure 4.1, combined with student reflections on their own inquiry processes, provides a way for students to revise their mental models around scientific method.

Students at the high school level have varying degrees of experience with designing scientific experiments. Although it is reasonable to expect high school students to understand the general procedure for planning experiments with controlled variables, it is likely that they will have difficulty identifying all the important variables. Furthermore, students are more likely to control those variables that they believe will affect the result (AAAS 2001). The nature of variables in scientific investigations can be explored in activities that allow the students the freedom to conduct experiments as they choose. In the discussion that emerges from their effort, you may call attention to the wide variety of variables present in the situation and the creativity each team exhibits.

In everyday life, high school students develop logical conclusions based on evidence (AAAS 2001), but many struggle with identifying and applying scientific evidence appropriately (McNeill and Krajcik 2007). Some

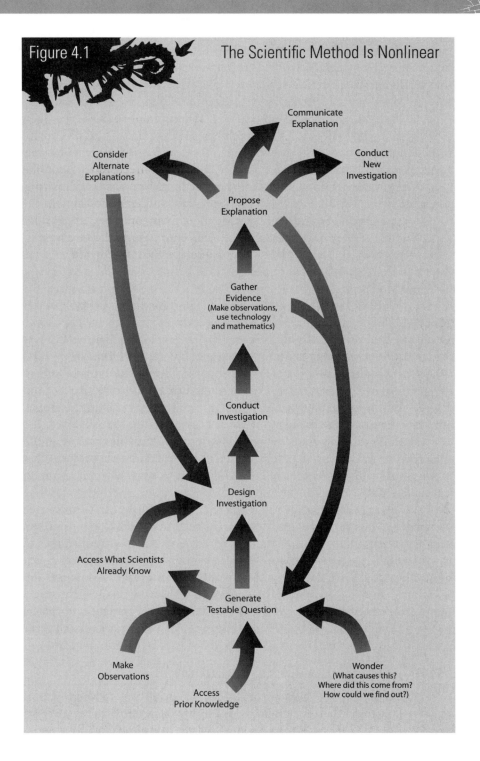

Figure 4.1

The Scientific Method Is Nonlinear

may also show a tendency to base conclusions on personal experiences rather than on scientific evidence (AAAS 2001). Students may believe that evidence selected from prior or secondhand knowledge provides an equally sound basis for scientific conclusions as information produced by experimentation provides (AAAS 2001). High school students are likely to recognize the inadequacies in conclusions drawn from invalid or insufficient data, but they will probably need prompting and practice to state their reasoning clearly (AAAS 2001).

To help students develop the ability to make and critique explanations, you must first allow adequate time for discussion and analysis following an inquiry experience. Students benefit even more from following a scaffolded approach to developing explanations. This approach includes assessing what constitutes evidence, identifying inferences that can be drawn from the evidence, verbalizing the logical reasoning that allows the inferences to be drawn, and articulating the explanation (claim, evidence, and reasoning) that summarizes the whole phenomenon being investigated (Kuhn et al. 2006; McNeill et al. 2006).

Providing students with a method for developing and evaluating explanations also helps them think critically about claims in general. Students may think that if a claim is reported or published it is true. Students who practice evaluating explanations will be more likely to examine reports for evidence from the design or results of a study to decide whether the claims are valid.

When conducting investigations, students display bias. For example, they tend to look for and accept evidence to explain the hypothesis that is consistent with their prior beliefs. They tend to distort or fail to generate evidence that is not in keeping with their preconceived ideas (AAAS 2001). They may also display the belief that all questions can be answered by science, when in fact science is limited to providing evidence only for testable questions. Allowing students to develop questions, and to identify those that are most easily testable, helps them begin to appreciate the limitations of scientific inquiry. The postexperiment discussion is also key in helping students recognize the presence of bias in science. By showing the variety of data collected and the conclusions drawn from similar investigations across one classroom, you can help students understand that scientific inquiry strives to avoid bias but that bias may be unavoidable.

Prior Conceptions About Evolution

Research into the benchmarks on biological evolution for high school students suggests that understanding evolution is tied to the students' understanding of the nature of science and their general reasoning abilities (AAAS 2001). Students with strong reasoning skills are equipped to examine critically the theory of evolution in light of the scientific evidence as well as alternative explanations they may encounter outside of school (AAAS 2001).

Natural selection is often misunderstood by middle and high school students who are confused by the different meanings and uses for the word *adaptation* (AAAS 2001). Students generally understand the everyday use of the word in which individuals and cultures adapt deliberately or through nonheritable processes. In contrast, biological adaptations are heritable and change over the course of generations in response to selective pressures from the environment (AAAS 2001). As a result, Lamarckian ideas are frequently a part of students' mental models before evolution instruction, and they are remarkably persistent (Crow 2004). Watch students closely for signs that they believe adaptations result from a conscious effort or overall purpose or design (AAAS 2001). To give students an opportunity to confront Lamarckian ideas in their mental model, you may have students examine the evidence for an evolutionary event and evaluate whether the Darwinian or the Lamarckian explanation better accounts for the evidence.

You may also find that students are unfamiliar with the ideas that adaptation in one generation may turn out to be insignificant or maladaptive in a subsequent generation and that natural selection does not favor only the fastest, strongest, and largest animals. Offering students multiple and varied examples of selection, documented in real time, helps them construct a more accurate view of selection.

The unifying principle of evolution also provides an opportunity for students to explore the widely accepted scientific explanation for the diversity of life on Earth. While many students resist accepting that evolution explains how species, including humans, are generated, the teacher's role is to present the evidence for this process while respecting students' varied beliefs. One clarification you can make is that while evolutionary explanations describe how species are generated, the process of evolution does not explain the origin of life.

Expect many students to have the prior conception that humans evolved from apes and to picture modern apes as the common ancestor to which scientists refer. High school and college-age students have great difficulty interpreting the evolutionary trees used to illustrate common ancestry and relationships between species. They fail to recognize that internal nodes represent ancestors, they misinterpret how the tree depicts time, and they do not use the lines connecting organisms as indications of relationship. Students' understanding of these diagrams is critical to their formation of an accurate mental model of evolution, but their learning must be scaffolded for them to develop the skills of reading traits from a tree, deducing ancestral traits, and reconstructing trees (Meir et al. 2007).

Many people have difficulty comprehending the expanse of time involved in producing the biodiversity we see today. Most people recognize that historical and geological events happened long ago but appear to conceive events in broad categories such as "extremely ancient," "moderately ancient," and "least ancient." Students struggle with sequencing events within these categories, and they may even think that events such as the origin of Earth and life occurred simultaneously (Libarkin et al. 2005; Trend 2001). Teachers may find that scaffolding students' learning about the relative order of important biological and geological events, before introducing absolute dates and dating methods, may be a more successful sequence with students unfamiliar with deep time (Trend 2001).

Concepts related to evolution, more than any of the other unifying principles, are challenging for some students not only because of conceptual difficulties but also because of real or perceived conflicts with students' beliefs. This aspect of teaching evolution is addressed in chapter 8.

Prior Conceptions About the Interaction and Interdependence of Life

The Project 2061 benchmarks for the Interdependence of Life standard note that students likely already recognize that species depend on one another and on the environment for survival. Activating students' prior knowledge of food webs, the water cycle, and sunlight dependency helps you guide them to construct a more sophisticated understanding of ecosystems, such as the kinds of relationships that organisms share and the complexity of food webs. Even at the high school level, however, students may hold a linear view of organismal interaction and are unlikely to recognize interactions other than predator-prey relationships (McComas 2002). Therefore, teachers cannot take students' prior understanding of the words *ecosystem* and *food web* for granted.

Conceptual and reasoning difficulties around ecosystem topics frequently stem from inadequate student mental models about matter and energy. If students fail to recognize that plants use carbon derived from carbon dioxide to build structures, they will express confusion when studying the cycling of carbon and other forms of matter through communities. Similarly, if students think that, once eaten, food energy disappears, they will struggle with understanding how energy flows through communities. Having students identify the sources of energy and matter in communities and tracing their transformation and flow through specific examples may help students overcome this conceptual difficulty and reinforce correct conceptions about matter and energy that they hold.

Students also may not understand the scientific meaning of the word *community*, because some hold the idea that communities are made of similar living things (Krebs 1999). A case in point is that while microbes play essential and multifaceted roles in ecosystems, these roles are frequently overlooked in biology instruction. Drawing out the microbial contribution to the flow of energy and matter through ecosystems helps provide balance to student conceptions of biological diversity as well as counter the common prior conception that most microbes cause disease.

Students' understanding of population dynamics, even following instruction, may tend toward extremes, like the idea that populations always grow until limits are reached and then crash (McComas 2002). Activities illustrating the maintenance of largely stable populations could help counter this prior conception.

Instruction around the unifying principle of the interaction and interdependence of life leads naturally into instruction related to environmental problems. When considering these, you may encounter the prior conception that an imbalance or change in species composition in an environment is always bad, or that, when biological communities are changed by humans, they are damaged forever (Krebs 1999). Examples of ecosystem resilience and recovery are essential if students are to place environmental problems and solutions into perspective. Furthermore, students benefit from opportunities that allow them to analyze various philosophies about the environment and distinguish these from the science of ecology. Frequently, the two are conflated, causing confusion about what instruction is purely scientific and what involves the application of science within the context of values to human decision making (Krebs 1999). This explains the controversial nature of some topics. See chapter 8 for more discussion and examples of different types of controversy in biology teaching.

Prior Conceptions About Genetic Continuity and Reproduction

Reproduction and inheritance are areas many students find fascinating. Nevertheless, high school students continue to have several prior conceptions about both reproduction and the inheritance of characteristics. The authors of *Making Sense of Secondary Science* summarize several incorrect ideas about reproduction that are common among middle school and high school students (Driver et al. 1994). Students often equate sexual reproduction with copulation. For example, many students consider in vitro fertilization an example of asexual reproduction. They do not understand that sexual reproduction is the fusion of specialized cells from two parents that does not necessarily require physical contact between the parents. Students also often assume that males of all species are larger and stronger than females and that the offspring produced by asexual reproduction are weaker than those produced by sexual reproduction.

The Project 2061 *Atlas of Science Literacy* (AAAS 2001) identifies several incorrect ideas that middle school students and some high school students often have about genetics and inheritance. Terminology is often a source of confusion for students when studying genetics (Pearson and Hughes 1988). Students often believe that *mutation* and *recessive* have negative connotations. Furthermore, they often associate the phrase *have the gene* with genetic disorders. Taking the example of cystic fibrosis, students may not integrate their prior knowledge that everyone has every gene in every cell. It is only when certain genes are mutated that there may sometimes be a condition such as cystic fibrosis. Students also struggle to understand that even if a person has a mutated gene, he or she will not necessarily develop a disorder, depending on the particular disease. To help address these problems, you should carefully define terms you use related to genetics and continue to use them in a very precise manner.

Some students believe that the characteristics of each parent are "blended" in their offspring. Other common, incorrect prior conceptions about heredity are that offspring inherit characteristics from just one parent, either the mother or the same-sex parent, or that certain characteristics are inherited solely from the mother and others are inherited solely from the father (AAAS 2001). Using a modeling activity for meiosis that begins with a small set of chromosomes, introduces students to crossing over, and ends after "fertilization" can help students recognize that genes are discrete entities inherited from both parents. The genes from each parent combine to form particular characteristics.

X-linked traits are also an area of confusion for many students. Students should understand that females may also inherit genes associated with X-linked traits from either their mothers or their fathers, or both. The incorrect idea that some characteristics produced by the environment can be inherited over several generations frequently persists among high school students (AAAS 2001). Students should understand the correct notion that populations have preexisting variations, some of which may be favored by changing environmental conditions. Over many generations, the favored variations become more prevalent in a population.

Research studies have found that upper middle school and high school students have some understanding that genes carry translatable information (AAAS 2001). They are less likely to understand that all cells carry all

DNA but that only certain genes are expressed based on the type of cell and its function.

Prior Conceptions About Growth and Differentiation

Ideas about growth and differentiation in living systems challenge students to consider development as more than simply a process of becoming larger. The benchmarks for students in grades 9–12 include understanding that embryonic development unfolds as a succession of mitotic cycles that result in increasing numbers of cells. Remarkable time-lapse images of developing organisms that can help dispel the common prior conception that embryonic growth occurs as a result of cells getting larger rather than by an increase in the number of cells are now frequently available online.

Students may eventually integrate their mental model of matter and energy with an understanding of animal growth, but often fail to do so with respect to plants. For example, students may state that "plant food" from the soil (as they have seen added to houseplants) is used for growth but that carbon dioxide is not needed. They may think that plants need sunlight for warmth rather than to supply energy needed for growth (Barman et al. 2006). Ironically, watching plants grow is a classic science lab that many students have experienced. Revisiting prior learning about matter and energy during activities related to animal and plant growth may help students construct appropriate mental models about the growth of all organisms.

In addition, students in grades 9–12 should come to understand that small differences in the environment in which embryonic cells develop cause them to develop slightly differently by activating or inactivating different parts of the genetic code (AAAS 2001). Most high school students, however, have little understanding of what determines differences between cells, particularly in light of the idea that nearly all cells contain a full complement of the organism's genetic code. Though there is limited research in this area, scaffolded activities that connect cellular and tissue features with specific genes that are turned "on" and "off" help students develop this understanding.

The benchmarks for grades 9–12 include understanding that the decisions of one generation may come to bear on another generation. But students have rarely made the connection between individual responsibility and human development. Activities that illuminate how human choices can lead to developmental errors or cancer can help students in their construction of a more sophisticated mental model.

In humans, development can be broadly understood to encompass the entirety of a lifetime. The Project 2061 *Atlas of Science Literacy* (AAAS

2001) identifies several incorrect prior conceptions related to how culture affects behavior. For example, research suggests that students tend to over-generalize information about racial and cultural differences. In fact, there is no biological basis to racial classifications (Marks 1996). Students benefit from the opportunity to compare human development among cultures. These learners are more likely to abandon the belief that some human cultures are biologically subordinate, which enhances their ability to reason about different worldviews (AAAS 2001).

Prior Conceptions About Energy, Matter, and Organization

The unifying principle of energy and matter in living systems is an area many students find challenging. It also is challenging for the teacher because the many incorrect prior conceptions are difficult to dislodge. The Project 2061 *Atlas of Science Literacy* identifies several incorrect prior conceptions related to matter and energy that high school students commonly have. Although students are likely to understand, at least vaguely, that food provides energy for their activities, they are less likely to understand that food also is the source of the molecules—the matter—they use for growth (AAAS 2001).

High school students tend not to recognize that the molecules in food must be transformed before they are incorporated into their bodies (AAAS 2001). They are likely to believe that the protein in the food they consume is directly incorporated into their muscles, instead of understanding that proteins and other nutrients are broken down into subunits, which are then rebuilt into the specific proteins and other macromolecules that make up their bodies. To address these prior conceptions, you could have students create models or animations or write stories that trace the path of matter through the body.

Concepts about food, nutrients, and macromolecules are often taught in a unit on diet and exercise. Related to this, students may also believe that muscle turns into fat or fat into muscle. Cells do not change from one type to another, however. Furthermore, the number of muscle and fat cells do not change in response to exercise, weight loss, or weight gain. Muscle and fat cells do change in size.

A common misunderstanding among high school students (as well as many adults) is that plants obtain food from the soil. It is difficult for students to replace this understanding with the correct conception that plants use carbon dioxide (an invisible gas) from their environment and energy from sunlight to make their own "food" internally (AAAS 2001). Furthermore, students have a number of difficulties with photosynthesis. One prior conception arises from the terminology used. Using the term *dark reactions* leaves students with the idea that this part of photosynthesis occurs only at night or in the dark (Lonergan 2000). You may address this by using the term *Calvin cycle* or *light-independent reactions* when referring to this process. Students also often have the misunderstanding that photosynthesis occurs during the day and cellular respiration occurs at night. In fact, plants carry out respiration continuously.

Although high school students understand that dead organisms and waste products from organisms decay, they may not realize that decomposition requires the activity of other living organisms (AAAS 2001). Students are frequently uncertain what happens to matter when it decays (AAAS 2001). It is useful to help them follow the transformations of matter from one component of an ecosystem to another to dispel the incorrect notion that matter is created and destroyed within each component.

Prior Conceptions About the Maintenance of a Dynamic Equilibrium

Students' understanding of dynamic equilibrium, or homeostasis, must include comprehension of the various elements involved as well as the ability to relate these processes to one another. For this reason, students often gain a partial understanding of the topic but find it difficult to have a complete understanding.

Much of students' prior knowledge of the concept of homeostasis likely is in the context of disease, in which balance is disrupted. According to the research into the benchmarks, upper-elementary students may believe that germs cause all illnesses (AAAS 2001). However, research also shows that as students grow older their understanding and beliefs grow to include the ideas that illness can be caused by malfunctioning internal organs and systems, poor health habits, and genetics (AAAS 2001). Related to this, students may also have the idea that most bacteria cause illness (Williams and Gillen 1991), but their knowledge should include information on bacteria that help maintain homeostasis in processes like digestion.

It is important to ensure that students understand the role and meaning of homeostasis in relation to other typical body processes as well. One prior conception students may have is that homeostasis represents a particular number or fixed value. For example, they may feel that blood sugar must return to a specific value after eating, at which point the level has returned to homeostasis. Other examples of prior conceptions can be seen if we look at students' responses to questions about the body after exercise. Some students indicated that increases in heart and breathing rates during exercise are attributed to the exercise itself, while others responded that blood is needed to continue exercising or that blood itself requires the increase in oxygen (Westbrook and Marek 1992).

You can do several things to help students learn about homeostasis. First, you can break down the process into the different variables and allow students to gain comprehension of each of these elements separately (Westbrook and Marek 1992). Then, work to relate the elements to provide the big picture of the process. In addition, homeostasis is a concept that students are often expected to learn without the benefit of concrete experience. Student investigations through case studies or experiments can give students the opportunity to experience the concrete results of this abstract physiological phenomenon (Westbrook and Marek 1992).

Conclusion

Students' prior knowledge is an important part of the learning process as it interacts with knowledge taught in the classroom. There are times, however, when prior concepts can cause undesirable results, sometimes to the point of preventing students from grasping new information that is presented. To address this, you must first become aware of and diagnose prior conceptions before beginning a lesson. Many of the most common prior conceptions were addressed throughout this chapter, but you should also make an effort to learn about the specific conceptions held by your own students. This may come in the form of a pretest, class discussion, or individual interviews.

Once prior conceptions have been identified, you should structure the learning environment in a way that provides students with opportunities to test their beliefs and prove the correct concepts to themselves. Inquiry-oriented learning that allows students time for discussion, cooperation, and engagement is often an effective means of establishing correct information and discounting misinformation. Strategies have been offered throughout this chapter on how to address particular misunderstandings.

As students begin to reshape their thinking, it is important for you to revisit prior conceptions a number of times. Often students' prior ideas have been ingrained for a long time, and discovering the correct concept on one occasion may not fully dislodge the inaccurate conception.

Helping students re-create their mental model of concepts is a difficult task. It often takes time away from other activities in the classroom. By addressing prior conceptions and allowing students to perform their own tests to support the correct ideas, however, you can help students learn correct concepts and ways of thinking. This is a way of learning that is not possible while incorrect prior knowledge is firmly held.

SECTION I REFERENCES

Adams, A. D., and P. B. Griffard. 2001. Analysis of alternative conceptions in physics and biology: Similarities, differences, and implications for conceptual change. Paper presented at the annual meeting of the National Association for Research in Science Teaching, St. Louis.

Aikenhead, G. S., and O. J. Jegede. 1999. Cross-cultural science education: A cognitive explanation of a cultural phenomenon. *Journal of Research in Science Teaching* 36 (3): 269–287.

American Association for the Advancement of Science (AAAS). 2001. *Atlas of science literacy.* Washington, DC: AAAS.

———2005. High School Biology Textbooks: A Benchmarks-Based Evaluation. At *http://www.project2061.org/publications/textbook/hsbio/report/default.htm.*

American Association of University Women (AAUW). 1992. *How schools shortchange girls.* Washington, DC: AAUW.

Ausubel, D., J. Novak, and H. Hanesian. 1978. *Educational psychology: A cognitive view.* New York: Holt, Rinehart, and Winston.

Barman, C. R., M. Stein, S. McNair, and N. S. Barman. 2006. Students' ideas about plants and plant growth. *American Biology Teacher* 68 (2): 73–79.

Bransford, J., A. Brown, and R. Cocking. 1999. *How people learn: Brain, mind, experience, and school.* Washington, DC: National Academy Press.

BSCS. 2006. *BSCS biology: A human approach.* Dubuque, IA: Kendall/Hunt.

Bunce, D. M., and D. Gabel. 2002. Differential effects on the achievement of males and females of teaching the particulate nature of chemistry. *Journal of Research in Science Teaching* 39: 911–927.

Bybee, R. W. 2001. Teaching about evolution: Old controversy, new challenges. *Bioscience* 51 (4): 309–312.

Clewell, B. C., and P. B. Campbell. 2002. Taking stock: Where we've been, where we are, where we're going. *Journal of Women and Minorities in Science and Engineering* 8: 255–284.

Cohen, D. K., and D. L. Ball. 2001. Making change: Instruction and its improvement. *Phi Delta Kappan* 83 (1): 73–77.

Committee on Undergraduate Science Education. 1997. Misconceptions as barriers to understanding science. In *Science teaching reconsidered: A handbook*, eds. Committee on Undergraduate Science Education, 27–32. Washington, DC: National Academy Press.

Creswell, J. L., and R. H. Exezidis. 1982. Research brief—Sex and ethnic differences in mathematics achievement of black and Mexican American adolescents. *Texas Technical Journal of Education* 9 (3): 219–222.

Crow, L. 2004. Lamarck is sitting in the front row. *Journal of College Science Teaching* 34 (1): 64–65.

Dill, B. T. 1983/1994. Race, class, and gender: Prospects for an all-inclusive sisterhood. In *The education feminism reader*, eds. L. Stone and G. M. Boldt, 42–56. New York: Routledge. Repr. *Feminist Studies* 9 (1): 130–50.

Driver, R., A. Squires, P. Rushworth, and V. Wood-Robinson. 1994. *Making sense of secondary science: Research into children's ideas*. New York: Routledge.

Gadgil, A. J. 1998. Drinking water in the developing countries. *Annual Review of Energy and the Environment* 23: 253–286.

Gillibrand, E., P. Robinson, R. Brawn, and A. Osborn. 1999. Girls' participation in physics in single sex classes in mixed schools in relation to confidence and achievement. *International Journal of Science Education* 21: 349–362.

Griffard, P. B., and J. H. Wandersee. 1999. Challenges to meaningful learning in African-American females at an urban science high school. *International Journal of Science Education* 21: 611–632.

Haberman, M. 1991. The pedagogy of poverty versus good teaching. *Phi Delta Kappan* 73: 290–294.

Hanson, S. L., and E. P. Johnson. 2000. Expecting the unexpected: A comparative study of African-American women's experiences in science during the high school years. *Journal of Women and Minorities in Science and Engineering* 6: 265–294.

Harding, S. 2001. After absolute neutrality: Expanding science. In *Feminist science studies: A new generation*, eds. M. Mayberry, B. Subramaniam, and L. H. Weasel, 291–304. New York: Routledge.

Haussler, P., and L. Hoffmann. 2002. An intervention study to enhance girls' interest, self-concept, and achievement in physics classes. *Journal of Research in Science Teaching* 39: 870–888.

Houston, B. 1985/1994. Should public education be gender free? In *The education feminism reader*, eds. L. Stone and G. M. Boldt, 122–134. New York: Routledge. Repr. *Educational Theory* 35 (4): 359–370.

Hueftle, J. J., S. J. Rakow, and W. W. Welch. 1983. *Images of science*. Minneapolis: University of Minnesota, Science Assessment and Research Project.

Johnson, D. W., R. T. Johnson, and K. A. Smith. 1991. *Active learning: Cooperation in the college classroom*. Edina, MN: Interaction Book Company.

Johnson, D. W., R. T. Johnson, M. B. Stanne, and A. Garibaldi. 1990. Impact of group processing on achievement in cooperative groups. *Journal of Social Psychology* 130 (4): 507–516.

Kahle, J. B., J. Meece, and K. Scantlebury. 2000. Urban African-American middle school science students: Does standards-based teaching make a difference? *Journal of Research in Science Teaching* 37 (9): 1019–1041.

Keller, E. F. 1985. *Reflections on gender and science.* New Haven, CT: Yale University Press.

Kowalski, S. M. 2008. Students, language, and physics: Discourse in the science classroom. Paper presented at the meeting of the National Association for Research in Science Teaching, Baltimore.

Krebs, R. E. 1999. *Scientific development and misconceptions through the ages.* Westport, CT: Greenwood Press.

Kuhn, L., L. O. Kenyon, and B. J. Reiser. 2006. Fostering scientific argumentation by creating a need for students to attend to each other's claims and evidence. In *Seventh annual international conference of the learning sciences*, eds. S. A. Barab, K. E. Hay, and D. T. Hickey, 370–375. Mahwah, NJ: Lawrence Erlbaum Associates.

Kurth, L. A., C. W. Anderson, and A. S. Palincsar. 2002. The case of Carla: Dilemmas of helping *all* students to understand science. *Science Education* 86: 287–313.

Labudde, P., W. Herzog, M. P. Neuenschwander, E. Violi, and C. Gerber. 2000. Girls and physics: Teaching and learning strategies tested by classroom interventions in grade 11. *International Journal of Science Education* 22 (2): 143–157.

Lee, C. D. 2003. Why we need to re-think race and ethnicity in educational research. *Educational Researcher* 32 (5): 3–5.

Lee, O. 1999. Science knowledge, world views, and information sources in social and cultural contexts: Making sense after a natural disaster. *American Educational Research Journal* 36 (2): 187–219.

Lee, O., and M. A. Avalos. 2002. Promoting science instruction and assessment for English language learners. *Electronic Journal of Science Education* 7 (2): 99–122.

Lemke, J. L. 1990. *Talking science: Language, learning, and values.* Norwood, NJ: Ablex Publishing.

Libarkin, J. C., S. W. Anderson, J. D. Science, M. Beilfuss, and W. Boone. 2005. Qualitative analysis of college students' ideas about the Earth: Interviews and open-ended questionnaires. *Journal of Geoscience Education* 53 (1):17–26.

Lonergan, T. A. 2000. The photosynthetic dark reactions do not operate in the dark. *American Biology Teacher* 62: 166–170.

Loucks-Horsley, S., K. Stiles, and P. Hewson. 1996. Principles of effective professional development for mathematics and science education: A synthesis of standards. *NISE Brief* 1 (May): 1–6.

Lynch, S. J. 2000. *Equity and science education reform.* Mahwah, NJ: Lawrence Erlbaum.

Marks, J. 1996. Science and race. *American Behavioral Scientist* 40 (2): 123–133.

Marx, R. W., P. C. Blumenfield, J. S. Karjcik, B. Fishman, E. Soloway, R. Geier, and R. T. Tal. 2004. Inquiry-based science in the middle grades: Assessment of learning in urban systemic reform. *Journal of Research in Science Teaching* 41 (10): 1063–1080.

Mau, W., M. Domnick, and R. A. Ellsworth. 1995. Characteristics of female students who aspire to science and engineering or homemaking occupations. *The Career Development Quarterly* 43: 323–337.

McComas. 2002. The ideal environmental science curriculum: I. History, rationales, misconceptions and standards. *American Biology Teacher* 64 (9): 665–672.

McNeill, K. L., and J. Krajcik. 2007. Middle school students' use of appropriate and inappropriate evidence in writing scientific explanations. In *Thinking with data*, eds. M. Lovett and P. Shah, 233–266. Mahwah, NJ: Lawrence Erlbaum Associates.

McNeill, K. L., D. J. Lizotte, J. Krajcik, and R. W. Marx. 2006. Supporting students' construction of scientific explanations by fading scaffolds in instructional materials. *Journal of the Learning Sciences* 15 (2): 153–191.

Meir, E., J. Perry, J. C. Herron, and J. Kingsolver. 2007. College students' misconceptions about evolutionary trees. *American Biology Teacher* 69 (7): e71–e76.

Modell, H., J. Michael, and M. Wenderoth. 2005. Helping the learner to learn: The role of uncovering misconceptions. *American Biology Teacher* 67 (1): 20–26.

Morse, M. P., and American Institute of Biological Sciences (AIBS). 2001. *A review of biological instructional materials for secondary schools.* Washington, DC: American Institute of Biological Sciences.

National Research Council (NRC). 1996. *National Science Education Standards.* Washington, DC: National Academy Press.

National Science Foundation (NSF). 1999. *Women, minorities, and persons with disabilities in science and engineering: 1998.* Washington, DC: NSF.

Palincsar, A. S., S. J. Magnusson, K. M. Collins, and J. Cutter. 2001. Making science accessible to all: Results of a design experiment in inclusive classrooms. *Learning Disability Quarterly* 24: 15–32.

Pearson, J. T., and W. J. Hughes. 1988. Problems with the use of terminology in genetics education: 1. A literature review and classification scheme. *Journal of Biological Education* 22 (3): 178–182.

Posner, G. J., K. A. Strike, P. W. Hewson, and W. A. Gerzog. 1982. Accommodation of a scientific conception: Toward a theory of conceptual change. *Science Education* 66 (2): 211–227.

Powell, J. C., J. B. Short, and N. M. Landes. 2002. Curriculum reform, professional development, and powerful learning. In *Learning science and the science of learning*, ed. R. W. Bybee, 131–136. Arlington, VA: NSTA Press.

Rosser, S. V. 1995. Reaching the majority: Retaining women in the pipeline. In *Teaching the majority: Breaking the gender barrier in science, mathematics, and engineering*, ed. S. V. Rosser, 1–21. New York: Teachers College Press.

———. 1997. *Re-engineering female friendly science.* New York: Teachers College Press.

———. 2000. *Women, science, and society: The crucial union.* New York: Teachers College Press.

Sadker, M., and D. Sadker. 1994. *Failing at fairness: How America's schools cheat girls.* New York: Maxwell Macmillan International.

Sandoval, W. A., and K. Morrison. 2003. High school students' ideas about theories and theory change after a biological inquiry unit. *Journal of Research in Science Teaching* 40 (4): 369–392.

Schmidt, W. H., C. C. McKnight, L. S. Cogan, P. M. Jakwerth, and R. T. Houang. 1999. *Facing the consequences: Using TIMSS for a closer look at U.S. mathematics and science.* Boston: Kluwer Academic.

Shakespeare, P., P. Kelleher, and L. Moxam, L. 2007. Soft skills, hard skills, and practice identity. Paper presented at the World Conference of Cooperative Education, Singapore.

Shulman, L. S. 1986. Those who understand: Knowledge growth in teaching. *Educational Researcher* 15 (2): 4–14.

Slavin, R. E., and E. Oickle. 1981. Effects of cooperative learning teams on student achievement and race relations: Treatment by race interactions. *Sociology of Education* 54 (3): 174–180.

Smith, C., S. Carey, and M. Wiser. 1985. On differentiation: A case study of the development of the concepts of size, weight, and density. *Cognition* 21: 177–237.

Spencer, R., M. V. Porche, and D. L. Tolman. 2003. We've come a long way—maybe: New challenges for gender equity in education. *Teachers College Record* 105 (9), 1774–1807.

Sweller, J. 1999. *Instructional design in technical areas.* Camberwell, Victoria, Australia: Acer Press.

Thompson, C., and J. Zeuli. 1999. The frame and the tapestry: Standards-based reform and professional development. In *Teaching as the learning profession*, eds. L. Darling-Hammond and G. Sykes, 341–375. San Francisco: Jossey-Bass.

Trend, R. D. 2001. Deep time framework: A preliminary study of U.K. primary teachers' conceptions of geological time and perceptions of geoscience. *Journal of Research in Science Teaching* 38 (2): 191–221.

United Nations. 1966. International covenant on economic, social and cultural rights. Office of the United Nations High Commissioner for Human Rights: *www.unhchr.ch/html/menu3/b/a_cescr.htm.*

Vygotsky, L. S. 1968. *Thought and language.* Trans. and ed. A. Kozulin. Cambridge, MA: MIT Press.

Westbrook, S. L., and E. A. Marek. 1992. A cross-age study of student understanding of the concept of homeostasis. *Journal of Research in Science Teaching* 29 (1): 51–61.

Williams, R. P., and A. L. Gillen. 1991. Microbe phobia and kitchen microbiology. *American Biology Teacher* 53 (1): 10–11.

Wivagg, D., and D. Allchin. 2002. The dogma of "the" scientific method. *American Biology Teacher* 64 (9): 645–646.

Section II

Introduction

Invitations to Inquiry

Teaching science as authoritative facts and dogma has an extremely bad effect on students' attitudes toward science and scientists. That method divorces the conclusions of science from the data and the conceptual frameworks that give the conclusions meaning. As a consequence, students can learn an unintended lesson: Science is unreliable and unrelated to reality. Consider students who have the impression that science consists of unalterable truths. Five or 10 years after graduation, they discover that much of what they learned has become obsolete and has been replaced.

Unprepared for the changes and unaware of what produced them, students doubt the soundness of their textbooks and teachers. The doubt can become a doubt of science itself and of professional competence in general. The former students have no recourse but to fall into a dangerous relativism or cynicism. Many students do not learn to discriminate the conceptual from the physical. For them, a change in scientific knowledge is unexpected and incomprehensible because it is a change in what they believed to be fixed and certain. Because they do not understand that some of the things they were taught were not literal facts, but rather data embodied and organized into ideas, these students cannot account for the changes. They are further confused by statements that refer to things they never learned at all. These experiences can reinforce their impression that science is whimsical or mysterious and has no relevance to everyday realities.

Teaching science as inquiry can prevent these consequences and show students how knowledge arises from the interpretation of data. Students learn that the interpretation of data—even the search for data—proceeds from a foundation of concepts and assumptions that changes as knowledge grows. Students learn that knowledge changes and changes for good reason: We know more than we knew before. They also learn the converse: Although present knowledge may be revised, present knowledge is not false. Present knowledge in science is based on the best-tested data and concepts we currently possess. Merely telling students how knowledge arises from data and how it changes is not enough. Students must experience science in operation, not talk about science as only a summation of what has been demonstrated.

Chapter 5

What Is Inquiry?

Section II

Scientific inquiry refers to the diverse ways in which scientists study the natural world and propose explanations based on the evidence derived from their work. Inquiry also refers to the activities of students in which they develop knowledge and understanding of scientific ideas, as well as an understanding of how scientists study the natural world.
—*National Research Council,* National Science Education Standards, *1996, p. 23*

To a scientist, *inquiry* refers to an intellectual process that humans have practiced for thousands of years. The history of inquiry in American science education, however, is much briefer. Until about 1900, science education was regarded as getting students to memorize a collection of facts. In fact, many of today's teachers and students can confirm that this approach is still with us. In 1910, educator and philosopher John Dewey criticized this state of affairs in science education. He argued that science should be taught as a way of thinking. According to this view, science should be taught as a process (NRC 2000). During the 1950s and 1960s, educator Joseph Schwab (1966) observed that science was being driven by a new vision of scientific inquiry. In Schwab's view, science was no longer a process for revealing stable truths about the world but instead reflected a flexible process of inquiry. He characterized inquiry as either "stable" or "fluid." Stable inquiry involves using current understanding to "fill a … blank space in a growing body of knowledge." Fluid inquiry involves the creation of new concepts that revolutionize science.

So that science education would reflect the modern practice of science more accurately, Schwab advocated placing students in the laboratory immediately. There, students could ask questions and begin the process of collecting evidence and constructing explanations. Schwab described three levels of openness in laboratory instruction. At the most basic level, the educational materials pose questions and provide methods for students to discover relationships for themselves. At the second level, the materials again pose questions, but the methods of discovering relationships are left to the students to devise. At the third, most sophisticated level, the materials present phenomena without posing questions. The students must generate their own questions, gather evidence, and propose explanations based on their work (Bybee

2000). This approach stands in contrast to the more typical one, in which a teacher begins by explaining what will happen in the laboratory session.

The Nature of Scientific Inquiry: Science as a Way of Knowing

An important aspect of scientific inquiry is that science is only one of many ways that people explore, explain, and come to know the world around them. There are threads of inquiry and discovery in almost every way that humans know the world. All of the ways of knowing contribute to humanity's general body of knowledge. Each way of knowing addresses different issues and answers different questions. Science is a way of knowing that accumulates data from observations and experiments, draws evidence-based conclusions, and tries to explain things about the natural world. Science excludes supernatural explanations and personal wishes.

In some ways of knowing, the meaning of statements or products is open to interpretation by any viewer. Science is different because it is characterized by a specific process of investigation that acquires evidence to support or reject a particular explanation of the world. Although the meaning of the evidence can be debated, the evidence itself is based on careful measurement and can be reproducibly collected by any individual using appropriate techniques.

Inquiry and Learning

Several years ago, the National Research Council (NRC) released the report *How People Learn* (NRC 1999). It brought together findings on student learning from various disciplines, including cognition, neurobiology, and child development. Research demonstrates that experts tend to solve problems by applying their knowledge of major concepts, or big ideas. Novices tend to seek simple answers consistent with their everyday expectations about how the world works. Science curricula that stress depth over breadth provide the time necessary for students to organize their understanding in such a way that they can see the big picture as the experts do.

Some of the findings from the NRC report that are relevant to inquiry are summarized in an addendum to the *National Science Education Standards* titled *Inquiry and the National Science Education Standards* (NRC 2000). A brief description of these findings follows:

1. *Understanding science is more than knowing facts.* According to noted biologist John A. Moore (1993), science is a way of knowing. More than a collection of facts, science is a process by which scientists learn about the world and solve problems. Scientists, of course, have many facts at their disposal, but how these facts are stored, retrieved, and applied is

what distinguishes science from other ways of knowing. Scientists organize information into conceptual frameworks that allow them to make connections between major concepts. They are able to transfer their knowledge from one context to another. The conceptual frameworks affect how scientists perceive and interact with the world. They also help scientists maximize the effectiveness of their use of inquiry.

Students may perceive science not as a way of knowing about their world but rather as facts that must be memorized. They may view parents, peers, and the media as their primary sources of information about what is happening and what should happen. It is important for students to distinguish science as a way of knowing from other ways of knowing by recognizing that, with science, they can find evidence-based answers to questions.

2. *Students build new knowledge and understanding based on what they already know and believe.* The knowledge and beliefs that students bring with them to the classroom affect their learning. If their understanding is consistent with the currently accepted scientific explanation, it can serve as a foundation upon which they can build a deeper understanding. If, however, students hold beliefs that run counter to prevailing science, it may be difficult to change their thinking. Usually students have an understanding that is correct within a limited context. Problems arise when they attempt to apply this understanding to contexts that involve factors they have not yet encountered or considered.

They should know that decisions should be based on empirical evidence rather than on the perception of evidence. Simply telling students the correct answer is not likely to change their way of thinking.

But inquiry-based instruction provides opportunities for students to experience scientific phenomena and processes directly. These direct experiences challenge deeply entrenched misconceptions and foster dialogue about new ideas, moving students closer to scientifically accepted explanations.

3. *Students formulate new knowledge by modifying and refining their current concepts and by adding new concepts to what they already know.* Two things must occur for students to change their conceptual framework. First, they must realize that their understanding is inadequate. This happens when they cannot satisfactorily account for an event or observation. Second, they must recognize an alternative explanation that better accounts for the event or observation and that is understandable to them.

4. *Learning is mediated by the social environment in which learners interact with others.* This finding goes beyond the idea that two heads are better than one. As is also true for scientists, students do not construct their understanding in isolation. They test and refine their thinking through interactions with others. Simply articulating ideas to another person helps students realize what knowledge they feel comfortable with and what knowledge they lack. By listening to other points of view, students are exposed to new ideas that challenge them to revise their own thinking.

5. *Effective learning requires that students take control of their own learning.* Good learners are metacognitive. This means that they are aware of their own learning and can analyze and modify it when necessary. Specifically, students must be able to recognize when their understanding conflicts with evidence. They must be able to identify what type of evidence they need in order to test their ideas and to modify their beliefs in a manner consistent with that evidence.

6. *The ability to apply knowledge to novel situations (that is, to transfer learning) is affected by the degree to which students learn with understanding.* Ideally, students solidify their learning by applying their understanding to new contexts. They receive feedback from experiences in these new situations and modify their learning accordingly. This process is facilitated by their doing tasks they see as useful and that are appropriate to their skill level. Allowing adequate time for students to acquire new information and make connections to their prior knowledge is essential.

The NRC research findings point out similarities between students' natural curiosity and methods of inquiring about the world and scientists' more formal approach to problem solving. As both children and adults learn, they pass through similar stages of discovery. As stated in *How People Learn:*

> An alternative to simply processing through a series of exercises that derive from a scope and sequence chart is to expose students to the major features of a subject domain as they arise naturally in problem situations. Activities can be structured so that students are able to explore, explain, extend, and evaluate their progress. Ideas are best introduced when students see a need or a reason for their use—this helps them see relevant uses of knowledge to make sense of what they are learning (Bransford et al. 1999, p. 139).

Inquiry in the Classroom

Inquiry-based instruction offers an opportunity to engage student interest in scientific investigation, sharpen critical-thinking skills, distinguish science from pseudoscience, increase awareness of the importance of basic research, and humanize the image of scientists. The process by which students acquire their understandings and abilities of inquiry continues during their school career. The practice of inquiry cannot be reduced to a simple set of instructions.

The science classroom changes as we learn more about how people learn and what constitutes effective teaching practices. Hands-on experiments should receive less emphasis than forming explanations based on evidence and communicating scientific understanding to others. Applying the results of experiments to scientific arguments demonstrates a more complete understanding of scientific inquiry than simply ending an investigation once a result is obtained.

Students who engage in inquiry develop

- an understanding of scientific concepts,
- an appreciation of how we know what we know in science,
- an understanding of the nature of science,
- skills necessary to become independent inquirers about the natural world, and
- tendencies to use their understanding and abilities in science when analyzing new information.

Inquiry is more than just the processes of science. It is an area of science content. The *NSES* (NRC 1996) details specific standards related to both the abilities necessary to do scientific inquiry and the understandings about scientific inquiry. If students meet the standards for abilities necessary to

Table 5.1	Abilities Necessary to Do Scientific Inquiry: Grades 9–12

- Identify questions and concepts that guide scientific investigations.
- Design and conduct scientific investigations.
- Use technology and mathematics to improve investigations and communications.
- Formulate and revise scientific explanations and models using logic and evidence.
- Recognize and analyze alternative explanations and models.
- Communicate and defend a scientific argument.

Source: National Research Council. 1996. *National science education standards.* Washington, DC: National Academy Press.

Table 5.2	Understandings About Scientific Inquiry: Grades 9–12

- Scientists usually inquire about how physical, living, or designed systems function. Conceptual principles and knowledge guide scientific inquiries. Historical and current scientific knowledge influence the design and interpretation of investigations and the evaluation of proposed explanations made by other scientists.
- Scientists conduct investigations for a wide variety of reasons. For example, they may wish to discover new aspects of the natural world, explain recently observed phenomena, or test the conclusions of prior investigations or the predictions of current theories.
- Scientists rely on technology to enhance the gathering and manipulation of data. New techniques and tools provide new evidence to guide inquiry and new methods to gather data, thereby contributing to the advance of science. The accuracy and precision of the data, and therefore the quality of the exploration, depends on the technology used.
- Mathematics is essential in scientific inquiry. Mathematical tools and models guide and improve the posing of questions, gathering data, constructing explanations and communicating results.
- Scientific explanations must adhere to criteria such as: a proposed explanation must be logically consistent; it must abide by the rules of evidence; it must be open to questions and possible modification; and it must be based on historical and current scientific knowledge.
- Results of scientific inquiry—new knowledge and methods—emerge from different types of investigations and public communication among scientists. In communicating and defending the results of scientific inquiry, arguments must be logical and demonstrate connections between natural phenomena, investigations, and the historical body of scientific knowledge. In addition, the methods and procedures that scientists used to obtain evidence must be clearly reported to enhance opportunities for further investigation.

Source: National Research Council. 1996. *National Science Education Standards*. Washington, DC: National Academy Press.

do scientific inquiry, they have some proficiency in the skills that scientists use to investigate the natural world. When students meet the standards for understandings about scientific inquiry, they demonstrate a recognition of why scientists work in the way they do and what makes scientific inquiry different from other types of knowledge. The National Science Education Standards for the abilities and understandings about inquiry that students in grades 9–12 should meet are included in tables 5.1 and 5.2.

The Five Essential Features of Inquiry

If you asked a group of people what inquiry-based learning experiences look like in the classroom, you would get as many answers as people in the group. In *Inquiry and the National Science Education Standards*, the National Research Council (2000) specifies five essential features of inquiry teaching and learning that apply across all grade levels:

1. *Learners are engaged by scientifically oriented questions.* Scientists recognize two primary types of questions. The *existence* questions often ask why: "Why do some animals have hair?" and "Why do we sleep?" *Causal* questions ask how: "How does a mountain form?" "How does an insect breathe?" Although science can usually answer causal questions, it cannot always answer existence questions. The teacher plays a critical role in guiding students to questions that can be answered with means at their disposal. Sometimes this simply involves changing a "why" question to a "how" question.

2. *Learners give priority to evidence, which allows them to develop and evaluate explanations that address scientifically oriented questions.* Scientists obtain evidence as scientific data by recording observations and making measurements. The accuracy of data can be checked by repeating the observations or making new measurements. In the classroom, students use data to construct explanations for scientific phenomena. According to the NSES, "explanations of how the natural world changes based on myths, personal beliefs, religious values, mystical inspiration, superstition, or authority may be personally useful and socially relevant, but they are not scientific."

3. *Learners formulate explanations from evidence to address scientifically oriented questions.* This element of inquiry differs from the previous one in that it stresses the path from evidence to explanation, rather than the criteria used to define evidence. Scientific explanations are consistent with the available evidence and are subject to criticism and revision. Furthermore, scientific explanations extend beyond current knowledge and propose new understanding that extends the knowledge base. In a similar way, students who generate new ideas by building on their personal knowledge base also extend their knowledge and understanding.

4. *Learners evaluate their explanations in light of alternative explanations, particularly those reflecting scientific understanding.* Scientific inquiry differs from other forms of inquiry in that proposed explanations may be revised or thrown out altogether in light of new information. Students can consider alternative explanations as they compare their

results with those of others. They should become aware of how their results relate to current scientific knowledge.

5. *Learners communicate and justify their proposed explanations.* Scientists communicate their results in enough detail that other scientists can attempt to reproduce their work, providing science with an important vehicle for quality control. Other scientists can use the results to investigate new but related questions. Students, too, benefit by sharing their results with their classmates, giving them an opportunity to ask questions, examine evidence, identify faulty reasoning, consider whether conclusions go beyond the data, and suggest alternative explanations.

Full Versus Partial Inquiry

Inquiry lessons can be described as either full or partial with respect to the five essential features of inquiry described in table 5.3. Full inquiry lessons use each element, although any individual element can vary according to how much direction comes from the learner and how much comes from the teacher. For example, inquiry begins with a scientifically oriented question. This question may come from the student, the student may choose the question from a list, or the teacher may simply provide the question.

Inquiry lessons are described as partial when one or more of the five essential features of inquiry are missing. For example, if a teacher demonstrates how something works rather than allowing students to discover it for themselves, then that lesson is regarded as partial inquiry. Lessons that vary in their level of direction develop students' inquiry abilities. When teachers first introduce young children to inquiry lessons, the children are not developmentally or academically ready to benefit from full inquiry lessons. Partial or guided inquiry lessons usually work for them. Guided inquiry may also work well when the goal is to have students learn a particular science concept. In contrast, a full or open inquiry is preferable when the goal is to have students hone their skills of scientific reasoning.

Misconceptions About Inquiry-Based Instruction

Despite the consensus found in educational research, teachers may have different ideas about the meaning of inquiry-based instruction. At one extreme are teachers who believe they are practicing inquiry by posing questions to their students and guiding them toward answers. At the other extreme are teachers who feel they are not practicing inquiry unless they allow their students to engage in a lengthy open-ended process that directly mimics scientific research. Given these two extremes, it is not surprising that misconceptions about inquiry-based instruction abound. Some of the more prevalent misconceptions have been wrongly attributed

| Table 5.3 | Essential Features of Classroom Inquiry and Their Variations | | | |

Essential Feature	Variations			
Learner engages in scientifically oriented questions.	Learner poses a question.	Learner selects among questions, poses new questions.	Learner sharpens or clarifies a question provided by the teacher, materials, or other source.	Learner engages in a question provided by the teacher, materials, or other source.
Learner gives priority to evidence in responding to questions.	Learner determines what constitutes evidence and collects it.	Learner is directed to collect certain data.	Learner is given data and asked to analyze.	Learner is given data and told how to analyze.
Learner formulates explanations from evidence.	Learner formulates explanations after summarizing evidence.	Learner is guided in process of formulating explanations from evidence.	Learner is given possible ways to use evidence to formulate explanation.	Learner is provided with evidence.
Learner connects explanations to scientific knowledge.	Learner independently examines other resources and forms the links to explanations.	Learner is directed toward areas and sources of scientific knowledge.	Learner is given possible connections.	
Learner communicates and justifies explanations.	Learner forms reasonable and logical argument to communicate explanation.	Learner is coached in development of communication.	Learner is provided broad guidelines to use to sharpen communication.	Learner is given steps and procedures for communication.

More ← — Amount of Learner Self-Direction — → Less
Less ← — Amount of Direction From Teacher Material — → More

Source: National Research Council. 2000. *Inquiry and the National Science Education Standards: A guide for teaching and learning.* Washington, DC: National Academy Press.

to the NSES. These mistaken notions about inquiry deter efforts to reform science education. The materials in this handbook are designed to dispel misconceptions about inquiry-based instruction.

Misconception 1: Inquiry-based instruction is the application of the "scientific method." Teachers have a tendency to teach their students in the same way that they were taught. Many teachers learned as students that science is a method for answering questions and solving problems. They were told that the process of science can be reduced to a series of five or six simple steps. This concept of the scientific method in American science education goes back to John Dewey during the first part of the 20th century. In reality, there is no single scientific method. Scientists routinely use a variety of approaches, techniques, and processes in their work. The notion that scientific inquiry can be reduced to a simple, step-by-step procedure is misleading and fails to acknowledge the creativity inherent in the scientific process.

Misconception 2: Inquiry-based instruction requires that students generate and pursue their own questions. For some teachers, open-ended inquiry seems to best mirror the process of inquiry practiced by scientists. They may believe that if open-ended inquiry is not possible then they should resort to more traditional forms of instruction. In fact, no single form of inquiry is best in every situation. In many instances, the goal is that students learn some specific science content. In such cases, the questions themselves, not their sources, are most important. Even if the teacher provides the student with a question, an inquiry-based approach to the answer is still possible.

Misconception 3: Inquiry-based instruction can take place without attention to science concepts. During the 1960s, it became fashionable to promote the idea of process over substance. Teachers were sometimes told that they (and their students) could learn the process of inquiry in isolation and then apply it on their own to subject matter of their choice. This elevation of process over substance, however, ignores lessons learned from research on student learning, which tell us that students first begin to construct their learning using their prior knowledge of the topic and then inquire into areas that they do not yet understand. The *NSES* clearly indicates that students need to learn both scientific concepts and the abilities of and understanding about scientific inquiry. People who have expertise in a field need both a deep understanding of subject matter content and facility with inquiry processes to solve problems and develop new understanding.

Misconception 4: All science should be taught through inquiry-based instruction. Inquiry-based instruction is a tool used by teachers to help them attain educational goals for their students. Despite its usefulness, inquiry is not the most appropriate tool for every instructional situation. Teaching science, as well as the practice of science, requires varied approaches. Using any single method exclusively is less effective than using a combination of methods. Ultimately, using a single method becomes boring for the student. Inquiry-based instruction is perhaps most appropriate when teaching concepts that do not conform to common student preconceptions or that require students to analyze discrepant information. Students tend to need more time to construct their understanding of abstract concepts than they need for understanding of more concrete information.

Misconception 5: Inquiry-based instruction can be easily implemented through use of hands-on activities and educational kits. Hands-on lessons and materials help teachers implement inquiry-based instruction in the classroom, and they also help students focus their thinking in appropriate areas. There is no guarantee, however, that student learning will go beyond performing the tasks at hand. It is possible for a student to successfully complete an experiment and yet not understand the science concept the experiment is designed to teach. With inquiry-based instruction, students must actively participate by gathering evidence that helps them develop an understanding of a concept. Teachers must evaluate how well the lesson or materials incorporate the essential features of inquiry and use them accordingly.

Misconception 6: Student interest generated by hands-on activities ensures that inquiry teaching and learning are occurring. Student engagement in the topic is a critical first step in learning. Many students certainly prefer hands-on activities to sitting through a lecture, but their enthusiasm does not necessarily translate into learning. The teacher must assess the students' level of mental engagement with inquiry; challenge naive conceptions; ask probing questions; and prompt students to revise, refine, and extend their understanding.

Misconception 7: Inquiry-based instruction is too difficult to implement in the classroom. Teachers unfamiliar with inquiry-based instruction may be uncomfortable trying something new. They may reason that they were not taught using these methods and question why it should be any different for their students. Common excuses for not using inquiry are that it takes too much time, does not work with large classes, or does not work with less-capable students. These attitudes typically result from improper use of inquiry methods rather than from any inherent problem with the inquiry approach itself. When teachers understand the essential features of inquiry, its flexibility in the classroom, and students'

willingness to embrace it, they usually come to regard it as an essential strategy in their teaching.

Inquiry and Professional Development

> The current reform effort … requires a substantive change in how science is taught. … An equally substantive change is needed in professional development practices.
>
> —National Research Council, *National Science Education Standards*, 1996, page 56

Recognizing that inquiry is a critical part of the science curriculum is only one step toward improving the level of inquiry in the science classroom. Another aspect of elevating inquiry is the need for ongoing professional development programs that help teachers enact a vision of the inquiry-based classroom, support the implementation of new classroom materials, and coordinate assessment priorities with an emphasis on inquiry.

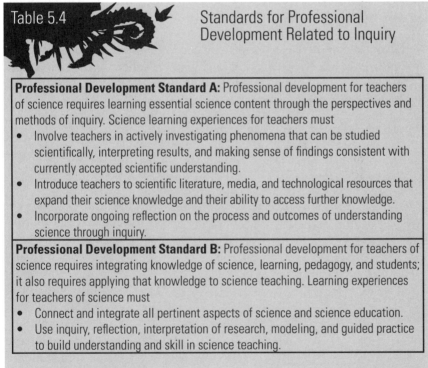

Table 5.4	Standards for Professional Development Related to Inquiry

Professional Development Standard A: Professional development for teachers of science requires learning essential science content through the perspectives and methods of inquiry. Science learning experiences for teachers must
- Involve teachers in actively investigating phenomena that can be studied scientifically, interpreting results, and making sense of findings consistent with currently accepted scientific understanding.
- Introduce teachers to scientific literature, media, and technological resources that expand their science knowledge and their ability to access further knowledge.
- Incorporate ongoing reflection on the process and outcomes of understanding science through inquiry.

Professional Development Standard B: Professional development for teachers of science requires integrating knowledge of science, learning, pedagogy, and students; it also requires applying that knowledge to science teaching. Learning experiences for teachers of science must
- Connect and integrate all pertinent aspects of science and science education.
- Use inquiry, reflection, interpretation of research, modeling, and guided practice to build understanding and skill in science teaching.

Source: National Research Council. 1996. *National Science Education Standards*. Washington, DC: National Academy Press.

In addition to specifying the abilities and understandings that students should develop, the NSES also outline professional development standards for teachers that involve inquiry. These standards are outlined in table 5.4.

Teachers need opportunities to build their knowledge. Like their students, teachers need to view learning as a lifelong process. Because ongoing scientific research leads to continuing changes in our understanding of the world around us, an understanding of inquiry is important for an understanding of how science is done and what conclusions can be drawn from scientific studies. Professional development programs that effectively help teachers improve their use of inquiry in the classroom share four characteristics:

- They offer coherent opportunities for teachers to learn over time.
- They allow and encourage collaboration between people, including teachers and scientists.
- They are committed to giving teachers the knowledge and abilities needed to address the science literacy needs of all their students.
- They view inquiry as a set of abilities and understandings that the teachers themselves need to have as well as a way to learn subject content.

Becoming an effective science teacher is a continual process starting with preservice experiences and stretching throughout a teaching career. As teachers learn, they can translate their own experiences with inquiry into better learning experiences for their students.

Chapter 6

Getting Started With Inquiry: Six Invitations*

An understanding of scientific inquiry is not just something that helps your students pass science class in high school. If students develop an understanding of how science inquiry is done and how it contributes to understanding the natural world, they will be better prepared to analyze and interpret information throughout their lives. Science is involved when we make decisions about our health, the products we use, and how we as a society invest in our futures. Merely telling students how knowledge arises from data and how it changes is not enough. Students must experience science in operation rather than just talk about science only as a summation of what has been demonstrated.

The invitations to inquiry that follow are one useful means to helping students develop a deeper understanding of how science is done and what we can learn from science. They are teaching units that expose students to small samples of inquiry—samples suitable to their competence and knowledge.

Each invitation focuses on one or more of the essential features of inquiry (see chapter 5, p. 63). During the invitation, students engage in analyzing the development of scientifically oriented questions, giving priority to evidence, formulating explanations, and connecting explanations to other knowledge or to the importance of communicating and justifying explanations as a critical part of advancing scientific knowledge. Each invitation has a psychological structure that uses the types of communication and interaction that occur within groups. For example, some material is structured to invite contributions from students with different abilities, thus fostering cooperation. Other materials encourage dialogue between students and teachers.

Student participation in inquiry serves two objectives. First, students discover that science is something more than merely learning what others already know. They find that science is an activity of the mind, a challenge to the imagination, and an endeavor that rewards thought and invention. Second, through participating in inquiry activities, students develop skills in interpreting data and in understanding scientific knowledge.

---

*The title of this chapter in the first edition of the *Biology Teachers Handbook* was "Invitations to Enquiry." The invitations were the work and passion of Joseph Schwab, who brought this innovation to the BSCS program to teach inquiry in two ways: "First, it poses example after example of the process itself. Second, it *engages the participation* of the student in the process" (Schwab 1966). In this fourth edition we continue the tradition of featuring the invitations, using the currently more accepted form of *enquiry: inquiry* with an "i." The invitations in this edition are based on the original ones but connected to more current understandings about the teaching of inquiry as elaborated in *Inquiry and the National Science Education Standards* (NRC 2000).

Ease and Difficulty

We present six invitations. Your students may or may not have studied the content area involved before beginning an invitation. The content in each invitation is interesting and relevant, but it is not of primary importance. Some invitations are simpler than others. In some cases, you may think that the scientific problem or question is too simple for high school students. By taking a seemingly simple problem, however, students can focus on understanding inquiry.

Methods of Using the Invitations to Inquiry

Each invitation has two components. One component is composed of information for students. The other component contains the student materials along with annotations and information for the teacher. The teacher materials are presented in bold type. These materials indicate the purpose and content of the invitation and the suggested answers to questions.

Place and Time of Use

You can use the invitations as independent learning experiences or in conjunction with laboratory exercises. You can select them on the basis of the biological subject matter they discuss or for their relevance to the aspect of inquiry that a particular laboratory experience illustrates. In addition, you can use the invitations in conjunction with classroom work. Not only will your discussion of the biological subject matter be strengthened by work on the invitation, but the invitation also may shed additional light on the textbook treatment.

Guidelines for Using the Invitations

We recommend the following guidelines for using each invitation to inquiry:

1. Read each invitation before starting it with your students.
2. Note whether the invitation requires that you prepare duplicated materials or that you present it orally.
3. Pose the problem in the invitation and invite students' reactions.
4. Deal with the students' responses as they arise, asking diagnostic questions that will help them understand why certain responses are less well reasoned than others and will help them review the logic that justifies well-reasoned responses.
5. The goal of the invitations is not to obtain the right answer immediately. Rather, it is to invite students to use their information and intelligence in an effort to discover the answer. Honor each answer a student gives by discussing how well reasoned it is—not whether it is right or wrong.
6. Avoid giving answers prematurely by carefully considering when to include some of the teacher or summary material to illustrate the invitation.

Invitation to Inquiry 1: Seed Germination

Student Information

SCIENCE INQUIRY EMPHASIS

- Asking scientifically oriented questions (asking testable questions)
- Formulating explanations

A researcher who was interested in the conditions under which seeds would best germinate placed several grains of corn on moist blotting paper in each of two glass petri dishes. The researcher placed one of these dishes in a room with no light source and the other in a well-lighted room. Both rooms were the same temperature. After four days, the researcher examined the grains. All the seeds in both dishes had germinated.

How would you interpret the data from this experiment? Do not include data that you have obtained elsewhere; restrict your interpretation to the data from this experiment alone.

_____

_____

_____

_____

What factor was clearly different in the surroundings of the two dishes? What specific problem led the researcher to design this particular plan for the experiment? State the problem as precisely as you can.

_____

_____

_____

_____

In view of the problem you stated, look at the data again. What interpretation can you make?

_____

_____

_____

_____

Although light is not necessary for the germination of corn seeds, different amounts of light can speed up or slow down germination. How might the experiment check this possibility?

_____

_____

_____

_____

_____

Plan an experiment to test the effect of temperature on germination. Make sure your plan clearly states the question your experiment will test.

_____

_____

_____

_____

_____

_____

_____

_____

_____

_____

_____

_____

_____

_____

_____

_____

_____

_____

_____

_____

_____

Invitation to Inquiry 1: Seed Germination*

Teacher Annotations and Information

SCIENCE INQUIRY EMPHASIS

- Asking scientifically oriented questions (asking testable questions)
- Formulating explanations

Invitation 1 asks students to improve the question that is tested in an experiment. It also asks students to consider the validity of one interpretation of data. Finally, it asks students to apply what they have learned to another situation.

A researcher who was interested in the conditions under which seeds would best germinate placed several grains of corn on moist blotting paper in each of two glass petri dishes. The researcher placed one of these dishes in a room with no light source and the other in a well-lighted room. Both rooms were the same temperature. After four days, the researcher examined the grains. All the seeds in both dishes had germinated.

How would you interpret the data from this experiment? Do not include data that you have obtained elsewhere; restrict your interpretation to the data from this experiment alone.

The researcher designed the experiment to test the light factor. Some students may say the experiment suggests that moisture is necessary for the sprouting of grains. Others may say it shows that a warm temperature is necessary. If such suggestions do not arise, introduce one as a possibility. Suggest the weakness of these ideas by asking students if the data suggest that corn grains require a glass dish to germinate. Probably none of your students will accept this. Show them how the data on moisture or warmth are no different from the data available on glass dishes. In neither case are the data evidence for such a conclusion.

Researchers occasionally take calculated risks in interpreting data, but they do not propose interpretations for which there is no evidence. This invitation illustrates an obvious misinterpretation.

What factor was clearly different in the surroundings of the two dishes? What specific problem led the researcher to design this particular plan for the experiment? State the problem as precisely as you can.

*Invitation 3 in *Biology Teachers Handbook*, 3rd edition

The researcher designed the experiment to test the necessity of light as a factor in germination. The invitation began with a general question: "Under what conditions do seeds germinate best?" This is not the most useful way to ask a question for scientific inquiry because it does not indicate where and how to look for an answer. A question is useful in a scientific problem when it is specific enough to suggest what data are needed to answer it. For example, asking, "Do seeds germinate better with or without light?" points to what data are required. We need to compare germination in the light with germination in the dark. General questions are not bad, but they must lead to a solvable problem.

This invitation also introduces the role of a clearly formulated problem in controlling the interpretation of the data. Investigations that lead to significant advances in understanding have clearly defined, scientifically oriented questions.

In view of the problem you stated, look at the data again. What interpretation can you make?

The evidence indicates that light is not necessary for the germination of some seeds. Tell your students that light is necessary for some other seeds, such as Grand Rapids lettuce, but may inhibit the germination of others, such as some varieties of onion.

Although light is not necessary for the germination of corn seeds, different amounts of light can speed up or slow down germination. How might the experiment check this possibility?

Counting the number of germinated seeds per day in lighted and unlighted dishes would provide some evidence.

Plan an experiment to test the effect of temperature on germination. Make sure your plan clearly states the question your experiment will test.

This type of experiment requires setting up the same moisture and light conditions but varying the temperature for different containers of seeds.

Invitation to Inquiry 2: Natural Selection

Student Information

SCIENCE INQUIRY EMPHASIS

- Formulating explanations
- Asking scientifically oriented questions (asking testable questions)

People working with dairy cattle at an agricultural experimental station noticed a large population of flies in the barn where the cattle lived. The population of flies was so large that it affected the animals' health. So the workers sprayed the barn with a recently developed insecticide called Fly-Be-Gone. They found that the insecticide killed almost all of the flies.

A week or so later, however, the number of flies was again large. The workers again sprayed with the same insecticide. The result was similar to that of the first spraying. Most of the flies died.

A week later, the population of flies increased again, and again the workers sprayed the insecticide in the barn. This sequence of events was repeated four or five times; then it became apparent that the Fly-Be-Gone was becoming less and less effective in killing the flies, until it finally appeared to be useless. Construct several different hypotheses to account for these facts.

_____

_____

_____

_____

_____

The workers made a large batch of the Fly-Be-Gone insecticide solution when they first sprayed the insecticide. They used this same batch of insecticide solution in all the sprayings. One worker suggested that the insecticide solution might decompose with age. Propose at least two different ways to test this hypothesis.

_____

_____

_____

_____

_____

The workers made a fresh batch of Fly-Be-Gone and used it once again on the large fly population at the experimental station's barn. Only a few flies died after spraying with this fresh insecticide solution.

The workers then used the same fresh batch of Fly-Be-Gone on a fly population at another barn several miles away. The results were like those originally seen at the experimental station—most of the flies died. Thus, the workers obtained two quite different results with a fresh batch of Fly-Be-Gone. Moreover, the weather conditions at the time of the effective spraying at the distant barn were the same as when the workers sprayed without success at the experimental station.

Examine the major components of this problem:

1. The "something" used (the Fly-Be-Gone insecticide)
2. The conditions under which the something was used
3. The way in which the something was used
4. The "thing" on which the something was used (the flies)

Thus far, all the hypotheses and actions deal with a few of these components. Which ones?

_____
_____
_____
_____
_____

What components in the list have you not used to form your hypotheses?

_____
_____
_____
_____
_____

Consider the fourth component on the list. Use your knowledge of biology to think of something that might have happened within the fly population that would account for the decreasing effectiveness of Fly-Be-Gone as an insecticide.

_____
_____
_____
_____
_____

Some flies survive after application of Fly-Be-Gone, and others do not. Propose ideas that might explain why some flies survive and some die.

_____

_____

_____

_____

_____

Remember, the workers sprayed the experimental barn several times. After each spraying, the populations increased again. Suppose the flies that survive after insecticide use do so because they have a certain gene that makes them resistant to the insecticide. Think about the frequency of the gene in the original fly population. How does it compare with the frequency of that gene in the fly population after five applications of the insecticide? Predict how the frequency of that gene would or would not be different in the two populations.

_____

_____

_____

_____

_____

Invitation to Inquiry 2: Natural Selection*

Teacher Annotations and Information

SCIENCE INQUIRY EMPHASIS

- Formulating explanations
- Asking a scientifically oriented question

Invitation 2 emphasizes using data to formulate an explanation. Students also practice developing hypotheses or testable questions to solve a problem.

People working with dairy cattle at an agricultural experimental station noticed a large population of flies in the barn where the cattle lived. The population of flies was so large that it affected the animals' health. So the workers sprayed the barn with a recently developed insecticide called Fly-Be-Gone. They found that this killed almost all of the flies.

A week or so later, however, the number of flies was again large. The workers again sprayed with the same insecticide. The result was similar to that of the first spraying. Most of the flies died.

A week later, the population of flies increased again, and again the workers sprayed the insecticide in the barn. This sequence of events was repeated four or five times; then it became apparent that the Fly-Be-Gone was becoming less and less effective in killing the flies, until it finally appeared to be useless. Construct several different hypotheses to account for these facts.

Reasonable hypotheses include the following:

- **The composition of Fly-Be-Gone changes with the age of the solution.**
- **Fly-Be-Gone is effective only under certain environmental conditions that changed in the course of the work (for example, temperature and humidity).**
- **The flies that are genetically most susceptible to the insecticide were selectively killed.**

The last hypothesis should not be elicited at this point or developed if students suggest it.

---

*Invitation 13 in *Biology Teachers Handbook*, 3rd edition

The workers made a large batch of the Fly-Be-Gone insecticide solution when they first sprayed the insecticide. They used this same batch of insecticide solution in all the sprayings. One worker suggested that the insecticide solution might decompose with age. Propose at least two different ways to test this hypothesis.

One approach is to use sprays that are mixed or diluted at different times and then to test the different batches on different barn populations of flies. A different approach is to perform a chemical analysis of fresh and old insecticide solutions to determine whether changes had occurred over time.

Investigating problems using different approaches may contribute to the reliability of the conclusions drawn from each. Neither approach is perfect, but each makes a contribution.

The workers made a fresh batch of Fly-Be-Gone and used it once again on the large fly population at the experimental station's barn. Only a few flies died after spraying with this fresh insecticide solution.

They then used the same fresh batch of Fly-Be-Gone on a fly population at another barn several miles away. The results were like those originally seen at the experimental station—most of the flies died. Thus, the workers obtained two quite different results with a fresh batch of Fly-Be-Gone. Moreover, the weather conditions at the time of the effective spraying at the distant barn were the same as when they sprayed without success at the experimental station.

Examine the major components of this problem:

1. The "something" used (the Fly-Be-Gone insecticide)
2. The conditions under which the something was used
3. The way in which the something was used
4. The "thing" on which the Fly-Be-Gone was used (the flies)

Thus far, all the hypotheses and actions deal with a few of these components. Which ones?

The hypotheses so far have concerned only components 1 and 2.

What components in the list have you not used to form your hypotheses?

Students have not used components 3 and 4. Component 3 may be pursued as a further exercise if you wish. However, you should emphasize the major possibility contained in component 4.

Consider the fourth component on the list. Use your knowledge of biology to think of something that might have happened within the fly population that would account for the decreasing effectiveness of Fly-Be-Gone as an insecticide.

Students should recognize that some flies survive the application of insecticide. Ask the students to remember that after the first spraying, most, but not all, of the flies died. Ask them where the new population of flies (that grew after the first spraying) came from—that is, who were their parents?

Is it more likely that the parents were among the flies that died (more susceptible to the insecticide) or among the flies that survived (more resistant to the effects of the insecticide) after the spraying?

Some flies survive after application of Fly-Be-Gone, and others do not. Propose ideas that might explain why some flies survive and some die.

Accept reasonable ideas at this time. Students may suggest things like mutations, specific "protective" or "susceptibility" genes, or differences in the amount (dose) that individuals can tolerate (some individual flies may have received different doses of spray depending on where they were in the barn). The important thing is that students' ideas focus on differences among the flies themselves to explain why some live and some die.

Remember, the workers sprayed the experimental barn several times. After each spraying, the populations increased again. Suppose the flies that survive after insecticide use do so because they have a certain gene that makes them resistant to the insecticide. Think about the frequency of the gene in the original fly population. How does it compare with the frequency of that gene in the fly population after five applications of the insecticide? Predict how the frequency of that gene would or would not be different in the two populations.

If there are genetic differences among flies that influence their ability to survive after insecticide application, we would expect the resistance gene to become more frequent in the final population. Dead flies do not produce offspring or pass on their genes. Ones that survive after insecticide application may. After each application of insecticide, individuals that carry the resistance gene survive and individuals that do not carry the gene usually die. Over time, through natural selection, the individuals that are best suited to this imposed environment (the presence of Fly-Be-Gone insecticide) survive and reproduce.

Invitation to Inquiry 3: Predator-Prey and Natural Populations

Student Information

SCIENCE INQUIRY EMPHASIS

- Giving priority to evidence
- Formulating explanations

A biologist was studying the size of the populations of small rodents and owls in a certain geographical area to find out what factors tended to control the size of the populations. The rodent population declined during the study period because of a virulent disease that attacked the small rodents. Adult owls normally fed on the small rodents. When the number of these rodents was reduced, the adult owl population—approximately 14 individuals—remained unchanged. The number of newly hatched owls, however, was far less than in previous counts.

What might explain how the reduced food supply resulted in fewer newly hatched owls but no decrease in the number of adult owls?

_____
_____
_____
_____
_____

The possibilities that might cause the population of young to decrease appear to follow two different routes. What are they?

_____
_____
_____
_____

The reduction in owlet population may be due, then, to an increased infant mortality rate or to a decreased birthrate. How could you determine which of these possibilities was operating?

_____
_____
_____
_____
_____

Suppose there was a decreased birthrate. This reduction might occur in two ways: fewer eggs produced and fewer laid eggs hatched. What are the different ways that the reduction of food could affect the adult owls so that they produce these results?

_____

_____

_____

_____

_____

What would you need to study to obtain data that would help determine which of these possibilities is the case? Note that any of them may contribute to the reduced population size of the new generation of owls.

_____

_____

_____

_____

_____

Recall that the biologist wants to study what happened to the natural population of owls. Examine the evidence presented earlier. Suppose the biologist decided that the research team must not gather the data it needs about the possibility concerning poor development of sperm or eggs (produced in the testes and ovaries). Determine why the biologist made this decision.

_____

_____

_____

_____

_____

How could the biologist use the laboratory to get useful information on the sperm or egg cell production possibility?

_____

_____

_____

_____

_____

Suppose the biologist wanted to draw a conclusion about the natural owl population by studying the reproductive organs of caged owls and using data from that study. What is one serious objection to this method?

_____

_____

_____

_____

_____

Suppose there has been a change in mating behavior. A study of the owls' behavior showed they mated less often when there were fewer rodents to eat than when there was a plentiful food supply. The biologist decided from these data that the lowered frequency of mating caused the reduced size of the new generation. Explain why the biologist should not draw this conclusion from these data.

_____

_____

_____

_____

_____

Invitation to Inquiry 3:
Predator-Prey and Natural Populations*

Teacher Annotations and Information

SCIENCE INQUIRY EMPHASIS

- Giving priority to evidence
- Formulating explanations

Sometimes scientists are not able to obtain evidence in the optimal way. Circumstances can make some investigations inappropriate or unfeasible. Invitation 3 asks students to consider what scientists can and cannot learn when they need to rely on "second-best" data. In addition, students consider the idea that multiple factors may be involved in causing a phenomenon.

A biologist was studying the size of the populations of small rodents and owls in a certain geographical area to find out what factors tended to control the size of the populations. The rodent population declined during the study period because of a virulent disease that attacked the small rodents. Adult owls normally fed on the small rodents. When the number of these rodents was reduced, the adult owl population—approximately 14 individuals—remained unchanged. The number of newly hatched owls, however, was far less than in previous counts.

What might explain how the reduced food supply resulted in fewer newly hatched owls but no decrease in the number of adult owls?

A general answer is that the reduced food supply caused a decrease in the population. Point out that the decrease was differential, and press for possible ways in which the reduced food supply might have acted to produce this differential decrease. Some possibilities are that the underfed owlets were more susceptible to disease; the adult owls might have been eating some of their young; underfed female owls were producing fewer eggs; or a lower percentage of laid eggs hatched. Elicit or, if necessary, supply a variety of these or similar answers.

The possibilities that might cause the population of young to decrease appear to follow two different routes. What are they?

*Invitation 8 in *Biology Teachers Handbook*, 3rd edition

Some of the suggested possibilities increase the mortality among the owlets. Other possibilities decrease the birthrate. Students may not be familiar with the words *birthrate* and *mortality*. If so, this is a good context in which to introduce them.

The reduction in owlet population may be due, then, to an increased infant mortality rate or to a decreased birthrate. How might you determine which of these possibilities was operating?

The possibility of increased infant mortality requires either observing the owls in their nests or finding other evidence that the young owls were dying or being killed by their parents or predators. Time-lapse infrared photography could perhaps produce such evidence. It would be easier to check on lowered birthrate by counting the number of laid and newly hatched eggs.

Suppose there was a decreased birthrate. This reduction might occur two ways: fewer eggs produced and fewer laid eggs hatched. What are the different ways that the reduction of food could affect the adult owls so that they produce these results?

There are a number of possibilities: poor metabolism that affected the ovaries so that fewer eggs are laid; similar effects on the testes that led to a decrease in the percentage of fertilized eggs among the eggs laid; and no effect on the eggs or sperm but a reduced frequency of mating.

What would you need to study to obtain data that would help determine which of these possibilities is the case? Note that any of them may contribute to the reduced population size of the new generation of owls.

This question asks only what students should study and not what data they should obtain. Students may not yet know enough biology to

Table 6.1	Possible Answers Regarding Data Needed for Study

Hypothesis	Subject Requiring Study
Poor development of egg and sperm cells	Ovaries and testes of well-fed owls compared with owls of this population
Change in mating	Frequency of mating in the local owl population compared with owls in a similar environment that are amply supplied with food
Percentage of eggs hatching	Comparison of the number of eggs incubated with the number of eggs hatched

speculate responsibly about the precise data this study would require. In any case, possible answers are listed in table 6.1.

Recall that the biologist wants to study what happened to the natural population of owls. Examine the evidence presented earlier. Suppose the biologist decided that the research team must not gather the data it needs about the possibility concerning poor development of sperm or eggs (produced in the testes and ovaries). Determine why the biologist made this decision.

The owl population is so small that killing a few owls to study the reproductive organs would make a large, artificial change in the population.

In biological investigations, the data that would best throw light on a problem may not always be obtainable. Sometimes this inaccessibility results from limitations in technology. Other times, researchers refrain from obtaining useful data because the steps necessary to collect them would ruin the possibility of later investigations. Researchers reject the best data in favor of less-definitive data and then examine the shortcomings of the second-best data.

How could the biologist use the laboratory to get useful information on the sperm or egg cell production possibility?

The biologist could feed caged owls (obtained from other sources) good and poor diets and then examine development of sperm and egg cells.

Suppose the biologist wanted to draw a conclusion about the natural owl population by studying the reproductive organs of caged owls and using data from that study. What is one serious objection to this method?

There is a possibility that caging could, itself, lead to a significant change in egg and sperm cell production.

Suppose there has been a change in mating behavior. A study of the owls' behavior showed they mated less often when there were fewer rodents to eat than when there was a plentiful food supply. The biologist decided from these data that the lowered frequency of mating caused the reduced size of the new generation. Explain why the biologist should not draw this conclusion from these data.

The evidence indicates mating behavior may be one factor that reduces the size of the new generation. The evidence does not rule out the possibility that the other factors may also contribute.

This invitation introduces students to some specific aspects of biological research and to some of the steps of scientific inquiry. To bring these into sharp focus, review what has happened. A structure for this review is in table 6.2.

Table 6.2 — Some Aspects of Biological Research and Scientific Inquiry

Scientific Inquiry Includes	Example in This Inquiry
Identifying a problem to study	1. A study of a stable population was under way when a disease suddenly changed the population.
Exploring cause	2. The investigator saw the opportunity to study another problem—the cause of the drop in population in owls. 3. The investigator considered some possible causes.
Collecting data/evidence	4. The investigator then tried to see what data might throw light on whether these possible causes were operating. 5. The investigator found that obtaining the most desirable data about one possibility would spoil the population for further study. 6. The investigator considered substitute evidence.
Testing the likelihood of possible causes	7. The investigator tested another possibility and found that it operated.
Interpreting data	8. The investigator made an overreaching interpretation of the evidence.
Considering multiple causal factors	9. Other scientists (your students!) critiqued the interpretation.

You should emphasize certain aspects of this suggested review's structure. The invitation emphasizes one idea of great significance in biology: the importance of studying natural situations rather than only laboratory or experimental ones. Students should see that, for all the knowledge that comes from experimental manipulation, the careful study of undisturbed (natural) situations is also important in biological science.

Invitation to Inquiry 4: Light and Plant Movement

Student Information

> SCIENCE INQUIRY EMPHASIS
>
> - Formulating explanations
> - Connecting explanations

As you may know, plants tend to bend toward the light. This movement usually results in more leaf surface being exposed to the available light. The process by which the plant "captures" light energy occurs mainly within the leaves of plants.

In view of this information, formulate an answer to this question: Why do plants bend toward the light?

_____

_____

_____

_____

_____

There is a lack of evidence that plants perform "actions" on purpose. In view of this fact, how could you improve this phrasing, which many students use: "Plants bend to get more light"?

_____

_____

_____

_____

_____

About 100 years ago, the biologist Charles Darwin and his son Francis began investigating plants that bend toward the light. They noticed that canary grass seedlings that received light mainly from one side bent toward the light. Most of the bending took place near the bottom of the seedling, just above the soil. Other observations, however, suggested to the Darwins that the seedling tip might have something to do with the bending. Therefore, they performed the following experiment: With a razor, they cut off the tips of seven young seedlings. These, together with seven uncut seedlings, were exposed to light from one side only. The seedlings with intact tips bent sharply toward the light. The cut seedlings without tips did not bend.

Explain this experimental result. What may be the reason for the failure of tipless grasses to bend?

_____

_____

_____

_____

_____

The Darwins then took more seedlings and covered the tips of half of them with blackened paper. They left the tips of the other half uncovered. Both sets were exposed to light from one side. The uncovered seedlings bent toward the light, but those with covered tips did not.

In view of the previous experiment in which the tips were cut, what was the purpose of the experiment that covered the tips?

_____

_____

_____

_____

_____

Remember that the curvature occurs at the base of the seedling. Given the results of both experiments, what hypothesis can you now propose about the contribution of the tip of the seedling to bending?

_____

_____

_____

_____

_____

Invitation to Inquiry 4: Light and Plant Movement*

Teacher Annotations and Information

SCIENCE INQUIRY EMPHASIS

- Formulating explanations
- Connecting explanations

Invitation 4 concentrates on the interpretation of data. It emphasizes two points. The first is the question of teleology. One unacceptable form of teleological interpretation is contrasted with the acceptable functional interpretation. The second point is the significance of ablation experiments. This invitation emphasizes that most biological inquiry is focused on the *normal* organism. Data obtained by removal of an organ, for example, are often intended to help us know what the organ contributes when in its normal place and condition.

As you may know, plants tend to bend toward the light. This movement usually results in more leaf surface being exposed to the available light. The process by which the plant "captures" light energy occurs mainly within the leaves of plants.

In view of this information, formulate an answer to the question: Why do plants bend toward the light?

In an average class, at least one student will reply, in effect, "They bend to get more light so they will grow better" or even, "They grow toward the light so they will be healthy." From such an answer, the discussion should move toward two points. First, help the students see that such a formulation suggests—or even intends to assert—something like *intelligent* behavior, behavior that *consciously* anticipates future needs. If a fact, characteristic, or explanation is attributed to or directed by a specific purpose or goal, scientists refer to it as teleological.

With the concept of *teleology* clarified, continue the discussion by developing the point that we have no reasonable data to indicate that plants make goal-oriented "decisions." Further, the information we do have about the structural and organizational basis for intelligence in humans suggests that plants are not likely to have this competence. (In the case of some animals, there is a basis for supposing conscious,

---

*Invitation 14 in *Biology Teachers Handbook*, 3rd edition

intelligent behavior.) Other common teleological explanations for phenomena in the natural world include that giraffes developed long necks so they can reach the leaves on the tallest trees; bacteria have specific resistance genes so they will survive the use of antibacterial substances; and giant pandas eat only bamboo because they know that is what they can digest. Each of these statements indicates a purpose or a goal for the characteristic that would not be known or intended for the organism.

The second main point of the discussion should show that although teleological interpretations, which assign conscious purpose to the individual plant, may be unsound, other interpretations are sound and useful. That is, there is a contribution to our understanding of living things when we link the actions of a given part of an organism to what is achieved by this action as far as the organism as a whole is concerned. Plant movements may, indeed, be reasonably interpreted to have survival value or adaptive significance. The plant may well "profit" from its movements, that is, carry on some other activities more effectively with such movements than without them. Human examples of adaptive behavior may be cited: learning behavior, even in infants; the papillary reflex; various protective withdrawal reflexes; and inflammation in areas of local infection.

Teleological interpretations fell into disrepute in biology because they assign consciousness and intelligence when there is little ground for doing so.

There is a lack of evidence that plants perform "actions" on purpose. In view of this fact, how could you improve this phrasing, which many students use: "Plants bend to get more light"?

One possible rephrasing is, "Plants respond to light by bending toward it; this results in a more efficient use of the available light." This rephrasing shows little difference in meaning when compared with the previous statement.

About 100 years ago, the biologist Charles Darwin and his son Francis began investigating plants that bend toward the light. They noticed that canary grass seedlings that received light mainly from one side bent toward the light. Most of the bending took place near the bottom of the seedling, just above the soil. Other observations, however, suggested to the Darwins that the seedling tip might have something to do with the bending. Therefore, they performed the following experiment: With a razor, they cut off the tips of seven young seedlings. These, together with seven uncut seedlings, were exposed to light from one side only. The seedlings with intact tips bent sharply toward the light. The cut seedlings without tips did not bend.

Explain this experimental result. What may be the reason for the failure of tipless grasses to bend?

Some students may suggest that only the tip of the plant can "perceive" light. Others may suggest that the act of cutting, rather than the absence of a tip, may have interfered with the plant's bending. Overcautious students may go no further than to say that the absence of a tip somehow prevented bending. Encourage these students to add to their statements. You should point out that the aim of such experiments is to find out what the tip contributed to the bending process when it was present. The aim is not to find out what the absence of the tip leads to; removal of the tip, instead, provides clues or evidence of the function of the tip in the bending process.

This experiment employs a common technique in science—an ablation experiment. Most biological inquiry is focused on the normal organism. Data obtained by ablation, or the removal of an organ, are often intended to help us know what the organ contributes when in its normal place and condition.

The Darwins then took more seedlings and covered the tips of half of them with blackened paper. They left the tips of the other half uncovered. Both sets were exposed to light from one side. The uncovered seedlings bent toward the light, but those with covered tips did not.

In view of the previous experiment in which the tips were cut, what was the purpose of the experiment that covered the tips?

In the experiment in which the tips of the plants were cut, there are two reasonable but mutually exclusive possibilities—loss of some specific sensory function when the tip was removed and injury to the plant caused by the cutting of the tip. In the second experiment, the second possibility is eliminated since the tips were not cut.

Remember that the curvature occurs at the base of the seedling. Given the results of both experiments, what hypothesis can you now propose about the contribution of the tip of the seedling to bending?

This question is designed to expand and define the concept of a plant tip "perceiving." Some students may say again that only the tip reacts to light. If so, encourage them to make constructive guesses about how the tip's sensitivity results in base curvature. Many possibilities exist, depending on your students' knowledge of biology. They may suggest that light may lead to the production of a chemical in the tip that reaches and affects the base. All such suggestions that fit the data should be treated as valid possibilities. The Darwins' suggestion was "when seedlings are freely exposed to a lateral light, some influence is transmitted from the upper to the lower part causing the latter to bend" (Darwin 1880).

Invitation to Inquiry 5: Cell Nucleus

Student Information

SCIENCE INQUIRY EMPHASIS

- Giving priority to evidence
- Formulating explanations
- Communicating and justifying explanations

Animals and plants are made up of one or more very small living units called cells. Most types of cells contain a still smaller part called the nucleus. To determine whether the nucleus of a cell is necessary for life or whether the cell could live without a nucleus, biologists divided different types of cells into two pieces so that one piece contained the nucleus and the other piece did not.

All the cell pieces that did not have nuclei died. All the cell pieces that had nuclei soon re-formed into smaller but normal-looking cells. These cells then grew to their former size and in all other ways behaved exactly the same as cells that have not been divided.

How would you interpret this experiment and its result?

_____

_____

_____

_____

_____

Biologists repeated the experiment with a larger number of cells and over a period of several days. The results of this second experiment are shown in table 6.3.

Make an interpretation of the data about the importance of the nucleus. What is it about these data that makes you uneasy about your interpretation?

_____

_____

_____

_____

_____

Table 6.3 — Survival of Nucleated and Non-nucleated Cell Fragments (Results From the Second Experiment)

Day of the Experiment	# of Cell Fragments Surviving	
	Non-nucleated Fragments	Nucleated Fragments
0 (beginning)	100	100
1	81	79
2	62	78
3	20	77
4	0	74
10	0	67
30	0	65

Assume the biologists who performed the experiment made the following conclusion: "The experiment was judged satisfactory and was terminated at the 30th day. The data indicate that the nucleus normally is necessary for the continued life of the cell." What is wrong with this conclusion?

_____

_____

_____

_____

_____

How, then, can the biologists defend their statement? One experiment rarely, if ever, can prove a scientific statement beyond any shadow of doubt. There is always some doubt, and successive experiments try to remove one doubt after another.

_____

_____

_____

_____

_____

Review the data from the second experiment about the number of nucleated and non-nucleated fragments that survived (table 6.3). A more cautious scientist complained to the biologists that their interpretation of the data is unacceptable unless they give at least one reasonable explanation for the death of so many nucleated fragments. Defend the biologists and provide them with such an explanation. Recall how the nucleated fragments were obtained. For example, suppose you tried to nurture 10 baby chicks or 100 baby kittens. Would all of them survive to maturity?

Some cells normally contain no nucleus but live a long time. Suppose the biologists' interpretation of the results is right—in cells that have a nucleus, there is something in the nucleus that is indispensable for survival. How would you explain the healthy long lives of cells that do not have nuclei?

One example of non-nucleated cells is the mature human red blood cell. The nucleus degenerates during the development of this cell, as does the substance in the nucleus. In view of this information, how long would you expect such cells to live? Explain your answer.

Invitation to Inquiry 5: Cell Nucleus*

Teacher Annotations and Information

SCIENCE INQUIRY EMPHASIS

- Giving priority to evidence
- Formulating explanations
- Communicating and justifying explanations

Invitation 5 emphasizes the role of evidence in forming explanations. Students examine data, recognize factors that influence the interpretations that can be drawn from the data, and modify interpretations to improve their accuracy.

Animals and plants are made up of one or more very small living units called cells. Most types of cells contain a still smaller part called the nucleus. To determine whether the nucleus of a cell is necessary for life or whether the cell could live without a nucleus, biologists divided different types of cells into two pieces so that one piece contained the nucleus and the other piece did not.

All the cell pieces that did not have nuclei died. All the cell pieces that had nuclei soon re-formed into smaller but normal-looking cells. These cells then grew to their former size and in all other ways behaved exactly the same as cells that have not been divided.

How would you interpret this experiment and its result?

The evidence as stated will compel most students to conclude that the nucleus is necessary for the continued life of the cell. Even in this idealized situation in which all the data are artificially perfect, there are doubts we could raise and qualifications we could add to the interpretations. For example, the nucleus may be necessary only for the repair of injury—hence the death of the non-nucleated fragments. What held true for the types of cells that the biologists tested may not necessarily hold true for all cells. Point out that the conclusions should be restricted to cells that normally have nuclei.

Biologists repeated the experiment with a larger number of cells and over a period of several days. The results of this second experiment are shown in table 6.3.

---

*Adapted from Invitations 1 and 2 in *Biology Teachers Handbook*, 3rd edition.

Table 6.3 — Survival of Nucleated and Non-nucleated Cell Fragments (Results from the Second Experiment)

Day of the Experiment	# of Cell Fragments Surviving	
	Non-Nucleated Fragments	Nucleated Fragments
0 (beginning)	100	100
1	81	79
2	62	78
3	20	77
4	0	74
10	0	67
30	0	65

Make an interpretation of the data about the importance of the nucleus. What is there about these data that makes you uneasy about your interpretation?

These questions should ensure that students examine the data carefully before going on. Their answers may anticipate to some extent what follows.

Assume the biologists who performed the experiment made the following conclusion: "The experiment was judged satisfactory and was terminated at the 30th day. The data indicate that the nucleus normally is necessary for the continued life of the cell." What is wrong with this conclusion?

The conclusion goes beyond the data. Not only did some non-nucleated fragments live for three days, but a number of nucleated fragments died, some after one day, more after two days, still more in 10 days, and so on. If the biologists had extended the experiment for 60 days or more, many more nucleated fragments may have died.

How, then, can the biologists defend their statement? One experiment rarely, if ever, can prove a scientific statement beyond any shadow of doubt. There is always some doubt, and successive experiments try to remove one doubt after another.

In short, it is misleading to say that scientists draw a conclusion about a natural phenomenon from one experiment. Their summing up is really an interpretation of their data, which will be tested again either by repeating the same experiments or by conducting other experiments that extend and refine the interpretations.

Doubt can be cast on almost any statement that goes beyond the immediate and particular, such as "That one automobile in front of this house is black in this light, to my eye." Overcaution is just as much a

handicap to the growth of dependable knowledge as reckless overgeneralization. Scientific knowledge increases and becomes more dependable only as we interpret data, draw conclusions, and go on to other problems that these interpretations suggest. The lifeblood of science is ongoing inquiry that refines earlier conclusions, makes them more precise, and extends their scope.

Review the data from the second experiment about the number of nucleated and non-nucleated fragments that survived (table 6.3). A more cautious scientist complained to the biologists that their interpretation of the data is unacceptable unless they give at least one reasonable explanation for the death of so many nucleated fragments. Defend the biologists and provide them with such an explanation. Recall how the nucleated fragments were obtained. For example, suppose you tried to nurture 10 baby chicks or 100 baby kittens. Would all of them survive to maturity?

Help students see that the experiment itself probably induced fatal damage to some of the nucleated fragments and that some fraction of any population of living things likely will die in a given time from many common causes. Stress that data will be less than perfect, because many factors are uncontrollable.

Obviously, a better experiment could be designed. Invite students to attempt to improve the experiment even though problems of adequate sampling and control arise. You might ask students to work in teams of three or four to design an improved experiment. Teams can then share their ideas with other teams or with the class.

Some cells normally contain no nucleus but live a long time. Suppose the biologists' interpretation of the results is right—in cells that have a nucleus, there is something in the nucleus that is indispensable for survival. How would you explain the healthy long lives of cells that do not have nuclei?

Cells without nuclei may have a different structural organization that does not require the substances that are found in the nucleus and that are required by nucleated cells to survive. Another possibility is that the substance within the nucleus of a nucleated cell is not located within a discrete nucleus in a non-nucleated cell.

One example of non-nucleated cells is the mature human red blood cell. The nucleus degenerates during the development of this cell, as does the substance in the nucleus. In view of this information, how long would you expect such cells to live? Explain your answer.

Mature human red blood cells have a limited survival time—on average about three to four months. Students don't have data to answer this question, but they should recognize that factors other than simply having a nucleus may be involved.

Section II

Invitation to Inquiry 6: Thyroid Action

Student Information

> **SCIENCE INQUIRY EMPHASIS**
>
> • Formulating explanations
> • Connecting explanations
> • Communicating and justifying explanations

A two-lobed mass of tissue, called the thyroid gland, lies in the throat on the ventral (front) side of the trachea. To determine the function of this gland, biologist X performed the usual experiment for this type of research—removal of the gland from a number of animals of species A. For these control animals, the biologist surgically opened the skin and exposed the thyroid but did not remove the gland. The thyroid remained intact and in place. The biologist then looked for the differences between the two groups of animals. The following symptoms appeared in the animals without the thyroid tissue:

1. Muscular tremors, followed by severe muscle cramping (These symptoms disappeared after about 20 days.)
2. Lowered body temperature
3. Thickening of the skin and the appearance of soft, jellylike material throughout the body
4. Lethargy (Although the normal animals were playful and active, the animals without thyroid tissue sat huddled in one place most of the time.)

Biologist X then studied these symptoms closely to see if there might be an explanation. All the signs indicated the animals lacked the ability to use food. Biologist X interpreted symptom 1 as an indication of malnutrition of the nerves and the other symptoms as indications of a reduced ability to use food for energy in the body generally. The biologist tentatively interpreted the data to mean that thyroid tissue controlled the ability to use food materials.

Another biologist, Y, then announced the results of what appeared to be the same experiment performed on another, similar species of animal. Only symptoms 2, 3, and 4 appeared. There was no sign of the muscular tremors and spasms found by biologist X.

What might account for this difference in results? What major parts of the situation should you examine to find a possible explanation for the differences in results? Try for no more than three major parts.

_____
_____
_____
_____
_____

Identify some possible sources of the differences in experimental results. Try for one source in each of the three parts of the situation.

_____
_____
_____
_____
_____

Still a third biologist, Z, working on a third species, noticed two very small bits of tissue, one on each side of the thyroid mass. The bits of tissue were somewhat darker than the larger thyroid masses. Biologist Z removed thyroids from a few animals but left the small, dark bits of tissue in place. The animals then showed symptoms 2, 3, and 4 on the original list but not symptom 1.

In view of the results obtained by all three biologists, what tentative explanation might account for the differences in results reported by biologists X and Y?

_____
_____
_____
_____
_____

On hearing about the results of Y and Z, biologist X studied the tissues in the thyroid region of the original experimental animals but found no such darker bits. Biologist Y made a similar study and did find these darker tissues. In the species of animal used for this experiment, however, the bits were located well to one side of the thyroids and escaped removal for this reason. Biologist Y gave a name to these smaller, darker bits of tissue, _parathyroids,_ to suggest their location.

Make two assumptions based on these results. First, assume biologist X is correct in reporting no visible dark masses on the thyroid of the original experimental animals. Second, assume that all three species of experimental animals are so closely related that all of them have the same major organs, and that these organs function in much the same way in each species. Keeping all three experiments in mind, what might biologist X look for to explain the unusual results?

_____

_____

_____

_____

_____

Suppose the three biologists find the newly discovered parathyroids in their animals, although in differing locations in each species.

- What experiment should X now perform to clarify the difference in results?
- What other experiment should Y and Z now perform?
- If the assumptions so far are correct, what results should X discover?
- What results should Y and Z discover?

_____

_____

_____

_____

_____

How did reviewing and analyzing the work done by the others affect the work done by the three different biologists?

_____

_____

_____

_____

Different species, although very similar, may differ enough from one another that complications occur when researchers interpret the combined results of experiments performed on them.

Another very important point stems from the work done by biologist X on the animal that had parathyroid tissue inconspicuously buried within the thyroid tissue. Recall that removal of the thyroids by biologist X resulted in removal of the parathyroids as well. What X thought was an operation to remove one type of organ really was an operation that removed two types of organs. Later, biologist X attributed the symptoms partly to the removal of the thyroids and partly to the removal of the parathyroids. This is an example of cause and effect. Anything that happens (the effect) is brought about by something else (the cause).

Invitation to Inquiry 6: Thyroid Action*

Teacher Annotations and Information

SCIENCE INQUIRY EMPHASIS

- Formulating explanations
- Connecting explanations
- Communicating and justifying explanations

Invitation 6 asks students to analyze data from a scientific investigation. They then compare that data with data from other experiments. Students must revise and extend their explanations based on the new data.

Invitation 6 emphasizes some complications that arise in doing causal research in biology. A whole gland, such as the adrenal gland, can be treated as a cause. If the cause is removed, you can observe the consequences of the removal. The consequences can be interpreted as indicators of the normal effects of the adrenal gland. Although there is nothing erroneous about such an experiment and interpretation, it is incomplete. The researcher could divide the gland into parts, such as the medulla and cortex, and rerun the experiment using one part at a time.

Behind this progressive analysis of causes is the idea that somewhere we arrive at irreducible unit causes or causal elements. The possibility of such elemental causes, however, does not mean that grosser, composite causes, such as whole organs or tissue components of organs, are wrong or useless. On the contrary, they may be very useful, not only in medicine but also in research.

A two-lobed mass of tissue, called the thyroid gland, lies in the throat on the ventral (front) side of the trachea. To determine the function of this gland, biologist X performed the usual experiment for this type of research—removal of the gland from a number of animals of species A. For these control animals, the biologist surgically opened the skin and exposed the thyroid but did not remove the gland. The thyroid remained intact and in place. The biologist then looked for the differences between the two groups of animals. The following symptoms appeared in the animals without the thyroid tissue:

---

*Invitation 17 in *Biology Teachers Handbook*, 3rd edition

1. Muscular tremors, followed by severe muscle cramping (These symptoms disappeared after about 20 days.)
2. Lowered body temperature
3. Thickening of the skin and the appearance of soft, jellylike material throughout the body
4. Lethargy (Although the normal animals were playful and active, the animals without thyroid tissue sat huddled in one place most of the time.)

Biologist X then studied these symptoms closely to see if there might be an explanation. All the signs indicated the animals lacked the ability to use food. Biologist X interpreted symptom 1 as an indication of malnutrition of nerves and the other symptoms as indications of a reduced ability to use food for energy in the body generally. The biologist tentatively interpreted the data to mean that thyroid tissue controlled the ability to use food materials.

Another biologist, Y, then announced the results of what appeared to be the same experiment performed on another, similar species of animal. Only symptoms 2, 3, and 4 appeared. There was no sign of the muscular tremors and spasms found by biologist X.

What might account for this difference in results? What major parts of the situation should you examine to find a possible explanation for the differences in results? Try for no more than three major parts.

In this case, a convenient analysis of the situation is as follows: Somebody removed something from something. This yields a three-part division in which to search: the investigator's technique, the tissue removed, and the organism used as the experimental animal.

Identify some possible sources of the differences in experimental results. Try for one source in each of the three parts of the situation.

In the case of the two biologists, one of them may have damaged other structures in the animal while removing the thyroid. In the case of the removed tissue, it is possible that the tissue masses are only superficially alike. There may be physiological differences in spite of the anatomical similarity. In the case of the experimental animals, they may react differently to the normal output of the thyroid tissue, even though the tissue itself is much the same in the two species.

Still a third biologist, Z, working on a third species, noticed two very small bits of tissue, one on each side of the thyroid mass. The bits of tissue were somewhat darker than the larger thyroid masses. Biologist Z removed thyroids from a few animals but left the small, dark bits of tissue in place. The animals then showed symptoms 2, 3, and 4 on the original list but not symptom 1.

In view of the results obtained by all three biologists, what tentative explanation might account for the differences in results reported by biologists X and Y?

The obvious possibility is that biologist X removed both large and small tissues whereas Y removed only the large tissues.

On hearing about the results of Y and Z, biologist X studied the tissues in the thyroid region of the original experimental animals but found no such darker bits. Biologist Y made a similar study and did find these darker tissues. In the species of animal used for this experiment, however, the bits were located well to one side of the thyroids and escaped removal for this reason. Biologist Y gave a name to these smaller, darker bits of tissue, *parathyroids,* to suggest their location.

Make two assumptions based on these results. First, assume biologist X is correct in reporting no visible dark masses on the thyroid of the original experimental animals. Second, assume that all three species of experimental animals are so closely related that all of them have the same major organs and that these organs function in much the same way in each species. Keeping all three experiments in mind, what might biologist X look for to explain the unusual results?

Given the assumptions, the animals used by biologist X have parathyroids, and given the diversity of position of these glands reported by Y and Z, it is likely that they are in a third position in X's animals. Biologist X's failure to see them on reexamination might be because they are embedded within the thyroid masses. Hence, X should look for identifiably different tissue masses within the thyroid.

Suppose the three biologists find the newly discovered parathyroids in their animals, although in differing locations in each species.

- What experiment should X now perform to clarify the difference in results?
- What other experiment should Y and Z now perform?
- If the assumptions so far are correct, what results should X discover?
- What results should Y and Z discover?

Biologist X should now remove the thyroid alone and should find symptoms 2, 3, and 4 but not symptom 1. Biologists Y and Z (and biologist X also, for thoroughness) should remove the parathyroids alone and discover the nerve-muscle symptoms without symptoms 2, 3, and 4.

How did reviewing and analyzing the work done by the others affect the work done by the three different biologists?

Even though the three biologists worked on different species of animal, they understood that they could learn from one another's work. For some results, the work on other species helped support the findings of the different researchers. In other cases, researchers looked for ways to explain the different results from the different investigations.

Different species, although very similar, may differ enough from one another that complications occur when researchers interpret the combined results of experiments performed on them.

Another very important point stems from the work done by biologist X on the animal that had parathyroid tissue inconspicuously buried within the thyroid tissue. Recall that removal of the thyroids by biologist X resulted in removal of the parathyroids as well. What X thought was an operation to remove one type of organ really was an operation that removed two types of organs. Later, biologist X attributed the symptoms partly to the removal of the thyroids and partly to removal of the parathyroids. This is an example of cause and effect. Anything that happens (the effect) is brought about by something else (the cause).

Chapter 7

An Invitation to
Full Inquiry*

Section II

Scientific inquiry is not a rigid series of steps but rather a process and a set of characteristics that distinguish science from other ways of knowing. Anyone can use the habits of mind that characterize scientific inquiry to think scientifically about any issue. Features such as requiring evidence and natural explanations, blending logic and imagination, explaining outcomes, predicting future results, and identifying and avoiding bias typify a scientific inquiry or study. The invitations to inquiry in chapter 6 are a way to help students develop an understanding of inquiry as well as the specific skills of inquiry.

In the full inquiry experience in this chapter, students will put all these skills of inquiry together as they think like scientists and apply critical-thinking skills to evaluate new information that they collect themselves. As an introduction to the experience, students first identify and analyze a news article that reports on a scientific phenomenon of interest to them. This allows students to practice applying their critical-thinking skills in a typical, real-world interaction with science. It also helps them choose a scientific question to investigate in a full inquiry of their own.

In full inquiry, students assume more direct roles in carrying out open-ended scientific investigations. A successful full inquiry requires learners to propose, design, carry out, analyze, and communicate the results of a scientific investigation. Each of the thinking steps involved in a successful inquiry is just as important as the hands-on step of doing an experiment. The opportunity to conduct a full inquiry provides a comprehensive way for students to apply and evaluate their critical-thinking and scientific-process skills. Students should feel more independent in their work and learning than in other investigations typically completed in the biology course. It is likely that students will conduct the majority of the work outside of class hours.

The techniques and processes promoted in this full inquiry are similar to those required by many science fairs. If you usually ask students to complete science fair projects, review the steps and suggestions that follow and consider using them as a template for meeting that goal. We strongly encourage you to include a full inquiry in your biology course to allow students an in-depth, realistic experience of scientific inquiry. We recommend, however, that you do not begin a full inquiry earlier than midway through the school year and not until after students have honed their inquiry skill by completing all or several of the invitations to inquiry in chapter 6. Keep in mind that students will need six to eight weeks to

---

*Adapted from BSCS. 2006. Explain: Being an Experimental Scientist. In *BSCS biology: A human approach*, student edition, 394–397, and teacher edition, 351–359. Dubuque, IA: Kendall/Hunt.

National Science Teachers Association

execute a full inquiry. Although much of the work for this full inquiry activity will be completed outside of class, you will need to set aside several class periods across the six to eight weeks to review and approve students' plans and check their progress.

Preparing for the Full Inquiry

Begin planning for the full inquiry several weeks before you introduce it to your students. The critical issues you will need to consider are materials and equipment, safety, and assessment.

Materials and Equipment

Part of planning a reasonable investigation involves being realistic about materials. You will probably want to limit expenses for materials acquired outside of class. You may find it useful to supply students with a list of available or appropriate materials with which to work. You will also need to monitor their choice of materials to ensure safety, as described in the following section. Make sure students understand that you reserve the right to deny their investigation if you believe the materials and equipment they need are too expensive or unsafe.

The projects will vary in the type and amount of advance preparation necessary. As you approve each step, keep in mind the variations of the experiments so you are not caught short of supplies or space. If you want students to display their results, arrange for the necessary display area. You also may want to build in class time for students to present their results to one another.

Safety

One of the central features of this activity is that students develop their own procedures. This makes it challenging to provide specific safety notes or to advise on precautions. It is essential, therefore, for each student to submit a written experimental design that shows not only comprehension of the concepts involved and a complete procedural plan but also a safety plan. The safety plan should demonstrate a student's awareness of the hazards inherent in the procedures and the precautions necessary to prevent harm.

It is your responsibility to review each student's safety plans carefully, discuss any necessary changes, and approve the revised plan before a student begins work. Be sure that the students show in their written plans that they are familiar with and understand the hazards and precautions of each chemical and all equipment with which they plan to work. Similarly, be sure the students demonstrate that they are familiar with any biohazards that may be associated with biomaterials they use and that they honor the necessary precautions. Hazards include, but are not limited to, electrical shock, sharp edges, recently bent or fire-polished hot glass tubing, other hot surfaces (such as hot plates), blending equipment, bright lights, and loud noises. Be sure that students identify any such hazards and plan for the appropriate precautions. Review basic information about laboratory safety with students before they begin any independent work.

The hazards and precautions of chemicals that may be used in each independent inquiry are summarized on their container labels and are described in more detail in the material safety data sheet (MSDS) for each chemical. Do not allow a chemical to be used without knowledge of the hazard and precautionary information. If you do not have an MSDS for a chemical, do not use the chemical or a mixture of chemicals until you have obtained the information. (Obtain Material Safety Data Sheets from your supplier; all suppliers of hazardous chemicals are required by law to provide this information to their customers.) MSDS information also can be found on the web at *www.setonresourcecenter. com/MSDS/index.htm*.

Appendix C summarizes common safety issues in the high school biology laboratory and how to accommodate them. This appendix summarizes information related to biology laboratories from the National Science Teachers Association (NSTA 2004) publication *Investigating Safely*. This book is an excellent, in-depth, and highly readable laboratory safety guide for high school teachers in all areas of science.

Note: Even with an adequate safety plan, if students' experiments involve dangerous chemicals or procedures, be sure they work under adult supervision.

Assessment Plan

We recommend using a scoring rubric for evaluating students' full inquiries. A sample rubric that you can use as is or adapt to meet your specific needs is provided in table 7.1. You will get higher-quality projects if you distribute the rubric to students *before* they begin planning their investigations. Spend some class time examining the rubric and discussing what each row means.

After students have had time to thoroughly discuss each area of the scoring rubric, randomly call on them to develop a description of an excellent project. Elaborate these student descriptions with your own ideas about excellence. Students should clearly understand your expectations for successfully completing this inquiry.

Criteria	Excellent	Could Be Improved	Needs Substantial Improvement
Concept: Questioning, using inquiry, and communicating results	• Inquiry is based on an interesting and scientifically testable question that can be tested with the equipment available and techniques that can be conducted in this class. • Hypothesis and prediction are clearly stated and include an explanation.	• Inquiry is based on a scientifically testable question that needs additional equipment, techniques, or both to isolate one or two significant variables. • Hypothesis and prediction are briefly stated and explained.	• Inquiry is based on a question that is not scientifically testable. • Hypothesis and prediction are too brief and explained poorly or incorrectly.
Explanation: Explanation for scientific design and analysis based on the question being asked	• Inquiry is designed with reasonable and logical use of the concepts that are important for the chosen topic. • Explanation of the design makes good use of the vocabulary that is important to the experiment. • Experimental design uses appropriate controls. • Results are recorded clearly and accurately. • Analysis clearly refers to the question, hypothesis, and prediction. • Analysis relates two or more specific examples taken from the results to demonstrate a clear rationale for the conclusion drawn.	• Experiment is designed with reasonable use of the concepts that are important for the chosen topic. • Explanation of the design uses minimal vocabulary that is important to the experiment. • Experimental design uses appropriate controls, though not all key variables are controlled. • Results are recorded accurately. • Analysis briefly refers to the question, hypothesis, and prediction. • Analysis uses only one reference to a specific example in the results to demonstrate a clear rationale for the conclusion drawn.	• Experiment is designed without reasonable use of the concepts that are important for the chosen topic. • Explanation of the design incorrectly uses vocabulary that is important to the experiment. • Experimental design uses inappropriate controls, several key variables are not controlled, or both. • Results are recorded inaccurately. • Analysis lacks reference to the question, hypothesis, or prediction. • Analysis does not reference specific examples from the results.
Explanation: Connections	• Presentation clearly and accurately explains the inquiry's connections to the unifying principles of biology.	• Presentation generally explains the inquiry's connections to the unifying principles of biology.	• Presentation is overly brief or incorrectly explains the inquiry's connections to the unifying principles of biology.
Presentation: Hypothesis, procedure, results, and analysis; grammar and punctuation	• Presentation is well organized and complete (contains a hypothesis, procedure, results, and analysis). • Grammar and punctuation are used correctly, making it easy to understand what is meant.	• Presentation has some organization and is complete (contains a hypothesis, procedure, results, and analysis), but some parts are difficult to locate. • Grammar and punctuation are generally used correctly. Sometimes it is difficult to be sure what is meant.	• Presentation has little evident organization, it is incomplete (missing one of the following: hypothesis, procedure, results, and analysis), or both. • Grammar and punctuation are frequently used incorrectly. Often it is difficult to be sure what is meant.

Introducing the Full Inquiry Activity

Introduce your students to their full inquiry experience by asking them to bring in recent magazines, newspapers, or videos that relate news stories reported before you begin this experience.

Encourage your students to look for articles that have to do with any area of biology that interests them. Medical news is likely to be a common choice. If so, encourage a broad cross-section of stories related to the science of medicine.

Ask students to analyze the news article by answering the following questions. They should base their answers on both the information in the article itself and what they infer.

- What question did the scientists ask?
- What background information informed the scientists?
- What type of investigation did the scientists conduct?
- What tools did the scientists use?
- What results did the scientists get?
- What conclusions did the scientists draw?
- What new questions did the scientists ask?

You may want to limit the number of articles discussed by selecting several from those the students bring in. Then allow them to choose one for their small group to analyze together.

Many students likely will find their articles do not include information for answering all the questions. This realization is an important part of the activity. (In fact, if you preselect articles for them to read, you may want to make sure that the articles do not include enough information to answer all of the questions.) Most articles in the popular press that deal with science issues present significantly less information than is necessary to fully evaluate whether the science was good or poor.

Following discussion of the articles and responses to the questions in small-group or whole-class settings, ask students to write at least two scientific questions that they would like to research. Tell students that they do not have to use any ideas from the articles they analyzed. They can use questions of personal interest or questions prompted by their discussions. The intent of this question really is to get students thinking about science topics that interest them.

Conducting the Full Inquiry

In the full inquiry experience, students are required to work more independently than at other times. They will need to take full responsibility for all parts of a scientific inquiry. The full inquiry experience outlined here emphasizes the thinking steps. These thinking steps include posing a testable question, which then is restated as a hypothesis; designing an experiment with adequate controls; analyzing data and using it to draw logical conclusions; and planning how best to communicate results to an outside observer.

1. Asking the Question

Tell students to review the questions they wrote after they analyzed their news articles. Are those questions of sufficient interest for them to conduct an investigation? Are they testable questions? If not, can students rewrite them so that they are? If some students no longer find their questions interesting, or if they are unable to make the questions testable, encourage them to do library research about a topic of greater interest to them. The new information will provide useful background and may give students an idea for a testable question.

Direct students to write a paragraph that elaborates their question for you to review. Their paragraph should

- record the question in one or two sentences,
- explain why the question is significant by writing several sentences that describe what already is known about the topic that they wish to investigate,
- restate the question as a hypothesis that can be tested, and
- record which of the six unifying principles of biology (see table 7.2 and chapter 3 in this volume) is related to their hypothesis.

If your students struggle greatly to develop their own questions, discuss the areas in biology that most interest them. This discussion could be linked to the previous activity in which they read about an issue in a news article. You may also consider having a list of starter questions available to spark students' ideas about what they might want to investigate; however, try to get students to come up with their own questions before you offer yours.

After the students find their questions, they will need to restate them as testable hypotheses and explain their significance. For many students, the classic if-then construction is a useful tool for constructing hypotheses. For example, if a student asks, "What effect does the wavelength of light have on a flower's ability to bloom?" the question could be restated as, "If a

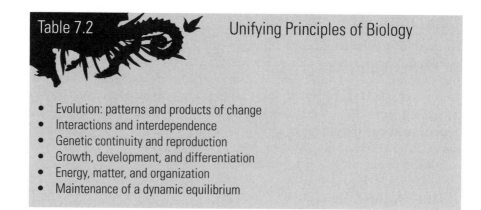

Table 7.2   Unifying Principles of Biology

- Evolution: patterns and products of change
- Interactions and interdependence
- Genetic continuity and reproduction
- Growth, development, and differentiation
- Energy, matter, and organization
- Maintenance of a dynamic equilibrium

flower is exposed to shorter wavelengths of light, then it will bloom earlier than other similar flowers exposed to longer wavelengths."

An important point: The question above is also an example of a meaningful question. Because plants require light for life, there is good reason to think that certain wavelengths of light may have better or worse effects on plant growth, development, or both. By contrast, plants do not require music for life, so there is no reason to think that rock music would benefit plant growth more than classical music. Students often have a hard time distinguishing between meaningful questions and trivial questions, and your guidance at this step can help set them in the direction of a rich and rewarding experience. Identifying the unifying principles that relate to the hypothesis will help the students place their inquiry in a broader biological context.

Although most of this step can be completed outside of class, you will want to check students' progress in class. When you review students' paragraphs, look for testable ideas, safe ideas, and connections to the unifying principles. This will be your last opportunity to identify insignificant or untestable questions that are not appropriate for this full inquiry. If a learner suggests building a model of a volcano or adding ethanol to a plant, help him or her see that such ideas do not test meaningful scientific questions. Encourage these learners to think of more-appropriate alternatives and provide suggestions as necessary.

2. Gathering Information

Direct your students to use the library, local scientists, the web, or other available resources to gather information related to their questions. Emphasize that scientists use data others have collected as well as data gathered directly through experimental investigations, and that students should also. Encourage students to be creative in locating diverse sources of information. Discourage use of the web (or any other resource) as the sole source of information. Science magazines, journals, and topic-specific books offer different types of information. Provide guidance for students in evaluating the credibility of their sources, particularly those from the internet (see chapter 13 for questions you should encourage students to ask about their sources).

3. Designing the Experiment

Assign students to write a page or two that describes their experimental design. The design should include

- a rationale that explains how the experiment will test the question and describes the controls and the role that they will play;
- a hypothesis that explains what students think the answer to the question may be and why they think so;
- a procedure that includes the materials they will need;
- a plan for analyzing their data; and
- a safety plan that records the precautions they will follow when they use chemicals, handle equipment, and handle biological hazards such as bacteria or yeast.

Be sure to tell students how much time they will have to plan, conduct, and complete their full inquiry and what materials and equipment are available to them. As learners write descriptions of their experimental designs, emphasize the need for a controlled experiment that consciously attends to safety issues. Depending on materials, space, and the nature of your students, you should clarify whether they should work alone, with a partner, or in a larger team.

4. Obtaining Teacher Approval

Arrange a procedure and time for reviewing students' plans with them. Discuss your impressions and suggestions that you have for improvements. Students should have your signed approval before they begin carrying out their experiment.

5. Conducting the Experiment

Once you have approved students' plans, they can begin their experiments. Much of this work will occur outside of class time; however, depending on safety issues and equipment needs, you may need to schedule time for some students to work in your classroom when you can supervise them. Remind the students to record their data in their science notebooks. You also may want to review the many methods for recording data: photographing; videotaping; sketching; and recording readings such as temperature, time, and growth.

6. Analyzing the Data

Instruct students to organize their data in a way that makes it easier to see patterns or understand what the data show them. This step will help them when they present their work to their classmates and others. In addition, encourage students to use appropriate statistics in their analyses. For example, many students include replicates in their experimental design, but simply report results for each individual within a treatment group rather than calculating and comparing means across treatment groups. You have an opportunity for a rich discussion of error and individual differences and for how to treat these differences in a way that does not compromise the conclusions drawn. In some cases, it may be appropriate for students to apply simple tests of significance, such as the chi-square test.

As students complete their experiments, ask them to be prepared to discuss their preliminary results in a peer review session. Students should decide what their data tell them and record their preliminary conclusions. They should describe any limitations of their experimental design and any unexpected results they may have found. Schedule class time for students to meet in small groups to share their findings and initial conclusions. (If the class has conducted team projects for the full inquiry, pair two or three teams together for sharing.) Encourage students to ask questions and make suggestions that help each researcher clarify the evidence that supports his or her conclusions and to present the findings most accurately and clearly.

7. Drawing Conclusions

Ask students to write a final page or two that explains what their conclusions indicate about the question they asked. Encourage them to do more than restate their results. Explain that results summarize data that has been gathered, whereas conclusions tie the results to the hypothesis. Students should support their conclusions by making specific references to their data. They should also describe how their work connects to the unifying principle most related to their inquiry. Students should state whether their hypothesis was supported or disproved and suggest how future experiments might reveal an even better understanding of the process or phenomenon being investigated. Look for evidence of thoughtful analysis and an effort to connect the inquiry with the larger conceptual picture of biology represented by one or more unifying principles.

8. Communicating Results

Determine a mechanism for students to communicate their results. Some possibilities for the presentations include the following:

- Private presentations such as verbal or written reports that are presented to the teacher
- Public displays in a hallway, a showcase, or the classroom
- Poster sessions to informally present findings to peers
- Oral presentations accompanied by PowerPoint slides
- Video or software presentations that can be viewed by a larger audience
- A science fair after school in the gymnasium or other large area

Student presentations should make it possible for someone else to understand what they did, why they did it, and what they found out. Where appropriate, encourage students to use graphs to display their data. Point out that graphs display a great deal of information in a small amount of space. Encourage students, as they listen to one another's present results, to look for evidence or examples that illustrate why the approach used for answering the question was scientific.

Wrapping Up the Full Inquiry Activity

Conclude the full inquiry experience by conducting a whole-class discussion that includes opportunities for students to reflect more generally on their experiences. Ask questions such as these:

- How did your inquiry depend upon or connect with technology, culture, history, and ethical issues? (For example, a full inquiry project that investigates the dependence of plant growth on particular wavelengths of visible light would rely on technology that enables the isolation of specific wavelengths of light.)
- What new hypotheses related to your original question did your investigation generate?
- What suggestions do you have for the direction of subsequent investigations?
- How do scientific approaches to knowing the world distinguish science from other ways of knowing the world?

Finally, encourage your students to make connections between their experiments and the unifying principles. This task reinforces the relevance of biology and the importance of science in society.

BACKGROUND INFORMATION

If you want more background about the methods of inquiry or a rationale for doing scientific inquiry, we recommend the following resources:

American Association for the Advancement of Science (AAAS). 1990. *Science for all Americans.* New York: Oxford University Press.

————. 1993. *Benchmarks for science literacy.* New York: Oxford University Press.

BSCS. 1993. *Developing biological literacy,* 2nd ed. Dubuque, IA: Kendall/Hunt.

————. 2006. *Why does inquiry matter? Because that's what science is all about!* Dubuque, IA: Kendall/Hunt.

National Research Council (NRC). 1996. *National Science Education Standards.* Washington, DC: National Academy Press.

————. 2000. *Inquiry and the National Science Education Standards.* Washington, DC: National Academy Press.

National Science Teachers Association (NSTA). 2004. *Investigating safely.* Arlington, VA: NSTA Press.

SECTION II REFERENCES

BSCS. 2006. *BSCS biology: A human approach.* Dubuque, IA: Kendall/Hunt.

Bransford, J., A. L. Brown, and R. R. Cocking. 1999. *How people learn: Brain, mind, experience, and school.* Washington, DC: National Academy Press.

Bybee, R. W. 2000. Teaching science as inquiry. In *Inquiring into inquiry learning and teaching in science,* eds. J. Minstrell and E. H. van Zee, 20–46. Washington, DC: American Association for the Advancement of Science.

Darwin, C. R. 1880. *The power of movement in plants.* London: John Murray.

Moore, J. A. 1993. *Science as a way of knowing: The foundations of modern biology.* Cambridge, MA: Harvard University Press.

National Institute on Drug Abuse (NIDA). 2001, May. Researchers find evidence that prenatal exposure to ecstasy can cause long-term memory loss and other impairments in offspring. *Journal of Neuroscience* 2001 (21): 3228–35.

National Research Council (NRC). 1996. *National Science Education Standards.* Washington, DC: National Academy Press.

————. 2000. *Inquiry and the National Science Education Standards: A guide for teaching and learning.* Washington, DC: National Academy Press.

National Science Teachers Association (NSTA). 2004. *Investigating safely: A Guide for High School Teachers.* Arlington, VA: NSTA Press.

Schwab, J. 1966. *The teaching of science.* Cambridge, MA: Harvard University Press.

Section III

Introduction

The Role of Controversy in Biology Education

Most teachers have an abiding interest in learning and a desire to work with their students. They place great value on their relationships with their students and nurture these connections carefully. Thus, it is with some trepidation that many teachers approach controversial topics, thinking that covering these topics will threaten those relationships. They may fear that controversy will place them on opposite sides of an issue from their students. Controversial topics also tend to provoke a wide range of comments and questions from students. Some teachers worry that these comments and questions will reveal gaps in their knowledge of content or pedagogy. Finally, teachers may worry that discussing areas of controversy will lead to confrontations with parents or even their school administrations. So why should biology educators teach about controversial topics? Section III of the *Biology Teacher's Handbook* provides a perspective on this question and explores the nature and proper use of controversy in the biology classroom.

We assert that controversy in the biology classroom is better viewed as an educational asset rather than as an obstacle to be avoided. Proper use of controversy in the classroom can promote student engagement, hone critical-thinking skills, and make connections with students' everyday lives. Scientific controversy is part and parcel of the general notion of scientific literacy. Most students will not grow up to be scientists, but they live in a society that heavily depends on science and technology. It is vital that all students acquire a foundational knowledge of science in order to navigate through their personal lives and to make informed decisions regarding scientific issues that they encounter.

127

In his book *Why Science?* James Trefil (2008) provides the following definition of scientific literacy:

> Scientific literacy is the matrix of knowledge needed to understand enough about the physical universe to deal with issues that come across our horizon, in the news or elsewhere. (28)

This definition helps clarify why teaching about controversial issues in the biology classroom is so important. The areas of science most likely to come across students' horizons when they serve as citizens are precisely those areas that engender controversy.

It is important to recognize crucial distinctions among the different types of controversies in biological education. Scientific issues can be controversial from three different perspectives: science, teaching, and application.

- *Science: The existing scientific knowledge does not support a single explanation.* When Charles Darwin first proposed natural selection, he believed evolution proceeded gradually, with selection operating on small variations. Francis Galton, however, believed that natural selection needed to act on large, discontinuous variations. The debate between these two views has continued for decades. Because both camps had data to support their views, the ideas were controversial. Modern genetic data are finally supplying empirical data to help resolve this controversy. (Note that this controversy is not about the basic theory of evolution by natural selection but about the rate at which this process can occur.) Studying why each camp held its views provides useful opportunities for students to learn about the nature of science.
- *Teaching: The existing scientific knowledge is not in dispute.* Rather, the controversy stems from people having different beliefs about what content is appropriate for the classroom. Human reproduction has been, and continues to be, controversial to teach in some areas. All parties agree on how babies are made, but they disagree about how much information to present at what age and what values such information may or not promote.
- *Application: Again, the scientific knowledge is not in dispute.* Instead, the controversy centers on the application of that knowledge. There is controversy about using stem cells to treat disease. In this case, there is general agreement about what a stem cell is, its ability to develop into any type of adult cell, and that stem cells are harvested from embryos. The controversy arises from different beliefs about the moral standing of the embryo.

Each of these categories presents distinct opportunities, challenges, and pitfalls in the classroom.

A brief history of controversies in biology education is presented in chapter 8, followed by brief, but more specific discussions of contemporary topics that may contain elements of controversy. Position statements from the National Science Teachers Association and National Association of Biology Teachers on specific controversial topics are included. The chapter concludes with suggestions on how to handle controversial topics in the classroom, including the perspective from the *National Science Education Standards* (NRC 1996).

Chapter 8

Perspectives on Contemporary Controversial Topics in Biology Education

Today, science and technology are moving at breakneck speed. As science advances, concerns about its unintended consequences increase. This situation makes it seem as though controversy in the biology classroom is a recent development. In fact, controversy and high school biology have always coexisted.

One of the most persistent controversies in biology education concerns the teaching of evolutionary theory. This is a case in which the science is clear: Evolution provides a scientific explanation for the diversity and similarities among living organisms. The controversy is whether, and how, the theory of evolution should be included in the biology curriculum. In 1925, a high school teacher in Tennessee named John Scopes was charged with breaking a state law by teaching evolution to his students. The famous trial that resulted became known as the Scopes monkey trial and served as the basis for the play and film *Inherit the Wind*. Scopes was convicted and fined, but his case was only the first shot fired in the battles over teaching evolution that continue to this day.

During the first half of the 20th century, controversy in the biology classroom was largely avoided through the practice of precensorship. Gerald Skoog (2008) has analyzed American high school biology textbooks from the 20th century. He found that in 1950, half (7 of 14) of textbooks did not include the word *evolution* in the text, glossary, or index. Furthermore, all of the reviewed books from this period that included evolution placed it in one of the final chapters. Later in that decade, the Nobel Prize laureate Hermann Muller lamented that "one hundred years without Darwin are enough."

As related in section V, BSCS was founded in 1958 in response to growing concerns about the state of science education in the United States and the Soviet Union's launching of *Sputnik I*. BSCS's first three textbooks for high school biology all used evolution as a central theme. The BSCS textbooks were very popular, and, in just five years, more than 2.25 million copies were in use. Other publishers noticed the success of these books, and soon evolution was being given a more thorough treatment in nearly all textbooks.

Throughout the rest of the 20th century, coverage of evolution remained in the popular textbooks, but not without controversy. Anti-evolution groups pressured publishers to remove coverage of the topic, or at least to remove the word *evolution* from the text. Today, evolution remains a mainstay of high school biology textbooks, but legal challenges to its instruction still confront school boards and teachers.

Another area of controversy that affected biology teaching during the 20th century was human reproduction. As with evolution, many publishers dealt with the controversy through precensorship—they simply left it out of the textbooks. BSCS textbooks took a different approach and included coverage of this sensitive topic. Our books featured diagrams and illustrations that had never before appeared in high school textbooks. This prompted one critic to declare that BSCS was the *Playboy* magazine of biology textbooks (BSCS 2007). It should be noted that these first examples of controversy in the biology classroom were not focused on the science itself. Instead, the controversies centered on how the scientific ideas interacted with issues of religion and values.

Aside from spurring specific reforms to represent evolution and human reproduction from a scientific perspective, the Sputnik launch generated attempts to develop scientific literacy more broadly across society. Previously, science instruction was often geared toward students who were already inclined toward careers in science research or medicine. The growing recognition of the importance of a scientifically literate citizenry led educators to elevate the importance of teaching the nature of science and how scientific ideas influence and interact with society. Controversies represent excellent opportunities to teach about both the nature of science and the interaction of science and society. Thus, one important outcome of reform movements in the late 1950s and early 1960s was an increased recognition of the important role controversies could play in science education.

Controversy in Today's Classroom

Open any good newspaper and you will find articles that describe events, studies, policies, and controversies related to biology. Table 8.1 lists topics within the life sciences that can provoke controversy. For each topic, some related questions are posed about controversies in each area. Questions from each of the three different types of controversies described in the introduction to section III (science, teaching, and application) are included.

This admittedly incomplete list illustrates that controversy can be found in the biology classroom at every level, from molecular biology to ecology. Some controversial issues are predominantly important to scientists. Many controversial issues are of concern, however, to businesspeople, politicians, economists, lawyers, physicians, farmers, clergy, and indeed all citizens. People from all walks of life encounter controversy (sometimes indirectly) in the course of their daily lives. For example, people must choose whether to eat meat or genetically engineered food, buy products from companies that use animal experimentation, and support the use of biofuels.

In a democratic society, people can make their feelings about controversial issues known in a variety of ways, such as voting, responding to media surveys, debating with family and friends, exchanging opinions via the web, and purchasing selected goods and services. When people make

Table 8.1   Controversy in the Biology Classroom

Life Science Topic	Questions of Controversy	Nature of Controversy
Global climate change	• To what degree are humans responsible for increasing carbon dioxide in the atmosphere?	Science
	• Should nations reduce their use of fossils fuels, and if so, how?	Application
	• Should the generation of nuclear power be increased to combat global warming?	Application
	• Is it wise to plow under more land to generate more biofuels?	Science and Application
Population	• Does everyone have the right of unrestricted reproduction?	Teaching
	• How do we balance the world's population and food resources?	Science, Teaching, and Application
	• What is the impact of standard of living choices on the carrying capacity of Earth?	Science
	• How many people can Earth sustain indefinitely?	Science
Biodiversity	• What is the best way to protect ecosystems while using natural resources?	Science and Application
	• What rate of species extinction is "natural"?	Science
	• Is the Endangered Species Act valuable and realistic?	Application
	• Who owns valuable products obtained from plants and animals?	Application

up their minds about controversial issues, they are influenced by a number of factors such as religious beliefs, family upbringing, political leanings, and their personal experiences as shaped by gender, age, ethnicity, socioeconomic status, and education. Sometimes people are unable or unwilling to conduct an objective analysis of an issue. They may respond emotionally with their gut reaction, or they may be ignorant about the scientific principles involved.

Gut reactions have shown themselves to be a poor basis for forming public policy. If society is to maximize the benefits of biomedicine while minimizing the negative effects, then it is vital to educate society's members so that public policy is well informed and effective in guiding change. People need a basic understanding of scientific principles and must be able to carry out a thoughtful ethical analysis. These ideas are recognized in the *National Science Education Standards* (NRC 1996, p. 199). The Science in Personal and Social Perspectives content standard (grades 9–12) states that:

> Understanding basic concepts and principles of science and technology should precede active debate about the economics, policies, politics, and ethics of various science- and technology-related challenges. …

> Individuals and society must decide on proposals involving new research and the introduction of new technologies into society. Decisions involve assessment of alternatives, risks, costs, and benefits and consideration of who benefits and who suffers, who pays and gains, and what the risks are and who bears them. Students should understand the appropriateness and value of basic questions—"What can happen?"—"What are the odds?"—and "How do scientists and engineers know what will happen?"

The rest of this chapter describes a few important areas of controversy that biology teachers encounter today. For most controversies, teachers can turn to position statements by professional societies for guidance and support. For example, more-detailed position statements may be found at the websites of the National Science Teachers Association *(www.nsta.org)* and the National Association of Biology Teachers *(www.nabt.org)*.

Controversial Topic 1: Evolution

The teaching of evolution is the first and most important area of controversy associated with the biology classroom. As stated previously, the power of evolutionary theory to explain the diversity and similarities of living organisms is not controversial among scientists. Scientists and educators alike recognize the fundamental importance of evolution to the study of biology. Consequently, they strongly resist any attempt to remove it from the curriculum or to include nonscientific explanations for the diversity of life on Earth. The position statement on teaching evolution from NABT (2004a) includes the following:

> As stated in *The American Biology Teacher* by the eminent scientist Theodosius Dobzhansky (1973), "Nothing in biology makes sense except in the light of evolution." This often-quoted declaration accurately reflects the central, unifying role of evolution in biology. The theory of evolution provides a framework that explains both the history of life and the ongoing adaptation of organisms to environmental challenges and changes.
>
> While modern biologists constantly study and deliberate the patterns, mechanisms, and pace of evolution, they agree that all living things share common ancestors. The fossil record and the diversity of extant organisms, combined with modern techniques of molecular biology, taxonomy, and geology, provide exhaustive examples of and powerful evidence for current evolutionary theory. Genetic variation, natural selection, speciation, and extinction are well-established components of modern evolutionary theory. Explanations are constantly modified and refined as warranted by new scientific evidence that accumulates over time, which demonstrates the integrity and validity of the field.
>
> Scientists have firmly established evolution as an important natural process. Experimentation, logical analysis, and evidence-based revision are procedures that clearly differentiate and separate science from other ways of knowing. Explanations or ways of knowing that invoke non-naturalistic or supernatural events or beings, whether called "creation science," "scientific creationism," "intelligent design theory," "young earth theory," or similar designations, are outside the realm of science and not part of a valid science curriculum.

The position statement from NSTA (2003b) on the teaching of evolution includes the following declarations:

> Science curricula, state science standards, and teachers should emphasize evolution in a manner commensurate with its importance as a unifying concept in science and its overall explanatory power.

> Science teachers should not advocate any religious interpretations of nature and should be nonjudgmental about the personal beliefs of students.

> Policy makers and administrators should not mandate policies requiring the teaching of "creation science" or related concepts, such as so-called "intelligent design," "abrupt appearance," and "arguments against evolution." Administrators also should support teachers against pressure to promote nonscientific views or to diminish or eliminate the study of evolution.

> Administrators and school boards should provide support to teachers as they review, adopt, and implement curricula that emphasize evolution. This should include professional development to assist teachers in teaching evolution in a comprehensive and professional manner.

> Parental and community involvement in establishing the goals of science education and the curriculum development process should be encouraged and nurtured in our democratic society. However, the professional responsibility of science teachers and curriculum specialists to provide students with quality science education should not be compromised by censorship, pseudoscience, inconsistencies, faulty scholarship, or unconstitutional mandates.

> Science textbooks shall emphasize evolution as a unifying concept. Publishers should not be required or volunteer to include disclaimers in textbooks that distort or misrepresent the methodology of science and the current body of knowledge concerning the nature and study of evolution.

Controversial Topic 2: Human Reproduction

Areas of biology dealing with human sexuality have been, and will continue to be, controversial to teach. Nevertheless, such information is among the most important and relevant to the everyday lives of students. The position statement on the teaching of sexuality and human reproduction from NSTA (2000) includes the following preamble:

> Sexuality and human reproduction are essential concepts in a comprehensive science program. The teaching of these subjects continues to be very important at all educational levels. Parents, as first teachers, need to be a collaborative partner in this process. The National Science Teachers Association, NSTA, regards instruction in sexuality and the biology of human reproduction to be necessary in the education of every person and to represent a legitimate component of any teaching program in the life and health sciences. We hold that education in this field is feasible at every curricular stage and can therefore begin at the earliest grade or level. In addition, we consider knowledge of human sexuality as a fundamental and natural characteristic of humans that is critical for understanding the attitudes and actions of individuals, families, communities, and nations.

Controversial Topic 3: Environmental Issues

As the human population grows, environmental issues are likely to become dominant areas of concern for our society. Issues such as global climate change, land use, availability of freshwater, loss of biodiversity, and pollution all touch on areas of controversy. The position statement on teaching about environmental issues from the NABT (2004b) has this to say:

> Environmental science explores the complex interactions among human populations and their environment. Consistent with the National Science Education Standards[1] (National Academy of Science, 1996), the National Association of Biology Teachers holds that environmental science is a vital component of an effective modern biology curriculum that seeks to prepare an informed citizenry. Biology teachers should recognize how the understandings gained through environmental science interact with local, national and global environmental issues. Meeting the environmental challenges that face humankind requires a knowledgeable citizenry that understands how relevant scientific information informs sound policy decisions.
>
> [1] See NRC 1996 in the references.

The position statement from NSTA (2003a) on environmental education includes the following declarations:

> Environmental education programs should foster observation, investigation, experimentation, and innovation. Programs should be developed with grade-appropriate materials and should use a range of hands-on, minds-on instructional strategies that encourage active learning.
>
> Environmental education programs and curricula should address student outcomes as specified in the *National Science Education Standards*, be grounded in sound research, and reflect the most current information and understandings in the field.
>
> All learners are expected to achieve environmental literacy and an appreciation for and knowledge of a range of environmental issues, perspectives, and positions.

All learners should be taught how to think through an issue using critical-thinking skills, while avoiding instructor or media bias regarding what to think about the issue.

Environmental education should provide interdisciplinary, multicultural, and multi-perspective viewpoints to promote awareness and understanding of global environmental issues, potential solutions, and ways to prevent emerging environmental crises.

Developers of environmental education programs should strive to present a balance of environmental, economic, and social perspectives.

Appropriate technologies should be used to enhance environmental education learning experiences and investigations.

Environmental education programs and activities should be fostered through both formal and informal learning experiences.

Collaborations among schools, museums, zoos, aquaria, nature centers, government agencies, associations, foundations, and private industry should be encouraged to broaden the availability of educational resources, engage the community, provide diverse points of view about the management of natural resources, and offer a variety of learning experiences and career education opportunities.

Controversial Topic 4: The Use of Animals in the Classroom

During the second half of the 20th century, animal rights became a growing topic of public debate. In 1975, the Australian ethicist and philosopher Peter Singer published the book *Animal Liberation*. In it, he argues that the capacity for suffering is the vital characteristic that determines if an organism is entitled to equal consideration with humans. According to this view, it is morally indefensible to eat meat or to use animals in experiments.

Although some people agree with Singer, most adopt a less extreme view and hold that it is morally justifiable to use animals in research that is designed to reduce human suffering. Scientists engaged in such research are morally and legally obligated to treat animals in accordance with rules designed to restrict their use and minimize their discomfort. In general, the research community is guided by the three Rs: refine, reduce, and replace. Scientists endeavor to refine their protocols in such a way as to minimize pain caused to animals; they design experiments to reduce the number of animals needed; and, wherever possible, they replace animal subjects with nonanimal alternatives.

The following is taken from the position statement on the use of animals in biology education by NABT (2003):

> The study of organisms, including nonhuman animals, is essential to the understanding of life on Earth. NABT recommends the prudent and responsible use of animals in the life science classroom. Biology teachers should foster a respect for life and should teach about the interrelationship and interdependency of all things.

> Classroom experiences that involve nonhuman animals range from observation to dissection. As with any instructional activity, the use of nonhuman animals in the biology classroom must have sound educational objectives. Any use of animals must convey substantive knowledge of biology and be appropriate for the classroom and for the age of the students. Biology teachers are in the best position to make this determination for their students.

> NABT supports these experiences so long as they are conducted within the established guidelines of proper care and use of animals, as developed by the scientific and educational community. NABT encourages the presence of live animals in the classroom with appropriate consideration to the age and maturity level of the students (elementary, middle school, high school or college).

Controversial Topic 5: Recombinant DNA Technology and the Human Genome Project

Recombinant DNA technology and the Human Genome Project are not controversial as such. They are included in virtually every high school biology textbook. The applications of the technology, however, can and do generate controversy. When recombinant DNA technology was first developed in the early 1970s, some scientists became concerned that the technology could potentially produce threats to human health and the environment. A group of scientists who were leaders in the field met for several days at the Asilomar Conference Grounds in California to discuss the risks and benefits of the emerging technology. They put together a system of self-regulation that was designed to classify what sorts of experiments could be carried out under what sorts of containment conditions. In 1976, the Asilomar recommendations became the basis for the first federal guidelines for the conduct of recombinant DNA research.

About 15 years later, when the Human Genome Project (HGP) began, its leadership recognized that the project would produce data that could potentially be misused. They decided to devote 3% (later raised to 5%) of the budget to the study of the ethical, social, and legal implications of the HGP. The primary area of controversy associated with the HGP is genetic privacy. Who should have access to an individual's genetic data: employers, insurance companies, law enforcement agencies, family members? Each of these stakeholders can make a case for why access to such data is in their best interest. Even today, the federal government is struggling to pass legislation that delineates how the interests of the individual are balanced with those of other stakeholders with regard to genetic data.

Controversy over genetic technology is not limited to humans. Scientists' ability to use recombinant DNA technology to insert a gene from one organism and place it into the genome of another species raises many ethical concerns. Genetically modified organisms (GMOs) are plants or animals that have had one or more genes added to or subtracted from their genomes. GMOs are the latest manifestation of people's desire to manipulate other organisms to solve problems. Although there is nothing inherently unsafe about GMOs, it is necessary to examine each use of the technology in order to assess its relative safety. For example, some plants have genes from other organisms inserted into their genomes, perhaps allowing the plant to grow under stressful conditions or to increase its nutritional value. In such cases, it is important to know if the modified plant can pass the gene or genes on to other species or if the gene or genes can produce proteins that might cause an allergic reaction in people who eat the plant.

Applications of recombinant DNA technology and the acquisition of human genetic data will only increase as the 21st century unfolds. As students mature, enter the workforce, and vote, they will be confronted with a multitude of scientific controversies. Many such controversies will involve medical issues that will affect their health care decisions. Other controversies will affect them less directly but will affect their quality of life in other ways. To the extent that students have experience dealing with controversy through objective analysis, they will be better positioned to function as citizens and voters.

How Can You Handle Controversial Topics in the Classroom?

Many teachers recognize that controversy can help engage students in biology topics. It is easy to make direct connections between the appropriate use of controversial topics and each of the major content themes that runs through a general biology course. Including controversial topics in high school biology has a number of advantages. Controversy

- can stimulate interest in biological topics by providing real-world contexts in which it is necessary to understand fundamental biological concepts;
- provides students with opportunities to hone their critical-thinking and inquiry skills;
- can highlight the importance of basic research to our health and well-being;
- can challenge students to consider the societal implications of science and technology;
- can help students learn to deal with moral ambiguity and disagreement,
- is amenable to multidisciplinary approaches; and
- is consistent with, and supports, the National Science Education Standards (NRC 1996).

The first step in handling controversy in a pedagogically appropriate manner is to decide the manner in which the topic is controversial. At the beginning of this section, three categories were represented: issues that are controversial among scientists, issues that are controversial to include in a science curriculum, and applications and uses of scientific technology that are controversial. You should handle each category differently in your classroom.

Controversies Among Scientists

Many teachers like to employ classroom strategies such as role-playing and debates to provide students with opportunities to frame questions, gather evidence, and make arguments. These techniques are especially helpful when students debate issues that are controversial within science. True controversies in science require students to carefully reflect on evidence and reasoning when forming explanations and alternative explanations. Developing explanations and considering alternative explanations are critical aspects of scientific inquiry.

For example, many beginning students think that natural selection is the only mechanism of evolution. There have been strong debates, however, that continue today, among evolutionary biologists about the relative importance of natural selection and genetic drift. Asking students to debate the relative importance of each mechanism would require students first to understand the two concepts and second to gather evidence in support of their claims. An outcome of such a debate would be a deeper understanding of how evolution works. An inappropriate debate in a science class would be to have one group of students represent a scientific idea such as evolution and another group represent an unscientific idea such as creationism or intelligent design.

Topics Controversial in a Science Curriculum

Teachers have a professional obligation to teach science accurately. The National Science Education Standards, as well as state and district standards, outline the concepts that the community of science educators believes is important for scientifically literate students to understand. Standards can act as an important mediator between teachers and members of special-interest groups that do not want specific content presented.

When you enter a new teaching situation, it is important to ask many questions of fellow teachers, administrators, and other members of the community to get a feel for topics that may be controversial locally. Knowing areas that may be controversial will allow you the time to develop a specific plan to address the concerns before being confronted by an angry student, parent, or administrator. A well-thought-out plan will help you avoid being defensive. Some teachers send letters home to parents before covering topics such as human reproduction. This letter should include an outline of the content that will be covered and the relevant state or local standards. Sending such a letter allows direct communication with parents and allows you to avoid the distortion of the message if it is first filtered through students.

Biology teachers should also recognize that there are local and national groups that will support them in teaching science accurately. Many states have strong science teacher associations, and often professors at local universities can be recruited for support. Nationally, NSTA, NABT, and the National Center for Science Education (which offers specific support for the teaching of evolution) are important resources.

In the classroom, establish a culture of scientific integrity. When discussing topics that may be controversial to students, tell students they need to understand how scientists think about the topic. For example, when teaching about evolution, it may be helpful to explain to students that you are primarily interested that they understand why scientists accept evolution as an explanation.

Controversial Applications and Uses of Scientific Technology

Students quickly become engaged when they discuss applications of science that are controversial. But it is important for them to master the relevant science concepts before they proceed to take and defend a position on a topic. Fortunately, it is not necessary for students become familiar with all the technical details of a given controversy. For example, in the stem cell debate, students should have the following scientific understandings before taking a position on the issue:

- During early development, the cells of the embryo become increasingly specialized and lose their ability to take on the function of any type of adult cell.
- Embryo cells retain the ability to develop into any type of adult cell until about the eight-cell stage and are therefore called stem cells.
- At the present time, stem cells are harvested from embryos, thereby destroying the embryos in the process. However, scientists are working to remove stem cells without destroying the embryo.

Only after students have this basic scientific understanding of stem cells can they take an informed position in the debate.

After learning the scientific concepts, students need to understand the value or moral decisions that need to take place. Teachers sometimes feel that the discussion of values is inappropriate in the science classroom or that it detracts from the learning of "real" science. The theme of this chapter, however, is based upon the conviction that there is much to be gained by involving students in analyzing issues of science, technology, and society. Society expects all citizens to participate in the democratic process, and our educational system must provide opportunities for students to learn to deal with contentious issues with civility, objectivity, and fairness. Students also need to learn that science intersects with life in many ways.

Ideally, students should be given a variety of opportunities to discuss, interpret, and evaluate basic science and health issues, some in light of their values and ethics. As they encounter issues about which they feel strongly, some discussions might become controversial. The degree of controversy depends on many factors, such as how similar students are in socioeconomic status, perspectives, value systems, and religious beliefs. In addition, your language and attitude influence the flow of ideas and the quality of exchange among the students.

Some science teachers are uncomfortable allowing students to discuss issues related to values. The following guidelines may help you facilitate discussions on issues that involve different moral or value judgments. This list should help you balance factual information with your students' feelings:

- Remain neutral. Neutrality may be the most important characteristic of a successful discussion facilitator.
- Encourage students to discover as much information about the issue as possible.
- Keep the discussion relevant and moving forward by questioning or posing appropriate problems or hypothetical situations. Encourage everyone to contribute, but do not force reluctant students to enter the discussion.
- Emphasize that everyone must be open to hearing and considering diverse views.
- Use unbiased questioning to help students critically examine all views presented.
- Allow for the discussion of all feelings and opinions.
- Avoid seeking consensus on all issues. Discussing multifaceted issues should result in the presentation of divergent views, and students should learn that this is acceptable.
- Acknowledge all contributions in the same evenhanded manner. If a student seems to be saying something for shock value, see whether other students recognize the inappropriate comment and invite them to respond.
- Create a sense of freedom in the classroom. Remind students, however, that freedom entails the responsibility to exercise that freedom in ways that generate positive results for all.
- Insist upon a nonhostile environment in the classroom. Remind students to respond to ideas instead of to the individuals presenting those ideas.
- Respect silence. Reflective discussions are often slow. If a teacher breaks the silence, students may allow the teacher to dominate the discussion.
- Respectfully identify when scientific ideas are misrepresented.
- At the end of the discussion, ask students to summarize the points made. Respect students regardless of their opinions about any controversial issue.

You do not need extra time to address controversy in the biology classroom. Most areas of controversy are aspects of science content that is normally taught in a biology course and are included in the *National Science Education Standards* (NRC 1996). Table 8.2 lists areas of controversy and their relevant science topics. Also included are the content Standards most appropriate to each area. You can use controversy to engage students in science content that they might otherwise regard as irrelevant to their lives.

Section III

Table 8.2 — Controversy and the NSES Grades 9–12 Life Science Content Standards

Area of Controversy	Most-Relevant NSES Content Standards	Corresponding Topic in High School Biology Curricula
Cloning; stem cells; sex selection	Content Standard C: The Cell Content Standard E: Understandings About Science and Technology Content Standard F: Personal and Community Health Content Standard F: Natural and Human-Induced Hazards Content Standard G: Science as a Human Endeavor Content Standard G: Nature of Scientific Knowledge	Developmental biology • Fertilization • Cellular differentiation Genetics • Mitosis • Meiosis
Genetic testing; gene therapy	Content Standard C: Molecular Basis of Heredity Content Standard E: Understandings about Science and Technology Content Standard F: Personal and Community Health Content Standard F: Natural and Human-Induced Hazards Content Standard G: Science as a Human Endeavor Content Standard G: Nature of Scientific Knowledge	Genetics • Inheritance (DNA) Biotechnology • Recombinant DNA Body systems
Vaccination	Content Standard C: The Cell Content Standard F: Personal and Community Health Content Standard F: Natural and Human-Induced Hazards Content Standard G: Science as a Human Endeavor	Body systems • Immunology Evolution • Adaptation
Genetic enhancement; genetically modified organisms (GMOs); biopiracy	Content Standard C: Biological Evolution Content Standard E: Understandings About Science and Technology Content Standard G: Science as a Human Endeavor Content Standard G: Nature of Scientific Knowledge	Genetics • Inheritance (DNA) Biotechnology • Recombinant DNA Evolution • Adaptation Ecology • Diversity
Environmental release of GMOs; invasive species (biological control)	Content Standard C: Interdependence of Organisms Content Standard E: Understandings About Science and Technology Content Standard F: Personal and Community Health Content Standard F: Natural and Human-Induced Hazards	Ecology • Human impacts • Competition Biotechnology • Recombinant DNA Evolution • Natural selection

Environmental release of GMOs; biofuels	Content Standard C: Matter, Energy, and Organization in Living Systems Content Standard E: Understandings About Science and Technology Content Standard G: Science as a Human Endeavor Content Standard G: Nature of Scientific Knowledge	Ecology • Human impacts Evolution • Natural selection Biochemistry • Cellular respiration • Fermentation
Informed consent; confidentiality; placebos; patents; organ donations	Content Standard C: Behavior of Organisms Content Standard E: Understandings About Science and Technology Content Standard F: Personal and Community Health Content Standard F: Natural and Human-Induced Hazards Content Standard G: Science as a Human Endeavor Content Standard G: Nature of Scientific Knowledge	Body systems Nature of science Inquiry Science, technology, and society
Animal models in research	Content Standard C: The Cell Content Standard F: Natural and Human-Induced Hazards Content Standard G: Science as a Human Endeavor Content Standard G: Nature of Scientific Knowledge	Body systems Nature of science • Models Evolution • Homology

Source: National Research Council. 1996. *National Science Education Standards*. Washington, DC: National Academy Press.

SECTION III REFERENCES

BSCS. 2007. *BSCS: The Continuing Story*. DVD. Produced by John Feldman. Spencertown, NY: Hummingbird Films.

Dobzhansky, T. 1973. Nothing in biology makes sense except in the light of evolution. *The American Biology Teacher* 35, 125–129.

Muller, H. 1959. One Hundred Years Without Darwin Are Enough. *School Science and Mathematics* 59, 304–305.

National Association of Biology Teachers (NABT). 2003. The use of animals in biology education. *www.nabt.org/sites/S1/index.php?p=60.*

———. 2004a. NABT's statement on teaching evolution. *www.nabt.org/sites/S1/index.php?p=65.*

———. 2004b. Teaching about environmental issues. *www.nabt.org/sites/S1/index.php?p=62.*

National Research Council (NRC). 1996. *National Science Education Standards*. Washington, DC: National Academy Press.

National Science Teachers Association (NSTA). 2000. NSTA position statement: The teaching of sexuality and human reproduction. *www.nsta.org/about/positions/evolution.aspx.*

————. 2003a. NSTA position statement: Environmental education. *www.nsta.org/about/positions/environmental.aspx*.

————. 2003b. NSTA position statement: The teaching of evolution. *www.nsta.org/about/positions/evolution.aspx*.

Singer, P. 1975. *Animal liberation.* New York: Ecco.

Skoog, G. 2008. The contributions of BSCS biology textbooks to evolution education. In *Measuring our success: The first 50 years of BSCS*, 45–71, BSCS. Dubuque, IA: Kendall/Hunt.

Trefil, J. 2008. *Why science?* New York and Arlington, VA: Teachers College Press/NSTA Press.

Section IV

Introduction

Creating a Culture of Inquiry in Your Biology Classroom

Section II of *The Biology Teacher's Handbook* provides a rationale for teaching scientific inquiry and some experiences—invitations to inquiry—to help students develop their inquiry skills. Section IV goes a bit further to help you create an entire culture of inquiry in your classroom. Each chapter in this section is a how-to for different aspects of the inquiry classroom.

Surviving the first few years of teaching often comes down to classroom management skills. Experienced teachers have many strategies that make their classrooms run smoothly and help them keep the focus on learning. Chapter 9 sets the stage for classroom management with outstanding veteran teachers answering what would be the questions of a new biology teacher. Read this chapter for great ideas for structuring collaborative learning in your classroom, prepping and running laboratory investigations, maintaining live animals in your classroom and conducting effective field trips. The veteran teachers also offer suggestions for new laboratory and classroom facilities, should your school have the opportunity for building new facilities.

Chapters 10 through 12 describe how to use common instructional strategies to foster inquiry: collaborative learning, science notebooks, and strategies for helping students understand science readings. Chapter 13 presents a classroom exercise to help students become critical evaluators of information they gather from books, articles, the internet, and other nontextbook sources.

In chapter 14, we discuss the value of using an instructional model that is consistent with a constructivist perspective on learning (see chapter 1) and we provide the example of the BSCS 5E Instructional Model. Much of any culture is determined by who talks and how that talk is structured and received; classroom cultures are also influenced by the way learning is assessed. Chapter 15 provides multiple strategies for encouraging scientific conversation in your classroom. Chapter 16 describes assessment strategies that are consistent with an inquiry culture, particularly formative assessment strategies.

Finally, some instructional materials are more supportive of a culture of inquiry than others. Chapter 17 outlines a substantive process and set of tools for analyzing instructional materials (AIM) for their emphasis on inquiry and the AIM Process and Tools. It is a particularly helpful chapter to read the year or two before your next adoption cycle. If you are interested in using AIM for identifying and selecting instructional materials that help you and your district achieve your goals for science learning, contact BSCS at *pdcenter@bscs.org*.

Chapter 9

How to Set Up and Manage Your Biology Classroom

There are a number of important practical aspects to setting up and managing a biology classroom. These include strategies for organizing students into groups, conducting laboratory work, maintaining live organisms in the classroom, leading field trips, and using educational technology effectively.

Teachers who discover workable answers to questions related to these aspects of the biology classroom find themselves spending less time to get better results from their students. Often, it is the teachers with years of experience who have found ways to work smarter, not harder. Chapter 9 represents the collective wisdom of several veteran science teachers, organized in an interview format. In the interview, you will find suggested answers for several key questions regarding biology course management. We begin with brief introductions to the teachers (all names are fictional).

The Veteran Teachers

Arthur has taught middle school and high school life science and environmental science for 32 years in a suburban school district. The schools where he has taught were large and comprehensive, offering many levels of biology to meet the needs of all types of students.

Brad taught biology in a small-town high school for the first five years of his 30-year teaching career. The remaining years were spent in a large urban school with an increasingly diverse population. He has taught all levels of biology, including several years of AP biology.

Carla has taught high school science for 13 years in two small rural schools. In both schools, more than 60% of the students are Hispanic, and more than 60% are on the free/reduced lunch program.

Dennis teaches in a midsize town with a single high school. For 17 years, he has taught a variety of science subjects, but most recently he has been teaching an integrated science course to 9th and 10th graders in which the life science piece is about a quarter of the curriculum.

Ellen entered the teaching profession after 20 years in the U.S. Navy. She has taught biology and integrated sciences to 9th graders in an inner-city high school for eight years. The student population is very diverse and transient, and many are receiving some level of public assistance.

Fran has taught biology and AP biology at a small rural school for 10 years. More than 60 percent of her students are Hispanic.

Strategies for Organizing Students Into Groups

New biology teacher (NBT): How can I arrange my classroom for group work?

Carla: That's a great question, because something as simple as the desk arrangement in your classroom can have an impact on the class dynamics. Rows of desks with the teacher at the front says to students, "The teacher is the giver of information." Clusters of desks around the room can say to students, "We are working together to understand this concept."

Fran: I always get rid of desks in any classroom I'm assigned and use only tables—regardless of the activity that we're doing. This facilitates interaction among the students and promotes cooperative learning.

Brad: I liked the seating arrangement back at the lab stations. It allows groups to sit together.

Arthur: If you don't have lab tables, push four desks together.

Dennis: That's what I do, because I don't have lab stations.

Arthur: And remember, work students in groups with more than just labs. Give them group assignments. Do prelab as a group and occasionally use a group grade.

NBT: **What are the best strategies for organizing students into groups?**

Dennis: I mostly put students into groups of three, because I've found that one person in a group of four always seems to be left out.

Arthur: Yes, group size is important. I switch kids around frequently so they don't get cliquish.

Dennis: I vary group size, too. Sometimes I use a group of four, then break it down further to two groups of two for times when I ask kids to share ideas and critique each other's work.

Conducting Laboratory Work

NBT: **I'm struggling with space and time for prepping labs. What suggestions do you have for efficient lab prep?**

Fran: As far as space goes, I know teachers who designate an area in the lab or classroom that is for teachers only. In this case, you would need to make sure that the area has some storage and perhaps a cabinet that locks.

Arthur: To help with the time issue, I always bundle lab equipment and supplies. Keep them on the same shelf or cupboard. Have the students prep as much as possible during the prelab. Then they know where and what it is that they're using.

Dennis: The way I did the bundling that Arthur talks about is to have bins. You can get them at department stores. Be sure you get the clear ones with covers so you can see inside without taking off the top.

Brad: To be efficient, I had to prep mostly before or after school or during planning periods. No surprises there. You do what you have to do.

Carla: I was like Brad most of the time. However, some years I was lucky enough to get a student aide. They were juniors and seniors who had taken several science courses. This can be helpful if you get the right student.

Dennis: Another tip involves teamwork. We have a group of four teachers who teach the same class, so we assign roles. One teacher gets the equipment out and does any photocopying, another is responsible for restocking the bins and putting things away, another teacher makes sure we're on target with timing and takes care of the end-of-year ordering. We switch roles when the need arises.

NBT: **What are some strategies for setting up on lab day, so that I can make maximum use of our short class periods?**

Fran: Have your plastic storage boxes for each lab station ready to go. Inside the box, include a list of supplies so that, before students leave for the day, they can make sure that they have returned all of the equipment for the next class.

Brad: I agree. Everything must be prepared and set up before class. I also require students to have read the lab before arriving in class. If it is obvious that they didn't, then that reflects on their lab score.

Dennis: I always have an agenda for the day on the board. My kids know to look at that the first thing. They get used to having responsibility and sort of like it. That responsibility includes remembering the prelab information.

Arthur: You're right. The prelab ensures that kids know what the equipment looks like. I always set up equipment in rows to avoid logjams and assign specific students as specialists in each lab group. The roles I use for lab group are the equipment, material, and safety specialists, so I don't have to repeat information before starting.

Fran: I assign each student a role, too. One of those roles is the materials manager, who helps me keep up with the material and makes sure that it all gets back into the proper place before my students leave for the day.

Carla: Student responsibility is very important. Make lab groups responsible for returning materials and equipment so you aren't cleaning up from the last class.

NBT: **I have few lab materials and virtually no lab equipment. I don't even have sinks or water in my classroom. How can I build up my supply of lab materials and equipment so I can do more labs in my course?**

Fran: I know exactly how you feel! I took a job a few years ago and ran into the same problem. The first thing you do is inventory what you have and then determine what equipment the students need for basic inquiry labs—electronic balances, graduated cylinders, stopwatches—and order those first. Then, throughout the years, you can build on your supplies. If funding is a problem, there are many small grants available that you can apply for.

Brad: But you also need to stress to the administration the importance of equipment for a science lab. This must be budgeted, and that's their responsibility. Then, look into grants like those from the state-level biology teachers' organization. In my state, they offer small grants to classroom teachers.

Arthur: Not everything has to be expensive stuff made by Pyrex and Corning. Use as much home stuff as possible. Collect baby food jars for beakers, and think about items that might be at students' homes that can substitute for lab materials and equipment. Even 10-power hand lenses can help make something more interesting. With all the home requests, it also illustrates your budgeting plight. I recall a home biology book that uses a lot of things from home. I'm sure Google will bring up lots.

Dennis: Start small and grow. That could mean beginning with a single apparatus and using it for demonstrations. Then gradually apply your budget to get a classroom set. If you need to, keep building until you get the number of classroom sets you need. But until you do, couple an online simulation with the demonstration so kids at least have to think about the data. Also, stagger lab days with another teacher so she uses the equipment one day and you use it the other.

Carla: Some of the things that are most difficult to keep in stock—and usually come out of the teacher's pocket—are items that can be purchased locally. I'm talking about string, cups, bowls, and so on. One year, I hosted a lab shower and put an invitation with a supply list in the local paper. Parents and community members brought the shower gifts to the lab, and I was stocked for the year. I served punch and cookies, of course.

Fran: And you can still do labs without sinks and water. When I had that problem, I had the student with the traveling scientist role just head down the hall to the restroom to get water when needed. This is the student who retrieves material for everyone in his or her group, as needed. If that's not possible, get one of the 5-gallon containers that have a dispenser and use that as needed. You can use buckets for disposal.

NBT: **What safety issues do I need to be aware of in setting up my classroom?**

Brad: Well, all of them, of course! We just can't afford to skimp on some things. I use some of the lab supply companies for safety information. They generally have that information, especially with chemicals and how to store them properly, in the back of their catalogs or as a separate free publication. Just ask them.

Dennis: I agree. But also there's the classroom management aspect. For example, my kids always want to see the flashy stuff again, only bigger and louder. Don't do it. Keep things small scale, and remember to have kids wear safety gear during demonstrations. Keep the solution concentrations under 1.0 molar, and go over the safety issues for each lab.

Arthur: You're right. Review the proper part of your safety plan every time before a safety issue comes up in a lab. That implies you have a safety plan. In bio labs, protection of eyes, lungs, skin, blood, clothing, and innocent bystanders are the big things to look out for. Check the school district guidelines. Those guidelines probably detail the procedures they're going to defend in court.

Carla: I think one of the best things you can do to help ensure that your students conduct themselves in a safe manner during labs is to establish that mutual respect in the classroom. Your tone and classroom management techniques go a long way to promote student attitude in the lab. Their attitude will then be reflected in the way they conduct themselves in the lab.

Note: See appendix C in this handbook, which lists safety issues for the biology classroom.

NBT: **My life is hectic. Sometimes I have to get labs ready at the last minute. What are some strategies for preparing ahead for labs, so I'm not scrambling like this?**

Fran: First of all, at the beginning of the academic year, go shopping and purchase or order what you anticipate you'll need—that requires thinking through and preparing a scope and sequence that includes possible activities. That way you're not at a big-box store at midnight the night before, desperately trying to improvise. Then, as you plan the unit, begin to gather supplies for each lab station and place them in a small plastic storage box—one box per station. The boxes can be set aside in your prep room, ready to be distributed on lab day. There are some labs that require unique materials that I gather and store in a labeled plastic storage box for the next year. In that box, I put the materials, along with a copy of the lab or activity so that it's ready for the next year.

Arthur: Doing prelab activities with students the day before can help. Bundle labs, as was said before. A lot of times, you just have to scramble because items have to be fresh, were just delivered, or you had to run out last period to get them. Somehow, bribe your department coordinator to get your schedule organized with a prep period before biology class. Modify paperwork on lab instructions immediately after you've completed the lab, when it's fresh in your mind. Then you are not wasting time trying to remember pitfalls from the year before.

Dennis: I keep coming back to teamwork. Share responsibilities with colleagues. Don't think you have to do everything alone. Also, get a set of often-used glassware and equipment in your classroom so it's right there just in case something breaks. That way, one mistake doesn't stop the learning of an entire group.

Brad: I keep my records of what worked and what didn't work in my planning book. I make notes of when I need to start preparing a particular lab and use them for planning the following year. This helps me set up a syllabus for the entire year.

NBT: **Once I have the lab equipment prepared and ready to set out in the classroom, how can I set up my classroom so students can get to everything they need for labs without bumping into each other?**

Dennis: Prebox all the equipment for each lab team so there isn't a lot of traveling around. Make sure tables are laid out so you have aisles and a clear path to the eyewash and exit doors.

Brad: I do the same thing: Put multiple setups throughout the classroom. I have four lab stations so I make four of everything. We could also use eight groups and use eight setups or have two groups share one setup. This minimizes the movement around the classroom.

Arthur: Move desks together into lab group sites. Put supplies or materials in opposite corners to minimize the number of times kids' paths cross.

Carla: If I have the time, I put bins at each lab station that contain the supplies for the activity. If not, I have supplies located on a table in the front of the room so that students can get their supplies. I keep a stackable plastic drawer unit at each lab station that contains frequently used lab supplies like weighing paper and stirring rods. Then they are always available and do not have to be gathered each time we do a lab.

Fran: If it's not possible to put the materials that they need at their station beforehand, I like to use bins of some sort, placed at a central location. Those bins might contain goggles, lab aprons, or other needed items. Rather than let everyone roam the room to get supplies, I assign one person per group to serve as the traveling scientist.

NBT: **How do I set up my classroom for efficient cleanup after labs?**

Fran: First of all, use a timer to let you know when you have about five minutes left in class (or however much time you think students will need to clean up). Once again, I assign one person in the group to be in charge of cleanup—that doesn't mean that person does all the cleanup; he or she just makes sure that the group takes care of business. Make sure that all students know where to dispose of broken glass, chemicals, and such.

Arthur: Plastic tubs, basins, and bottles substitute for limited sink space. Assign alternating lab partners the responsibility of cleanup so the burden isn't always on one person. Designate shelves and cabinets for specific equipment. Mark microscopes, dissection kits, and other similar supplies with a matching parking place on a designated shelf or cupboard spot. The lab or table group uses the same tools each time, so it's easier to follow up on damage, dirt, or improper return.

Dennis: My room doesn't have sinks, so I do what Arthur suggests by having beakers and buckets at each table for things like broken glass and waste solutions.

Brad: Assign each group responsibility for cleaning up its area and lab materials. Make this responsibility count in its grade.

Carla: Often the lab activity extends to the end of the class period, and there is no time for cleanup. The group must clean off the lab desk and store the dirty equipment for later cleanup. When this happens, the lab groups know that at least one person from their groups must come in during the day or after school to clean up.

NBT: **Sometimes lab equipment and materials seem to "disappear" during labs. How can I minimize this?**

Dennis: Decide your policy about breakage ahead of time and be consistent. I always thought that some breakage was a normal part of doing business and would replace equipment. But losing glassware or just not putting it back is different. The key is creating a sense of classroom community so that everyone cares what happens because it affects the next class.

Carla: This goes back to the mutual respect and tone that I mentioned earlier. The classroom climate that you can create will go a long way in solving this problem, too.

Arthur: I know it's a hassle, but I have them check in and check out expensive equipment.

Fran: I put a checklist at each station and do a quick check before releasing students from the lab.

Brad: Again, make each group responsible for its own equipment and number everything. Also give each group a list of the materials it is responsible for.

NBT: **We're building new classrooms. What's the best arrangement for a biology classroom to allow for doing labs, but also for whole-class instruction and individual and small-group computer use?**

Arthur: Use lab tables in the central area of the classroom for desks. Counter space on the periphery with class desks (the lab tables) in front and lab benches in the back, with water, gas, and sinks. Next door, have a computer lab or class set of laptops and then

place your storeroom and lab prep room between the two labs. Keep office space separate.

Brad: Arthur has the idea. Keep the classroom divided into a classroom area and a separate lab area.

Fran: I like that, too—lab benches around the periphery of the room and tables in the center (no desks). Computers should be placed at each lab station so that inquiry can involve technology such as data collection and probes.

Dennis: I agree, but keep in mind that small lab spaces are not safe. They create bottlenecks and decrease learning.

Carla: Yes, too many accidents occur if students are always bumping into each other. Err on the side of more space if you have that option.

Maintaining Live Organisms in the Classroom

NBT: **What are the advantages of keeping live organisms in your classroom? The disadvantages?**

Arthur: Live critters will encourage learning in some students and repulse others—which can be a good thing, too. For many students, it is their first experience with a particular species and it opens up new awareness never tapped. Repulsion can be turned into fascination as familiarity works its charms.

Ellen: I have quite a few aquariums, both fresh- and saltwater, that I keep in my classroom. I also have vivariums with different microenvironments for reptiles, amphibians, and insects. The students find all the animals an exciting addition to the classroom. These do require work to keep them looking good and healthy. Saltwater aquariums are very expensive, and I would not be able to keep them up and going without writing grants.

Brad: Advantages include observational opportunities for all my students as well as responsibilities for those students involved in their care. It also gives the students kind of a classroom mascot. Disadvantages can be that some students may have allergies.

Arthur: Sometimes the drawbacks do outweigh the benefits. As Brad says, allergies may be a problem. Phobias and special medical conditions can isolate a student or, at the other end, be cause for removal of a student.

Ellen: Despite the disadvantages, live organisms offer an opportunity for students to be intimate with a living creature. It is one of the most important ways of motivating my students. I have forged stronger relationships with my students as we discuss our mutual interests in keeping fish or reptiles. I use the aquariums to teach chemistry as well as biology. My marine science students set up river tanks and collect the specimens that are displayed. It is a great object lesson about the diversity found in nature and the need to protect our natural resources.

NBT: **What strategies do you use for keeping organisms alive and healthy in the classroom?**

Brad: Get good information on what is required for its care, often from a pet store. Don't get something that requires a lot of extra equipment or has specials needs that you cannot supply.

Ellen: I have students maintain the classroom specimens. At the beginning of the year, I do a presentation on all the different plants and animals in the classroom. I include basic requirements for each. The students fill out applications to be a caretaker for a semester. The application must show that they have done some outside research on the specimen in question. I try to rotate the jobs based on interest and motivation.

NBT: **What rules do you have regarding live organisms, and how do you enforce them?**

Brad: Absolutely no behavior that could injure or abuse the organisms is allowed. I spell out times when an organism can be taken out of the cage and handled.

Arthur: Post rules and reasons for those rules, such as "Wash hands before and after handling because …" and "After feeding, snakes need time to digest and defecate. Give them a day before handling." This provides learning for your students along with

safety and comfort for visitors. And, as Ellen explained above, it enables students to deal with the care responsibilities.

Ellen: In my classes, students may touch or interact with an animal only with prior permission. I use that as a reward for completing assignments. Reptiles—for example, snakes—may only be handled in the lab away from students who are afraid of them. The snake is fed mice during nonstudent hours—school board policy. I have found that the more students know about the care of the various plants and animals and the more responsibility they share for them, the more caring they become.

Leading Field Trips

NBT: **Why should I do field trips? It seems like such a hassle.**

Arthur: It is a hassle, but a field trip is often better remembered than that brilliant lecture on spirogyra you flawlessly delivered. And, just like other modes of instruction, you get better with repetition. There's nothing like really seeing the organism, habitat, or process you've been trying to hammer into their heads.

Ellen: We need to provide our students with life opportunities. I live only 18 miles from the ocean, but very few of my students have ever seen it. Fewer than 1 percent of them own library cards or have ever been to a library. We can't expand students' horizons without showing them beyond the borders of our classrooms.

Arthur: The topics you cover should be the major stimulus for ideas. Sometimes a field trip can be the entire presentation for a subject you want to purvey. The time you spend has to be justified by curricular appropriateness.

NBT: **I want to do field trips, but I don't have the resources for transportation or the time in one class period. I'm not allowed to pull students out of their other classes. Do you have advice for me?**

Arthur: Field trips don't have to be great, transported excursions. They can just be trips outside to collect specimens along the fence or to collect bacteria on door handles inside the school.

Ellen: Consider walking trips to collect leaves and learn how to do dichotomous keys, research trips to the library, and trips to a pond or ditch on the school grounds to collect organisms.

Brad: You can get ideas from your curriculum and what your community has to offer. Invite a speaker to the classroom (a sort of reverse field trip).

Ellen: If you don't have transportation, try the walking trips just suggested. Local churches may have buses you could use.

Arthur: The transportation issue is educational reality. Unorthodox funding, sponsorships, advertising, even bake sales have been used to overcome this roadblock. Creativity and energy input are always required.

Brad: If time is the issue, consider before- or after-school trips and weekend trips. And, as we said before, consider what you could do on the school grounds during a class period.

Ellen: Another idea is to make the field trip fit more than one subject area and sell the other teachers on the idea.

NBT: **OK, I've worked out the logistical details. Now, how can I maximize learning from field trips?**

Arthur: Do the field trip yourself before you take your class. Note things along the way. Walk through the exhibit, locale, venue, or facility. Write questions for everything you want students to observe or experience.

Ellen: Teach lessons related to the field trip before you go. And, as Arthur says, provide a list of the observations and evidence you want students to focus on.

Arthur: To help with the latter, many facilities have field trip guides available that are posted online or obtainable upon your preliminary visit. Make sure your helpers—chaperones, student aides, or other teachers—have copies of these and their answers. Be visible, engaged, and enthusiastic yourself. Encourage positive interaction. Follow up on the learning that should have occurred.

Brad: I agree. Give students assignments related to the trip, either to be done on the trip, afterward as homework, or in the classroom upon their return.

NBT: **How can I maintain discipline on field trips?**

Brad: Same as anything else—students need to know the expectations.

Arthur: Yes, be prepared. Make sure consequences and rewards are clear. Disorganization will promote unwanted student adventures.

Brad: If you need some extra help, recruit other teachers or parents.

Ellen: I use parents as chaperones.

Arthur: It helps to bring a lot of volunteer helpers. Invite the principal or a dean.

Using Educational Technology Effectively

NBT: **What advice do you have for using technology effectively in my classroom?**

Arthur: Naturally, this depends on what technology you have available. Canned labs on CDs can provide experiences beyond the equipment you have and also experiences with "live" organisms. Squeamish students are often more comfortable with gross experiences on a screen than in real life.

Brad: I use the computer primarily for data collection and analysis, for diagrams, and for short videos.

Ellen: A classroom projection system is ideal, especially if you have only one computer in your classroom. Project what is on your screen, either through an LED projector or a TV screen. You can explore websites, model note taking, and use presentation software.

Arthur: Technology online can make for great research resources and allows individualization within the discipline. The teacher must first differentiate between garbage and peer-reviewed material, however.

Ellen: I use a laptop, PC writer pens, and student response systems in conjunction with my projection system. I couldn't live without my PC writer pen. I constantly model what goes into students' science notebooks. This technology was all purchased with department fund-raising and matching grants.

NBT: **What are the characteristics of computer programs or web resources that most effectively support learning?**

Ellen: They must be interactive.

Brad: Those that involve some sort of problem solving. Usually any technology that involves simulations of difficult concepts is helpful in my teaching.

Arthur: I like programs that allow students to avoid uncomfortable hands-on experiences. Otherwise, I would lose those students in protest or just plain refusal. Be careful, however, that canned programs are not designed to sell copies rather than facilitate an aspect of your teaching. I find that all-encompassing programs can provide more fluff than substance. I think teachers are better off buying a program that hits a specific mark or fills a certain void for which there is not equipment, expertise, or budget— for example, microscopic observations, biome inventories, or biochemical observations. And I still find videos invaluable for taking students to a place that can't be reached from the school's locale or because of budget constraints.

Final Advice

We believe the advice of experienced teachers is an invaluable resource to you. This chapter provides a sample of the great ideas and insights from veteran teachers who have developed strategies that enhance learning in their classrooms. We close the chapter with one last piece of advice: Look around, and notice the teachers whose students seem to achieve particularly well. Look at what those teachers are doing in their classrooms. Ask them why they use the strategies they do, how they implement the strategies in their classrooms, and what the outcome is for their students. Choose the best of their strategies and the ones that match your instructional style, and put them to use in your own classroom.

Chapter 10

How to Use Collaborative Learning in Your Classroom[*]

Educators have been conducting research about the relative effects of cooperative, competitive, and individual learning for several decades. The research shows that collaborative learning experiences tend to promote higher achievement in learners than do the competitive or individual learning experiences. The benefits of collaborative learning include the following:

- Collaborative learning makes the learners responsible for seeking information and achieving a particular task.
- Collaborative learning strategies model the collaborative nature of the scientific enterprise.
- Collaborative learning is an effective technique for involving learners from groups that are underrepresented in science.
- Collaborative learning can be a powerful way to interest and motivate students who otherwise might not be interested in or excel in science.

Several factors may be important in making collaborative learning experiences more effective:

- The time learners spend in discussion with teammates promotes the discovery of new ideas and helps them develop and clarify existing ideas.
- The conflict of ideas that results when learners work in collaborative teams increases the learners' motivation to understand the material and, as a result, they tend to achieve more.
- As learners work with each other, they tend to like each other more, which increases their motivation to learn and to help others learn.

Two factors, consistently applied, are key to making collaborative learning a highly successful strategy: a defined team goal and individual accountability. If these two elements are not present, the effectiveness of collaborative learning experiences will diminish. In fact, the learners would simply be working in groups—not collaborative teams. Other elements are essential to collaborative learning:

- *Use of roles.* All team members have a distinct and useful responsibility to the team in any given collaborative activity.
- *Modified heterogeneous grouping.* In pure heterogeneous groups, the learners work with people whom they would not necessarily choose as teammates or who may differ from themselves in learning style, background, or ability. When using a modified heterogeneous group-

---

*Adapted from BSCS. 2006. *BSCS biology: A human approach, teacher resource CD.* Dubuque, IA: Kendall/Hunt.

ing approach, heterogeneity is tempered because minority students, female students, and students identified for special education services are always paired with at least one other student like themselves. The goal is to avoid spotlighting students who may feel singled out in a group because of differences.

- *Group autonomy.* The team looks to its members first, rather than to the teacher, to answer questions or solve problems that arise.
- *Positive interdependence.* The members of a team must rely on each other for critical pieces of information or to accomplish crucial jobs in order to finish an assignment.
- *Use of working-relationship skills.* The learners learn how to cooperate, how to work with other people who might be completely different, and how to manage their teams.
- *Distributed leadership.* All learners have the opportunity to function in some type of leadership capacity, thus calling on untapped strengths and talents.
- *Individual accountability.* Each team member is held responsible for knowing all aspects of the lesson or activity the team does.
- *Team self-assessment.* The team members evaluate themselves on their use of collaborative learning skills.

What are the features of an activity in which collaborative learning strategies are the most beneficial? Are all activities suitable for incorporating collaborative learning strategies? To decide if collaborative learning strategies will benefit the activity, consider the following criteria:

1. *The activity must have the potential for naturally occurring roles.* The activity should have naturally occurring roles—not contrived or artificial roles. Ideally, the roles are equivalent in responsibility and distribute the leadership. You can ensure that each student takes on a variety of roles over time and does not consistently choose only the roles with which he or she feels comfortable. When first incorporating collaborative learning strategies into the classroom, you may wish to assign roles for team members. After students become familiar with the idea of roles, team members can choose roles or the teams can decide how the roles will be chosen.
2. *The activity must have the potential for the natural incorporation of working-relationship skills.* Working-relationship skills range from encouraging participation from team members to asking other members of the team to justify their positions. These skills should be an integral part of the activity, as part of a procedural step, introduction, or dis-

cussion question. For example, in an activity in which the students should be discussing something, the working-relationship skill might be listening to everyone's ideas during a team discussion. Practicing a working-relationship skill should have a higher priority than making sure everyone has an opportunity to do a rote task, such as having the chance to control the computer mouse.

Using Collaborative Learning Strategies in the Classroom

The following ideas may help ensure greater success with collaborative learning in the classroom:

1. *Discuss with students the value of working collaboratively.* If students have not been exposed to collaborative learning strategies before, they may find the new procedures difficult. Discussing the value of collaborative learning as part of their work in science class will help students understand the abilities these procedures are developing. For example, employers value employees who can work together to solve problems or develop alternative solutions to problems. By working collaboratively now, students are developing an important skill for their futures.

2. *Pay attention to the size of the teams.* The nature of the activity, including the logical number of roles, will often influence the size of the teams. It is important to remember, however, that group size can affect the degree of interaction among students. For example, in groups of six or more, it may be difficult to have discussions that include every team member. In a larger group, some students may sit back and let more-vocal students dominate the conversation. Conversely, pairs may be too small a group for some activities—one student may overshadow the other, or the discussion may not be as rich as it could be because there are only two viewpoints in the group.

3. *Maintain the same groups for a period of time.* For teams to develop group autonomy, they must work together for an extended period of time. This may range from one month to six months. You may wish to change groups when you begin new units of study.

4. *Hold students accountable for their own learning.* The potential gains of incorporating collaborative learning strategies can be completely undermined if each student is not held responsible for knowing and understanding all aspects of an activity or lesson.

5. *Provide opportunities for self-assessment.* The members of a team need time as individuals and as a group to assess their progress as a team.

6. *Choose a working-relationship skill to emphasize in the activity.* Begin by reviewing the activity that students will participate in. In some cases, an activity will lend itself readily to particular skills. At other times, you may choose a working-relationship skill to focus on a particular problem that the class, or a team, is having.

Implementing Working-Relationship Skills

A long-term benefit of collaborative learning for students is that it develops skills that will be important for all individuals throughout their lives. By incorporating and emphasizing specific working-relationship skills, in tandem with the science content, students are practicing skills that will be important to them when they enter the workforce. If you help students understand the relevance of these working-relationship skills, they will often become more interested in the process and the content.

Working-relationship skills range from lower-level skills to higher-level skills. Table 10.1 provides examples of the skills categorized by level. When you select a working-relationship skill to emphasize in an activity, make certain your students have mastered the lower-level skills upon which the new skill depends. For example, before you use *sharing perspectives* as a working-relationship skill, the learners should have mastered the skills of *honoring individual differences*, *listening to teammates*, and any other beginning-level skills that deal with direct communication.

Once you have chosen a working-relationship skill, use the following steps to help maximize the benefits to the students:

1. Ask the learners, "Why is it important to deal with [skill]?" After encouraging each group to come up with a statement, solicit responses and record them on the board or an overhead transparency.
2. Ask the learners, "What could you say to team members as a way of exhibiting [skill]?" Solicit responses and record them on the board or transparency.
3. Ask the learners, "What does it look like when you use [skill]?" Again, solicit and record responses.
4. Move on to the science activity. Remind learners that they should use the working-relationship skill that they just discussed.
5. While the activity is in progress, move around the class and monitor the teams' use of the skill while also addressing learners' questions about the science content.
6. At the end of the class period, ask each team to rate itself (for example, on a scale of 1 to 10) on how well it dealt with the skill. Tell teams to write a justification for their rating. Teams should reach consensus on their score

Table 10.1		Working-Relationship Skills Ranked by Skill Level
Beginning-Level Skills	**Intermediate-Level Skills**	**Advanced-Level Skills**
Acknowledging contributions of team members	Practicing active listening	Advocating a position
Being accountable to the team	Challenging ideas, not people	Asking for justification
Contributing to the team effort	Checking for accuracy and understanding	Compromising
Dealing with distractions while staying on task	Contributing ideas	Dealing with specific problems
Encouraging the participation of other team members	Disagreeing in a positive way	Probing for understanding
Finishing on time	Managing and organizing team tasks	Setting goals
Giving guidance without giving answers	Paraphrasing	Synthesizing the team's ideas
Honoring individual differences	Providing constructive criticism	
Inviting others to talk	Questioning techniques	
Listening to teammates	Reaching consensus	
Maintaining calm	Sharing perspectives	
Seeking help from teammates	Summarizing	
Using agreement	Taking responsibility	
Using names while looking at the speaker	Using initiative	

and justification. Teams can use this evaluation for their own information and to guide them when they address another working-relationship skill. Teams do not need to share their ratings with the class.

7. Share with the class your observations about how teams addressed the working-relationship skill. Emphasize positive results. If you didn't notice a clear, positive example while observing a team, suggest that

perhaps you did not observe that team at the right time and that you will likely notice a positive example the next time.

8. Review the teams' self-assessments. If you find that a team's rating is not justified by the behaviors you observed, or if a team is having problems with a particular skill, meet with the team privately to work out ways to improve teamwork.

Strategies for Collaborative Learning Teams

Collaborative learning does not just happen. This section provides suggestions for forming collaborative learning teams and helping them work together effectively. We also provide some troubleshooting strategies and ideas for what to do with teams that finish their work early.

Ideas for Forming Teams

Creating modified heterogeneous teams can be challenging. The following tips might help:

- Always form teams before students enter the room for the day. Use creative methods for determining who is on which team. To achieve heterogeneity, you might start by listing students alphabetically, then by birth date, hair color, telephone number, or other nonacademic characteristic, and then number them by twos, threes, or fours to create new teams. Alternatively, put students' names into a hat and draw out names to form teams. Once you have randomly placed students' names into groups, check to make sure that no group has only one girl, minority student, or special-needs student. Rearrange the random groups as necessary to achieve modified heterogeneous teams. If it is impossible to avoid isolating a girl or a boy, minority student, or special-needs student in a group, then carefully consider the personalities of the other group members. Are the teammates likely to listen to the ideas of someone different from themselves? The most important thing is to think carefully about the personalities of students to make sure that all students will have the chance to participate in their groups. It is all right if the modified heterogeneous teams lead to groups of all boys, all girls, or all students from the same ethnic group. Just make sure to vary these more homogeneous groups in future team projects.
- If you need teams of two and your class is not evenly divisible by two, form one team of three. If you need teams of three and your class does not divide evenly by three, form one team of two. Try to choose students who can handle dual roles. If you need teams of four, have extra students form groups of three. Pairs will have difficulty completing

activities designed for teams of four. If you cannot form several teams of three easily, consider one or two teams of five.

- Keep a record of which students have worked together. By the end of the year, try to make sure that students have worked with as many diverse personalities as possible.
- If a team is down to one student due to absences, assign that student to another team temporarily. If a student is absent, but the remaining team members number more than one, this team should continue as normal. Teams that are short a member can usually function adequately for a short time.
- When students are absent, assign their teammates the responsibility of helping the absent student catch up. If this is impractical, arrange for all absent students to come in together and complete the activity as a new team.

What to Do When Teams Do Not Cooperate

Cooperation might not come naturally to every learner on a team. This reality of the classroom setting can make collaborative learning a challenge at times. How you handle the first signs of noncooperation can set the tone for future collaborative learning experiences. As you plan your strategies for improving the cooperative nature of each student and team, keep in mind the following:

- *Let students take responsibility for solving problems.* Avoid functioning as the source of solutions to all problems. Turn problems back to teams whenever possible. Practice being a consultant. Offer a variety of suggestions that students choose from. Ask the students what strategies they have tried and what alternatives they would like to try.
- *Remind the learners that it takes time to become proficient at collaborative learning.* It may take a long time for students who begin with poor working-relationship skills to make small improvements. Watch for signs of progress.
- *Establish a classroom environment of respect and acceptance for each person.* You can do this by modeling desired behaviors yourself. Do not tolerate negative remarks or put-downs. Identify strengths in each student and point those out as appropriate. Encourage students to do these things as well.

Although the above suggestions provide general guidance for dealing with problems, they are not concrete. The following list describes a number of concrete strategies you can use to assist learners who have trouble working with others:

- If a team is arguing and headed in a destructive direction, ask students open-ended questions that redirect the discussion. Return in a few minutes to check progress.
- If a team is having difficulty reaching consensus, ask if there is a way the members can combine the various suggestions, rather than choosing among them.
- Watch for use of working-relationship skills. If a team consistently is not using a skill, ask the members of the team to identify two ways they could use the skill. Monitor their interactions and watch for use of the skill.
- Assign jobs that build on students' strengths. For instance, a non-English-speaking student probably would function better as a materials manager than as a reader. You might pair a student who is a good negotiator with a student who has difficulty resolving conflict. Do not use this technique repeatedly. All students are capable of learning and doing each job.
- Coach individual students who are having trouble participating as team members. Try to give the student replacement behaviors for those that get her or him into trouble consistently. For example, a student who dominates group discussion and does not give others time to talk could learn to count to 10 after presenting an idea so that others can respond. Someone who makes many negative remarks could learn to say, "You could be right" or another positive phrase as an alternative response.
- Insist that teammates work together to resolve their differences and succeed at a task. Do not bail students out too early. They will often resolve the problem if you give them alternatives to consider and time to apply the alternatives. One common problem that teams can resolve is having one member of the team who does not contribute. Let the students resolve this problem before completing an investigation so that they can work together more constructively. You may need to give the team extra time to finish its work.
- If a team has a member who dominates discussions, consider distributing "talk tokens." Give each student three or four tokens; when a student talks, he or she puts a token in a bowl. After the student has used all of the tokens, he or she cannot talk again until all other team members have used their tokens.
- Ask teams that are having trouble to split up and observe other teams. While they are observing, they should record notes about how the

other teams function. Then they should reassemble the team to discuss what they observed, how that might be different from what they do, and how they might apply what they observed.

- Change teams only as a last resort. Usually a student who has trouble on one team also will have difficulty on the new one.
- When determining new teams, avoid assigning students who consistently clash to the same team. If such students end up on the same team, you may keep them together for a prescribed time, but avoid the combination later in the year.
- Model specific behaviors you expect learners to use. If you use a derogatory style of communicating, students are likely to do the same. If you show respect for each student, that also will encourage students to do so.

Planning for Teams That Finish Early

It is unlikely that teams will finish each activity at the same time. Just as you plan for individual students who finish early, you will need to plan for teams that finish early. The following ideas may provide helpful strategies for dealing with teams that finish before other teams:

- Spend time with the team, asking probing and clarifying questions. Sometimes teams finish early because they have rushed through an activity. Help students realize that getting finished is not the ultimate goal of the activities and discussions. Sometimes students need to know that the quality of thought is more important than the speed at which an activity is accomplished.
- If two teams finish early, have members report to each other what they did, why they did it, what their conclusions are, and what those conclusions mean. You can use this strategy for single teams by having them answer the same questions for each other, in their science notebooks, or by talking to you.
- Provide resources, such as trade books, science books, or computer software, that relate to the activities. Look for resources that enhance the concepts and skills introduced in the activity.
- Debrief teams that finish early. There is usually not enough time in a class discussion for all teams to report their procedures and results. You can get a sense of how well each student is doing if you talk to individual teams before a whole-class discussion.

How to Assess Collaborative Learning

Assessment of the use of collaborative learning in your classroom should occur on two levels: your students' progress in using working-relationship skills and your growing facility for implementing this instructional strategy. In this section, we provide suggestions for assessment at both of these levels.

Assessing a Learners' Ability to Use Working-Relationship Skills

Just as it is important for students to assess their progress in understanding science concepts, it is also important for students to assess their own abilities to implement working-relationship skills. Tables 10.2 and 10.3 provide sample forms that students can complete for this assessment.

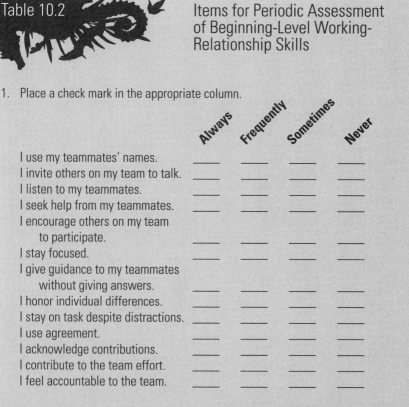

Table 10.2 — Items for Periodic Assessment of Beginning-Level Working-Relationship Skills

1. Place a check mark in the appropriate column.

	Always	Frequently	Sometimes	Never
I use my teammates' names.	____	____	____	____
I invite others on my team to talk.	____	____	____	____
I listen to my teammates.	____	____	____	____
I seek help from my teammates.	____	____	____	____
I encourage others on my team to participate.	____	____	____	____
I stay focused.	____	____	____	____
I give guidance to my teammates without giving answers.	____	____	____	____
I honor individual differences.	____	____	____	____
I stay on task despite distractions.	____	____	____	____
I use agreement.	____	____	____	____
I acknowledge contributions.	____	____	____	____
I contribute to the team effort.	____	____	____	____
I feel accountable to the team.	____	____	____	____

2. Describe a skill that you learned to use well in this unit. Why do you think you do a good job with this skill?
3. What skill did you have difficulty with? What made the skill difficult to use?
4. What skill is most important to your success? Explain.
5. What skill is most important to the success of your team? Explain.
6. How might you use the skill from question 4 outside of school?

Table 10.3 — Items for Periodic Assessment of Intermediate- or Advanced-Level Working-Relationship Skills

1. Place a check mark in the appropriate column.

Intermediate-Level Skills

	Always	Frequently	Sometimes	Never
I practice active listening.	___	___	___	___
I challenge ideas, not people.	___	___	___	___
I check for accuracy and understanding.	___	___	___	___
I disagree in a positive way.	___	___	___	___
I contribute my ideas.	___	___	___	___
I manage and organize team tasks.	___	___	___	___
I use paraphrasing for understanding.	___	___	___	___
I provide constructive criticism.	___	___	___	___
I use good questioning techniques.	___	___	___	___
I practice reaching consensus with my teammates.	___	___	___	___
I summarize information.	___	___	___	___
I use initiative.	___	___	___	___
I take responsibility.	___	___	___	___

Advanced-Level Skills

	Always	Frequently	Sometimes	Never
I advocate my positions.	___	___	___	___
I ask for justification.	___	___	___	___
I compromise.	___	___	___	___
I deal with specific problems.	___	___	___	___
I probe for understanding.	___	___	___	___
I set goals.	___	___	___	___

2. Describe a skill that you learned to use well in this unit. Why do you think you do a good job with this skill?
3. What skill did you have difficulty with? What made the skill difficult to use?
4. What skill is most important to your success? Explain.
5. What skill is most important to the success of your team? Explain.
6. How might you use the skill from question 4 outside of school?

Table 10.4 asks the learner to assess how his or her teammates and the team as a whole are progressing in using working-relationship skills. This perspective is important because it helps individuals on the team form a view of collective success. If all the team members feel that they have good skills, but the team is not working well, then the team needs to decide what other team dynamics need adjustment. Because this table allows learners to rate individual team members as well as the team as a whole, teammates can provide positive reinforcement for team members who may have had difficulties with some skills but have made good progress. Conversely, if a learner thinks that he or she is practicing good working-relationship skills, but everyone on the team thinks otherwise, then the individual may benefit from a frank discussion.

Table 10.4 — A Model Form for Individual Assessment of Team Members

Working-Relationship Skill	Individual 1	Individual 2	Individual 3	Individual 4	Team

1. Evaluate your individual team members and your whole team for how effectively they use working-relationship skills. Use a scale of 1–10, with 10 being the highest. Provide at least three pieces of evidence for your assessment.
2. What skill does your team use well? Provide enough evidence to support your claim.
3. What skill does your team need to improve upon? List two specific ways that you will work to improve that skill.
4. What did you accomplish in your team that you would have accomplished less effectively or efficiently by yourself?

Table 10.5	Sample Form for Tracking a Team's Use of a Working-Relationship Skill				
Working-Relationship Skill	Team 1	Team 2	Team 3	Team 4	Team 5

Table 10.5 is an example of a tool that you may use to evaluate how teams are doing. You can provide the view of an outside observer who may see positive changes and behaviors that the learners do not see.

Using instruments such as these models can help you develop a collaborative learning assessment package appropriate for your needs. You can modify the specific items on each form to fit your specific setting and the working-relationship skills used in each activity.

Assessing How Well You Implement Collaborative Learning

Collaborative learning may not come naturally to every learner on a team or to every teacher. If you are trying collaborative learning for the first time, you are likely to feel uncomfortable and unsure about whether you are proceeding properly. If you have used collaborative learning for a short time, you may feel that you are failing at implementing it more often than you are succeeding. Remember, however, that as with any other innovation, becoming successful takes time. Expect that you will need to continue to work on implementing the techniques before collaborative learning strategies feel natural for you.

As you continue to implement collaborative learning strategies in the classroom, you will need to monitor your progress. How well are your students exhibiting the skills of collaborative learning? Table 10.6 compares how collaborative learning differs from group work. A tool such as this can help you identify those collaborative learning elements that you feel you are executing consistently in your classroom and those that may need attention in the future.

Table 10.6	Differences Between Collaborative Learning Work and Group Work

Collaborative Learning Work	Group Work
• Learners have defined roles.	• Learners work in groups with no definite jobs.
• Teams are heterogeneous.	• Groups are homogeneous.
• Teams are autonomous; teams solve problems.	• Groups have no organized approach to solving problems.
• Teams practice and develop working-relationship skills.	• Groups use whatever interactive skills they have.
• Teams develop positive interdependence.	• Group tasks do not require interdependence.
• Teams share leadership.	• One leader always leads the group.
• Teams assess how they want to work together.	• Individual evaluation is what counts; group interactions are unimportant.
• Individuals are held accountable to the team.	• Individuals are accountable only to themselves.

Troubleshooting Implementation Problems With Collaborative Learning

As with other teaching strategies, collaborative learning may present problems that would influence your success with implementing each essential element

Table 10.7	Common Problems With the Implementation of Collaborative Learning

Collaborative Learning Element	Implementation Problems
Defined roles for students	• Each team member does not have an assigned role, so the work is uneven. • Teams are left to themselves to assign roles, and they assign the same roles to the same people all the time.
Modified heterogeneous teams	• Teams are not heterogeneous with respect to ability, gender, race, or other characteristic. • Learners choose their own teams and always choose to work with their friends. • Absences make it difficult to retain stable teams.
Team autonomy	• Learners count on the teacher to resolve issues rather than take the responsibility for solving their own problems. • Team autonomy is not recognized as highly valued. • One or more learners refuse to work on teams.
Working-relationship skills	• Learners do not know what is expected of them as they use working-relationship skills. They do not know what the skill would look like if it were working well (no models).
Positive interdependence	• Team members work individually, rather than cooperatively, to complete tasks. • Individual members can be successful without the entire team succeeding.
Distribution of leadership	• One team member always takes a leadership role.
Individual accountability	• Each individual on a team is not held accountable for what the team is learning and doing.
Team self-assessment	• Teams do not assess how well they displayed a specific working-relationship skill. • Learners do not give individual feedback about how well the team is working together.

of collaborative learning. Some of the common difficulties that may arise as you begin implementing collaborative learning strategies are presented in table 10.7. We provide specific ideas and ways to address the problems.

Defined Roles for Students

Do you assign distinct roles to each team member? Often, if you do not assign roles, some team members will remain idle while others do most of the work. *Do you appoint team members to certain roles?* If teams are left to themselves to assign roles, some team members may always assume the same roles.

Assigning team roles is vital to the function of collaborative learning in your classroom. These roles are part of what will enable you to move around the room and work with as many groups as possible to assess their progress. Without assigned roles, students often rely on the teacher to answer procedural questions and solve problems they are capable of handling themselves.

When you first begin implementing collaborative learning strategies, you may need to make sure that individuals on teams know what tasks are involved for each role in an activity or how each task should be carried out. Depending on the activity, students in each of these roles may need some guidance or instruction.

If you implement collaborative learning fully, one role that you may wish to include as a standard role in any activity is that of *communicator.* The communicator's task is to be aware at all times of what is happening in the group. This student is the only member of the team who can communicate with you or with another team. This forces team members to interact and make each other aware of difficulties they are having with an activity. It also makes your task of facilitating more manageable because only one member of each team will be asking for your input. Other possible roles include *taskmaster,* the person who keeps the team members on task; *supporter,* the person who encourages team members when difficulties arise; *summarizer,* the person who tells the group what has been done and what is left to do; *recorder,* the person who records ideas and answers; and *coordinator,* the person who divides the work to be done and assures that each member is doing the proper task.

Modified Heterogeneous Teams

Do you decide the makeup of collaborative teams? If students are left to choose their own teams, they usually will choose to work only with friends. This may cause management difficulties because friends are more likely to socialize and go off task than a more heterogeneous group of students. Do you expect students to work with others regardless of ability, gender, or race? Because of the increasing importance of cooperative interactions in our society, individuals need to master the skills of dealing with others regardless of how alike or different they may be. *Do you expect every student to fully participate in a group activity?* Because student-student bias is common, especially in science classrooms, it is important that all students feel they can relate to someone in their group. If students don't feel like they belong, it will be difficult for them to fully participate.

Team Autonomy

Do you turn problems back to the teams to solve? If learners can count on you to resolve issues, they will come to regard you as the source of solutions to all problems. Make the students take the responsibility for solving problems by turning the problems back to the teams whenever possible. Ask the students, "Have you asked everybody in your team?" or "Have you asked another team?" Ask the students what strategies they have tried and what alternatives they would like to try. If you need to give a response, offer a variety of suggestions from which students can choose.

If students are having trouble working with others, try some of these strategies. If a team is arguing and headed in a destructive direction, ask students open-ended questions that redirect the discussion. If a team is having difficulty reaching consensus, ask if there is a way the members can combine the various suggestions, rather than choose among them. Coach individual students who are having trouble participating as team members on one or two skills; try to give these students replacement behaviors for those that consistently cause them trouble. You might ask teams that are having trouble to split up, observe other teams, and take notes about how the other teams function. Then have team members use these notes to discuss how they might modify their own team interactions. Model the specific behaviors that you expect students to use.

Remember to use rewards and recognition to promote group autonomy. Psychologists have proposed that one fundamental human psychological need is to have a sense of oneself as competent and effective. Although this need is partially fulfilled by an individual's internal sense of accomplishment, it is enhanced by recognition for well-accomplished tasks.

For many learners, verbal recognition from the teacher is the best form of reward and recognition. You also might give teams that work well together the opportunity to lead a class discussion or conduct a demonstration. Other rewards that work well for high school students include displays of work, messages to parents, and increased responsibilities in the classroom.

Be sure that opportunities for reward and recognition are available for all collaborative teams. These opportunities can be based on the social functioning of the groups or on the completion of an assignment. Have teammates compete with each other to improve their team functioning and, occasionally, with other teams to achieve a sense of team behavior and belonging.

In the rare case of a student who flatly refuses to work in groups, you may want to suggest that she or he commit to a group for a limited time, such as a few weeks. If the student still resists teamwork, you may want to allow her or him to work individually. Make the student aware that working individually will require more work on her or his part. The student may eventually decide to participate in a team.

Working-Relationship Skills

Do you take the time to introduce, monitor, and provide feedback about the working-relationship skills as the students use them? Unless specific attention is given to the working-relationship skills, learners will not become adept at using them. Monitor students, formally and informally, to determine how well they are progressing. Record examples of specific comments or actions that reflect the students' use of the skill. Use the tally and comments to reinforce students who are using the appropriate skills.

Are students having difficulty using the working-relationship skills that you are emphasizing? Remember that learning new skills takes time and practice. Try to use a difficult skill more frequently. Conduct a whole-class discussion, asking students why they think the skill is so difficult to master. Have them conduct brainstorming sessions of new ways to address the skill, and then try some of the stronger suggestions.

If a team seldom uses a particular skill, ask one team member to take on the role of tracking the number of times the team uses the assigned working-relationship skill. Alternatively, have another team discuss how it uses the skill. Another strategy for a team that is not using a skill consistently is to ask members of the team to identify two ways they could use the skill. Monitor their subsequent interactions, and watch for use of the skill.

Remind the learners that it takes time to become proficient at using working-relationship skills. For students with poor skills, this could mean it will take all year for them to master a skill. Watch for small signs of progress, and recognize the students who demonstrate progress.

Structure lessons so that teams can identify their weak skills and practice them. Allow ample time for teams to evaluate their working-relationship skills. Encourage individuals or groups to commit to improving specific skills by signing a formal contract that you and the student or class design.

Positive Interdependence

Do the team members work individually, rather than cooperatively, to complete tasks? Collaborative teams require positive interdependence. If an activity does not offer this, look for ways to redesign the activity so that the group cannot succeed unless each team member completes his or her part in a given task. Jigsaw activities, in which an individual accomplishes one part of a task and then shares his or her results with other team members, are an effective way of reinforcing positive interdependence. In such activities, each team member gains specific knowledge or experience that enables the team to address a larger problem.

Can an individual member be successful without the entire team succeeding? If you find it difficult to restructure an activity to encourage positive interdependence, try building this element into follow-up assignments. You might have each team member complete a written assignment, but choose (randomly) only one of the assignments for grading. This will encourage team members to help each other prepare a good assignment. Using a similar technique, grade all assignments and then randomly choose one from each team for bonus points. A well-done assignment will result in more bonus points for each team member. Another option is to ask the teams to prepare a team response to an assignment and identify each team member's contribution.

Using team members as a source of solving problems is another way to encourage positive interdependence. You might ask, "What do your team members say about this question?" Another technique is to have the team divide the questions among group members so that, while the team is responsible for completing the whole section, each individual is responsible for one-fourth or one-third of the questions. When an oral response is needed from the team, tell the teams that you may call on any team member so every member should be prepared to respond. A technique for encouraging positive interdependence, which also involves thoughtful team evaluation, is to have teammates actually articulate (orally or in writing) each person's contribution and explain how the team would not have succeeded without each person's role.

In summary, if students always choose to complete assignments independently, they will forfeit opportunities to develop skills for working with others that will be important throughout their lives. If this is an area of continuing concern, use positive interdependence as a working-relationship skill on which teams must focus for a series of activities.

Distribution of Leadership

Does one dominant team member always take a leadership role? Monitor the team closely to assure that members switch roles as you direct. Look for more opportunities for jigsaw activities in which each team member becomes a leader in the area in which she or he has developed expertise.

Have students record their roles in their science notebooks so that you can quickly check whether they are rotating responsibilities.

Reexamine how the use of roles and positive interdependence is being implemented in your classroom. Sometimes weaknesses in these areas can lead to one team member who dominates the leadership role. You might keep track of those students who tend to lead more readily and assign them all to the same team the next time you switch teams. This will encourage the strong leaders to learn to share with each other and, at the same time, require that others take on the leadership roles in those groups without strong leaders. Another strategy is to take aside the leader of the group and privately work out a way to encourage her or him to take a secondary role for a set time period or for a specific activity. Some leaders can transfer to an encouraging role fairly easily. This change should allow someone else to fill the leadership role.

General Problems

Some other simple, quick strategies are as follows:

- *Homework helpers.* Have team members compare homework answers and record these answers. Collect one paper per team. If you use this strategy frequently, rotate whose paper you collect.
- *Sharing knowledge.* Before you begin an activity, ask teams to write down everything they already know about the topic. After they complete the activity, have the teams review what they wrote initially and discuss the new knowledge they gained.
- *Write a note.* Have each team member write a note that begins, "What I learned from this activity is …, but I still don't understand …" Have individuals trade notes with someone else on their team and write a reply to the note they received.
- *Turn to your neighbor.* After a lecture or whole-class discussion, ask learners to turn to their neighbor and point out or summarize a key point of what was said.

Once you feel comfortable using these simple strategies, go back to the more complete form of collaborative learning and try again. Give yourself time to become adept. As time passes, you will find yourself moving farther along the implementation continuum until eventually you find yourself incorporating collaborative learning as a natural part of your instructional style.

RESOURCES FOR COLLABORATIVE LEARNING

To learn more about collaborative learning, we recommend the following resources:

BSCS. 1994. *Middle school science and technology implementation guide.* Dubuque, IA: Kendall/Hunt.

Cohen, E. G. 1986. *Designing groupwork: Strategies for the heterogeneous classroom.* New York: Teachers College Press.

———. 1994. Restructuring the classroom: Conditions for productive small groups. *Review of Educational Research* 64 (1): 1–35.

Johnson, D. W., and R. T. Johnson. 1991. Group assessment as an aid to science instruction. In *Science assessment in the service of reform,* eds. G. Kulm, and S. M. Malcolm, 283–289. Washington, DC: American Association for the Advancement of Science.

Johnson, D. W., R. T. Johnson, and E. J. Houlbec. 1986. *Circle of learning: Cooperation in the classroom.* Edina, MN: Interaction Book.

Lundgren, L. 1993. *Cooperative learning resource guide.* Lake Forest, IL: Glencoe Division, Macmillan/McGraw-Hill School.

Slavin, R. E. 1987. *Cooperative learning: Student teams.* Washington, DC: National Education Association.

Chapter 11

How to Use Science Notebooks in Your Classroom

Many biology programs advocate the use of science notebooks or journals. Depending on the program, grade level, or teacher preference, notebooks can take one of many forms: a spiral notebook, a three-ring notebook, a bound composition or lab book, or a preprinted notebook from the publisher. Whatever the format, the important thing is that students have a place where experience, data, and language can come together to form meaning. From here on, we will refer to that place as a science notebook.

Why Are Science Notebooks Important?

The students' use of a daily science notebook is a small but important key to success. Used appropriately, notebooks can provide two major benefits. First, notebooks can document daily work. This daily routine helps the students focus on the task at hand and provide an organized record of their data. Second, notebooks can serve as a method for students to construct an understanding of concepts and build explanations. This provides a way for students to articulate what they do and do not understand.

Daily Documentation

Science notebooks help students organize and articulate their growing understanding. Using the notebook is integral to student participation and growth. Some typical uses for documenting information include the following:

- Recording data
- Taking notes
- Making sketches
- Organizing ideas through concept maps or other visuals
- Responding to questions in the activities
- Completing homework
- Keeping track of questions they may have
- Completing other assignments

Conceptual Development

Students should use a notebook throughout a course as a key piece in developing conceptual continuity and depth. Writing can be a powerful learning tool in science. Recording observations, thoughts, measurements, unanswered questions, and opinions in a notebook can help students construct science concepts for themselves. As they write about their hands-on experiences, they organize, reflect on, and clarify their thoughts so that they can better communicate their understanding. In addition, writing becomes a useful diagnostic and evaluative tool for teachers and parents. A student's notebook is a permanent and continuous record of what the student is learning and thinking.

Even when students are doing an activity or participating in a discussion that does not require written responses, encourage them to summarize what they learned or accomplished in class that day. Asking students to keep a daily record of their activities can provide you with a useful way to document their understanding. More important, the students can learn to monitor their own development by reviewing their work and identifying items that best represent their progress.

To help students focus on conceptual understanding, provide them with a way to focus on the big ideas or major concepts. You can accomplish this through a graphic organizer such as a concept development map or through a learning log that connects daily concepts to overarching unit concepts. Both of these notebook methods encourage students to track their conceptual learning in one place.

Communication With Parents or Guardians

An additional benefit of using student notebooks is that they provide a method of keeping parents or guardians informed. You might periodically assign homework that requires the students to take their science notebooks home and involve the parents or guardians in some activity. You might ask parents or guardians to initial the notebook following a discussion about class activities.

How Can Science Notebooks Be Organized?

Many students will need guidance on how to keep a notebook. Take time early in the program to inform students about what you think belongs in a science notebook and how you expect to use the notebook for assessment. A well-organized notebook can serve as a reference for students. Consider organizing notebooks into four sections: table of contents, conceptual development, daily entries, and personal glossary.

Table of Contents

Students should reserve room at the beginning of their notebooks to create and add to a table of contents. The number of pages reserved will depend on the length of the unit of study. For high school students engaged in a yearlong program, it may mean 10 to 16 pages. All pages of the science notebook should be numbered so that both the students and you can find appropriate pages quickly and easily.

Conceptual Development

Students should reserve room to keep track of how daily lessons relate to overarching conceptual understanding. They can represent this as a concept map or as an outline. Figure 11.1 and table 11.1 provide examples. The purpose is to provide a place for students to make conceptual connections.

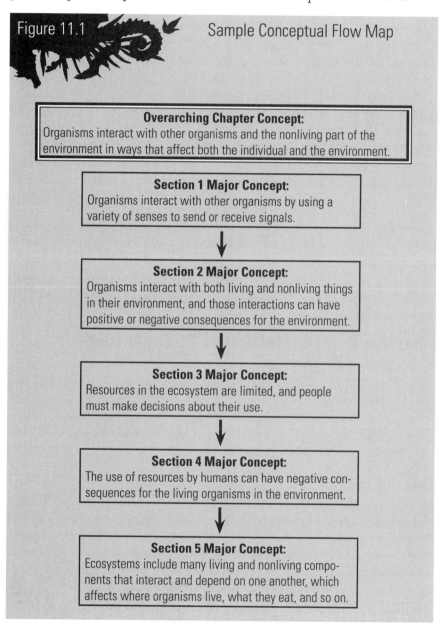

Figure 11.1   Sample Conceptual Flow Map

Overarching Chapter Concept:
Organisms interact with other organisms and the nonliving part of the environment in ways that affect both the individual and the environment.

Section 1 Major Concept:
Organisms interact with other organisms by using a variety of senses to send or receive signals.

Section 2 Major Concept:
Organisms interact with both living and nonliving things in their environment, and those interactions can have positive or negative consequences for the environment.

Section 3 Major Concept:
Resources in the ecosystem are limited, and people must make decisions about their use.

Section 4 Major Concept:
The use of resources by humans can have negative consequences for the living organisms in the environment.

Section 5 Major Concept:
Ecosystems include many living and nonliving components that interact and depend on one another, which affects where organisms live, what they eat, and so on.

Table 11.1   Sample Conceptual Flow Outline

Major Chapter Concept:
Traits are passed from one generation to the next in predictable patterns through the process of reproduction.

Section
1. Genetic information is passed from one generation to the next.

2. The laws of probability can be used to predict the outcomes of genetic crosses.
   a. The predicted outcomes of genetic crosses are more likely to match actual outcomes if the sample size is large.

3. Genetic information is transferred from one generation to the next in predictable patterns.
   a. Genes occur in multiple forms, called alleles, that confer variations in traits.
   b. Genes for different traits are inherited independently of each other.
   c. In many organisms, genes occur in pairs of alleles.
      i. If both alleles are the same, the individual is homozygous.
      ii. If the two alleles are different, the individual is heterozygous.
   d. Dominant alleles require only one allele in the pair for the trait to be apparent; recessive alleles must be present in two copies for the trait to be apparent.

4. Meiosis is the mechanism that
   a. gametes that have one-half of the genetic information from a parent.
   b. explains the predictable patterns of inheritance for many genes.

5. The probability of particular genotypic and phenotypic outcomes of a mating can be predicted by using Punnett squares.
   a. More-complete patterns of inheritance result from simultaneously following the inheritance of two traits.
   b. Genes on the X chromosome show a different pattern of inheritance because males have only one X chromosome while females have two.
   c. Crossing over during meiosis may separate alleles that are linked on the same chromosome.

6. Human traits exhibit a range of variation that is affected by natural selection.
   a. Genetic variations occur by mutations and the recombination of alleles.
   b. Complex traits exhibit continuous variation and are determined by multiple genes and environmental factors.

7. Traits are inherited from generation to generation by the process of reproduction, which also explains patterns of inheritance.

Table 11.2   Sample Personal Glossary Page

Term	Definition	Picture
Nucleotide (NOO klee oh tide)	These are the building blocks for DNA and RNA. They are made of a 5-carbon sugar that is linked to a phosphate group and a "base" that contains nitrogen.	**DNA nucleotide** cytosine (a nitrogenous base) deoxyribose (a 5-carbon sugar) phosphate
Ribosome (RY boh SOHM)	Ribosomes are small organelles where proteins are made. They are found in the cytoplasm of the cell (but they're made in the nucleus). They have a small subunit and a large subunit and are made of a combination of RNA and protein.	**ribosome**
Transfer RNA (tRNA)	These are adaptor molecules that translate the codons in messenger RNA and put the right amino acid in place in a protein. On one end, they can carry a specific amino acid, and on the other end they have three bases (the anticodon) that are complementary to the codons in the messenger RNA.	**transfer RNA** amino acid — met tRNA anticodon — U A C

Daily Entries

The daily entries section is a place for students to organize their daily class work. This section may include things like predictions, observations, procedures, data tables, graphs, discussion questions, diagrams, reflective notes, and daily summaries. You should emphasize honesty in record keeping rather than reaching correct conclusions. To help students organize the information so that it can be found more easily, ask students to

- date daily work;
- write in activity titles and textbook page numbers;
- label data tables, graphs, and charts; and
- write legibly.

In addition, students can use the daily entries section as a place to write their thoughts, ideas, and feelings about science. Encourage students to use their notebooks at anytime—not only when instructed to do so. This will reinforce the idea that notebooks are designed to help them construct their own understanding.

Personal Glossary

Ask students to reserve several pages at the backs of their notebooks to enter new terms. Students use the personal glossary individually, and its design should help each student retain word meanings. Encourage students to enter words that they find problematic. Explain that their glossaries are their responsibility to maintain and are important in helping them learn and retain scientific vocabulary.

One format for a glossary is a three-column chart (table 11.2). The first column lists the term; adding the pronunciation might be helpful. The second column includes the definition of the term; this should be a student-generated definition rather than one copied from a glossary or dictionary. The last column includes a visual representation of the term or a way that will help students remember the term.

How Can Science Notebooks Help Me Assess Student Understanding?

Notebooks should be a means for both teachers and students to assess understanding. Notebooks should not be graded, however; there are other opportunities for grading. Work in notebooks should provide opportunities for students to refine and clarify their thinking. Notebook feedback should be formative, providing hints and guidance. Do not expect a student's notebook to be a finished, edited product. To promote writing, allow students to be creative and take risks with their writing. Foster a supportive and accepting environment for "invented" spellings and grammatical errors. As you read a student's science notebook, respond to the quality of the thinking and observation. Periodically encourage students to revise selected notebook entries to improve their sentence structure, spelling, and grammar. When you focus on ideas and understanding, you model for students what is most important in science—the ability to think and reason.

Use these guidelines to help you use the students' notebooks as assessment tools:

- Review the notebooks frequently. This will demonstrate the importance you place on students' individual work and will identify students who might need additional assistance.
- Look for evidence of students' developing understanding and achievement of lesson outcomes. A quick review of each lesson's learning objectives and assessment indicators before reviewing the notebooks will expedite your review.
- Establish evaluation criteria together with students ahead of time, and stick to these criteria while assessing the notebooks. This provides students with the maximum opportunity to succeed.

How Can I Hold Students Accountable for Their Science Notebooks?

Remind students that their science notebook is first and foremost a place for them to organize their own learning and that they will get out of it what they put into it. It would be fabulous if every teacher had the time and energy to read and respond to every word in every student's notebook; however, that is highly unlikely. Of course, you will want to build in an effective accountability system without carrying hundreds of notebooks home to assess. There are some tools and strategies that can help you keep track of student notebooks and student learning:

- *Teacher checklist.* Checklists let you determine, at a glance, whether students are including appropriate information in their notebooks. Keep a list of information that you consider vital to every notebook. You can ask students to open their notebooks to a particular assignment. Then a quick walk through the class allows you to glance at student notebooks, checking that the information you want to see is included.
- *Peer checks.* Peer checks are a way to more specifically determine that students are including appropriate information in their science notebooks. At

the end of each chapter, provide students with a detailed list of things to look for in each other's notebooks. If the assignments are there (and appropriate), students can indicate where they found them (notebook page numbers), provide an "on time" stamp or sticker, and assign points. If there are discrepancies, you can double-check quickly based on the page numbers.

- *Open notebook quizzes.* Of course, there will be times when you want to look at student responses so that you can provide formative feedback. Open notebook quizzes assess student understanding without actually grading students' science notebooks. Consider assignments that provide you with student responses that allow you to monitor conceptual understanding. Ask students to copy their responses to only those assignments on the open notebook quiz. They can copy word for word or expand on their responses. We recommend that you provide students with formative feedback about exactly where they are in their understanding or with questions that will lead them to a better understanding rather than a grade, because this will help them focus on their learning rather than on grades. Holding open notebook quizzes acknowledges that notebooks are not graded but that they are an important student resource. Be selective about information that you want to read and respond to, most likely information that will help you monitor conceptual understanding. Assess what you care about.
- *Notebook rubric.* You may occasionally (perhaps once per unit) want to perform a global assessment of student notebooks. At the beginning of the unit, give students your notebook rubric so that they know your expectations (table 11.3). At the end of the unit, use the rubric to provide a score based on the rubric's criteria.

How Can Students Share Their Science Notebooks With the Class?

Encourage students to share what they have written in their science notebooks with you and with their peers. Some students will always be eager to read aloud from their notebooks during class discussions, but make sure each has a chance to read his or her notebook aloud at some point.

Sharing is important because it

- permits students to hear what others did and to learn by example,
- boosts self-esteem by giving the writer the opportunity to be the center of attention,
- provides another chance for students to reflect on what happened and what they learned during the lesson,
- encourages students to compare their ideas with those of others,

Table 11.3 Sample Notebook Assessment Rubric

Rubric: Journal Techniques

Criteria	Excellent	Could Be Improved	Needs Substantial Improvement
Permanence	• Journal is written in a spiral notebook and pages are not perforated to tear out. • All assignments that are done as handouts are neatly stapled or taped into the journal on a page that corresponds with the date of the work.	• Some assignments that should have been done in the journal were done on loose paper, but they are stapled or taped into the journal on a page that corresponds with the date of the work.	• Loose pages are placed in the journal and are not attached.
Legibility	• Handwriting is easy to read, and data are recorded in ink. • Journal entries include enough blank space that additional notes may be added.	• Handwriting is reasonably easy to read, and data are recorded in ink. • Journal entries are given enough space that they are easy to read.	• Handwriting, the color of the ink used, or both is difficult to read. • Entries are crowded into too little space.
Format	• Each entry begins with the date and textbook title for the activity. • Journal is written chronologically. • Each new activity starts at the top of a new page.	• Nearly all entries are dated and titled. • It is relatively easy for any reader to locate information in the journal.	• Journal has few dated entries and little organization.
Deadlines	• All assignments are completed on time.	• Nearly all assignments are completed on time, and all are finished by the time the journals are collected.	• Some assignments are missing or incomplete.
Observations	• Journal entries are neat records, with data and observations clearly recorded at the time of experimentation. • Data tables, units of measurement, and drawings are frequently used to clarify records.	• Journal entries are reasonably neat records, with data and observations included, though some were recorded after the experimentation was completed. • Data tables, units of measurement, and drawings are sometimes used to clarify records.	• Journal entries are difficult to understand because data and observations are incomplete or poorly recorded. • Observations appear to have been written after the experiment was completed.

Table 11.3

Sample Notebook Assessment Rubric (continued)

Rubric: Journal Techniques

Criteria	Excellent	Could Be Improved	Needs Substantial Improvement
Accuracy and Communication	• Observations are descriptive and to the point. • Drawings are included wherever appropriate. • Anyone who reads the journal can tell the difference between the student's actual observations and his or her ideas and speculations about what was observed. • Notes are written clearly and organized so that the student will still be able to understand them weeks or even months later. • Answers to analysis questions and essays are all written in the student's own words, in complete sentences, and well reasoned. • Accurate information is given, specific evidence is used to support responses at least three-fourths of the time, and the sources of the evidence are cited where appropriate.	• Observations and drawings are general. • Both observations and speculations are usually recorded, though it may not always be specified which they are. • Most descriptions and data will be easy to understand in the future. • Answers to analysis questions and essays generally explain the student's reasoning and logic, and they include accurate information. • Evidence is used to support responses at least one-half the time.	• Few observations or speculations are recorded. • Lack of detail makes it difficult to understand entries now, and it will be even more difficult in the future. • Answers to analysis questions and essays seldom refer to evidence for support.

Source: Adapted from BSCS. 2006. *BSCS biology: A human approach assessment DVD.* Dubuque, IA: Kendall/Hunt.

- allows students the opportunity to edit their own writing, and
- gives the teacher a chance to elaborate on concepts in which students are interested and to clarify concepts with which students are having difficulty.

Summary

Science notebooks can take many different forms. The important thing to remember is that they should provide a place where student experience, data, and language can come together to form meaning. This can happen when daily entries lead to conceptual understanding. Notebook organization is a tool to facilitate conceptual understanding. Checklists, peer checks, open-notebook quizzes, and rubrics can be used to facilitate students' accountability for their notebooks. Notebooks should be a vehicle for assessing student understanding and should be shared.

Chapter 12

How to Help Students Make Meaning From What They Read

Science for all is the goal set by the *National Science Education Standards* (NRC 1996). For many teachers, "all" includes a continuum of diverse students including gifted students, English language learners, special education students, and struggling readers. Helping students achieve high standards and gain conceptual understanding is difficult enough without the added challenge of language and literacy issues. Content area literacy is defined as the level of reading and writing skill necessary to read, comprehend, and react to appropriate instructional materials in a given subject area (Readence et al. 2004).

You may recall a time that a student said, "I read it, but I didn't get it." Santa et al. (1996) state, "Most students arrive at the science teacher's classroom knowing how to read, but few understand how to use reading for learning science content." Much of students' background has involved how to read fictional text. Students need opportunities to develop "reading to learn" strategies. Although many students may have the ability to read text, some lack the ability to comprehend and react to it. The strategies provided in this chapter are designed to support students in their efforts to comprehend and react to science text. The strategies are not meant to teach students to read.

We have two goals for including literacy strategies. First, we want to provide students with tools that help them engage in and comprehend science text. Second, we hope that students will be able to apply these tools when they are confronted with any difficult text. Neither of these goals can be met without the support of the classroom teacher. Literacy strategies are intended to be taught explicitly to students. We encourage teachers to model strategies for students as well as provide guided and independent practice. This additional support will provide more students with opportunities to learn, internalize, and apply strategies to support their learning.

Previewing the Student Text

Students often struggle with the organization of textbooks. They may not recognize text structures and supports, special features that are intended to cue and support the reader. They include things such as the table of contents, titles, subtitles, photographs, illustrations, graphs, bold type, icons, and hints in the margins.

It is a good idea to preview any text with your students. We encourage you to take your students on a tour of your science text, similar to the one that follows, before diving into the program. As your students continue to work with the text, remind them that text structures and supports are designed to help them learn.

What might a tour of the student book look like?

1. Locate the table of contents. How is a table of contents helpful?
2. Select a chapter.
   a. Look through the lesson, looking for titles, headings, and subheadings. What clues do the text sizes give you about the lesson?
   b. Look for bold-faced words. Why would some words be bold faced?
   c. Look for various text boxes. How are these readings different? How does knowing the purpose for reading help you to think about how you might read something?
   d. Look for visual clues, such as photographs, illustrations, charts, graphs, and icons. How can these clues help you learn?
   e. Are there any safety icons? How are they represented? Why are they important?
3. Look through another chapter. How is the layout of the chapter similar to the first chapter you looked at? How is it different?
4. How is this text organized to help you learn?

Literacy Strategies

"Readers wield a great deal of power when they learn how to harness purpose" (Tovani 2005). The goal of literacy strategies is to help students identify the purpose for reading for themselves. Effective readers often scan text to capture the intent of the reading and clarify a purpose for reading. Struggling readers may not have the tools to harness the purpose for reading. If students are unable to identify the purpose for reading, they likely are unable to organize their thoughts in a purposeful manner. To help students learn how to harness purpose, talk about the importance of identifying a purpose for reading. Encourage students to scan the text to clarify the purpose for reading so that they are aware of the kind of information they are seeking through their reading.

What Is the Purpose of Literacy Strategies?

Before students can make connections between the activities or investigations that they have engaged in and the important information in the text, they must be able to engage in and understand the text they are asked to read. Strategies can support readers in their efforts to comprehend and react to the text. Once students become familiar with an array of strategies, we hope that they can select and incorporate appropriate strategies as they read any material that is difficult for them to comprehend.

Who Should Use Literacy Strategies?

Your students probably fall on a continuum in their abilities to comprehend science text. Some of your students may be expert readers equipped with the tools to understand the text with little or no support. On the other hand, some of your students may be struggling readers who need explicit support to comprehend reading in science. You know your students, so incorporate strategies in a manner that makes the most sense for you and for them.

Organization of Literacy Strategies

The strategies are organized into three main categories: vocabulary, active reading, and reflection. Table 12.1 organizes the incorporated strategies by category.

Table 12.1	Three Categories of Literacy Strategies	
Vocabulary	**Active Reading**	**Reflection**
• 4-square chart • Concept definition map • Frayer Model • Semantic feature analysis • Verbal and visual word association • Word sort	• Anticipation guide • Directed reading/thinking activity (DR/TA) • K-W-L (what I Know; Want to know; Learn) • Parallel note taking • Read-aloud/think-aloud	• Discussion web • Generating interactions between schemata and text (GIST) • Questioning the author (QtA) • Read-encode-annotate-ponder (REAP) • Reflecting on my understanding • Role/audience/format/topic (RAFT)

Vocabulary Strategies

Science is inundated with technical terms. To comprehend science, students must master at least some of the vocabulary. The 4-square chart, concept definition mapping, Frayer Model, semantic feature analysis, verbal and visual word association, and word sort strategies described in this section will push your students beyond the memorization of definitions.

What Is the Purpose of Vocabulary Strategies?

Students need many opportunities to develop a useful science vocabulary. Words need to be introduced and discussed during activities. Students need frequent opportunities to read, write, and practice using important terms. Vocabulary strategies are intended to

- develop knowledge of new terms,
- develop deeper understanding of familiar terms,
- increase reading comprehension,
- improve range and specificity in writing, and
- help students communicate more effectively and accurately.

How Do You Assign Vocabulary Strategies?

In selecting vocabulary strategies, you need to consider the term or terms on which you are focusing. Some strategies (such as the concept definition map) are designed to help build a conceptual understanding. Some strategies (such as semantic feature analysis and word sorts) are designed

Figure 12.1   Example of a 4-Square Chart

Word	Examples
protein	*Enzymes*
	amylase
Definition	catalase
A very large biological molecule made up of hundreds of amino acids linked together in peptide bonds. Some proteins are enzymes that catalyze chemical reactions. Others have a structural function, such as the protein in hair and fingernails.	*Structural Proteins*
	keratin
	collagen
	Other Proteins
	hemoglobin
	insulin
Nonexamples	**Picture**
starch	
cellulose	
cholesterol	
DNA	

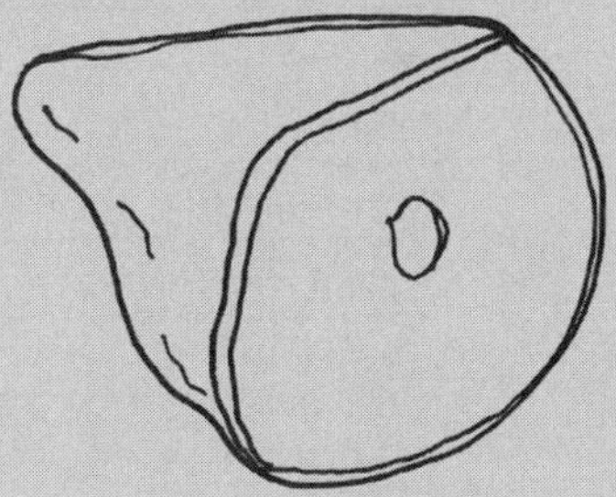

to show relationships, connections, or comparisons. Other strategies (such as the Frayer Model and 4-square chart) encourage deep understanding by asking for examples and nonexamples. Some strategies (such as the 4-square chart and verbal and visual word association) ask students to connect an image to the term. You need to think about your purpose for spending time with a term or terms and then incorporate a strategy that will help students achieve your purpose.

4-Square Chart. The 4-square chart (Eeds and Cockrum 1985) makes visual connections for students to the concept or term they are learning. The word and definition go in the top left square, examples go in the top right square, nonexamples go in the bottom left square, and a picture goes in the bottom right square (figure 12.1). The definition should be one that students develop rather than something copied from a dictionary or glossary. The examples and nonexamples help push students' thinking about the term. The picture serves as a nonlinguistic representation for students to associate with the term.

Concept definition map. The concept definition map (Schwartz 1988) is best used with key concepts (figure 12.2). The term being defined is connected to a broader concept or topic in science. Properties and characteristics, as well as examples, are used to help students explain their understanding of the term. Students write their own definition using their experiences, examples, and the properties they listed.

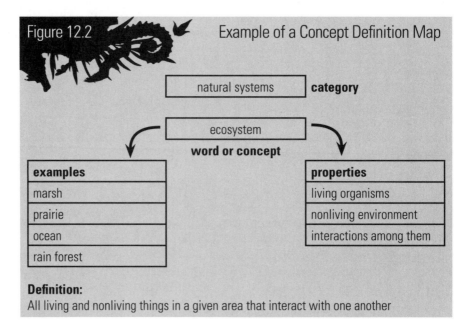

Figure 12.2   Example of a Concept Definition Map

natural systems   **category**

ecosystem

word or concept

examples	**properties**
marsh	living organisms
prairie	nonliving environment
ocean	interactions among them
rain forest	

Definition:
All living and nonliving things in a given area that interact with one another

Frayer Model. The Frayer Model (Frayer et al. 1969) provides a graphic organizer that asks students to organize their thinking about a term in four ways: definition, characteristics, examples, and nonexamples (figure 12.3). The definition goes in the top left square, characteristics go in the top right square, examples go in the bottom left square, and nonexamples go in the bottom right square. The definition should be one that students develop rather than something copied from a dictionary or glossary. The characteristics of the term should be things that are essential. The examples and nonexamples help push students' thinking about the term. The structure and thinking processes incorporated in this strategy provide an opportunity for students to build a deep understanding of the term.

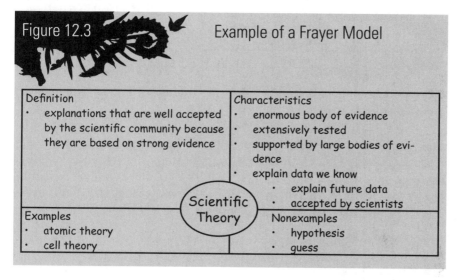

Figure 12.3   Example of a Frayer Model

Definition	Characteristics

• explanations that are well accepted by the scientific community because they are based on strong evidence	• enormous body of evidence
	• extensively tested
	• supported by large bodies of evidence
	• explain data we know
	   • explain future data
	   • accepted by scientists

Examples	Nonexamples
• atomic theory • cell theory	• hypothesis • guess

Scientific Theory

Semantic feature analysis. The semantic feature analysis (Johnson and Pearson 1984) is a grid that helps students learn the meaning of special vocabulary. Students define individual terms or concepts within a broader concept by analyzing the terms on a chart. Along the left side of the grid, members of the category are listed. Along the top of the grid, attributes (features) common to the broader concept are listed. An example of this is shown in table 12.2. Kingdoms are listed down the left side of the chart, while characteristics of the different kingdoms are listed across the top. Students examine attributes (features) common to the broader concept while looking at members. By checking off features found in each member, students are able to see how this member is similar to and different from the other members of the category. This strategy

Table 12.2 — Example of a Semantic Feature Analysis

Kingdom	Prokaryotic cells	Eukaryotic cells	Unicellular	Multicellular	Makes own food	Obtains food	Has nervous system	Reproduces asexually	Reproduces sexually
Bacteria	✓		✓		✓	✓		✓	
Animalia		✓		✓		✓	✓	✓	✓
Plantae		✓		✓	✓			✓	✓
Fungi		✓	✓	✓		✓		✓	✓
Protista		✓	✓	✓	✓	✓		✓	✓

helps students recognize similarities and differences among and between members of the same category.

Verbal and visual word association. The verbal and visual word association graphic organizer (Readence et al. 2004) incorporates nonlinguistic representations to help learners construct meaning, deepen understanding, and recall knowledge. This strategy includes a graphic organizer that challenges students to write the term (in their own words), define the term, draw a picture that will help them connect the term to the concept it rep-

Figure 12.4 — Example of a Verbal and Visual Word Association Chart

Term	Picture
Cerebrum sər ́·ē·brəm	
Your Definition	**Personal Connection or Characteristics**
the large part of the brain that is responsible for complex reasoning	The cerebrum would fill more than the brim of a hat.

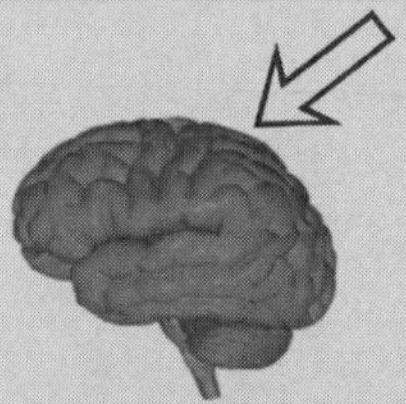

resents, and write or draw a personal association or characteristic that will help them to connect the concept to their life (figure 12.4).

Word sorts. The word sort strategy (Gillett and Temple 1983) helps students build conceptual understanding through sorting and classifying. Terms are written on cards (one term per card), and students are asked to group the terms into categories (figure 12.5). Teacher-generated categories are referred to as a closed sort. Student-generated categories are referred to as an open sort.

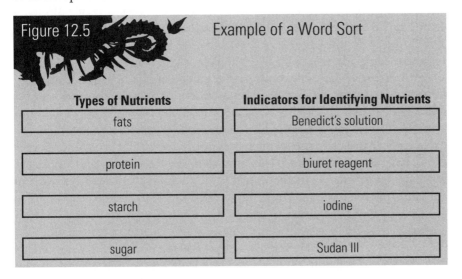

Figure 12.5   Example of a Word Sort

Types of Nutrients	Indicators for Identifying Nutrients
fats	Benedict's solution
protein	biuret reagent
starch	iodine
sugar	Sudan III

Active Reading Strategies

Reading is an active process. To comprehend science text, students must be engaged. The five strategies in this section are designed to help students actively engage in the text as they read.

What Is the Purpose of Active Reading Strategies?

Effective readers have developed strategies that help them make sense of text as they read. Struggling readers often perceive reading as simply word calling. Active reading strategies provide students with structures that

- activate prior knowledge and make predictions;
- surface misconceptions;
- locate, organize, and recall important information;
- make connections; and
- monitor comprehension.

These strategies help students realize that they should be thinking and making connections as they read.

How Do You Assign Active Reading Strategies?

Again, assigning a strategy depends on your purpose. Anticipation guides can help focus the reading on important concepts. K-W-L (what I Know, what I Want to know, and what I Learned) and DR/TA (directed reading/thinking activity) charts help activate prior knowledge and focus on learning. Parallel note taking provides a structure around which students can organize their thinking and recognize connections. Read aloud/think aloud is a way to model internal processes that should be taking place during the reading process.

Anticipation guide. The anticipation guide (Herber 1978) is a strategy that helps students activate prior knowledge. The guide also focuses and motivates student reading. The teacher creates four to six sentences around important concepts in the reading selected to support what the students are learning or review what students have already learned in class. The teacher then changes some of the statements to make them false and organizes the statements into a worksheet with columns for student responses before and after the reading (see figure 12.6). Students read to find out what the author says about each statement and then discuss what they learned from the reading and how their prior knowledge was supported or changed by the reading. It is extremely important that the statements be reviewed with the whole class following the reading to ensure that students have arrived at the appropriate answer, because there is a danger that misconceptions may be reinforced if understanding is not monitored.

Directed reading/thinking activity (DR/TA). The directed reading/thinking activity (Stauffer 1969) provides students with a structure around which to activate their prior knowledge and organize their thinking (figure 12.7). Before reading about a topic, students are asked to consider what they *know* they know, as well as what they *think* they know. This provides an avenue for a discussion, which may surface misconceptions. The next section, what they think they will learn, provides students with an opportunity to make predictions about what they will read; this helps set a purpose for reading. The last section, what they know they learned, encourages students to identify what they learned from their reading.

What I Know, Want to know, Learn (K-W-L). Many teachers are familiar with the three-column K-W-L (Ogle 1986, 1989) charts (figure 12.8). The "K" column provides an opportunity for students to think about what they already know about a topic before they begin to read. The "W" column provides a structure for students to think about what they "want to know" about the topic, allowing students to forecast what to look for as they read. The "L" column provides a structure for students to write what they have learned about the topic as they read. Because some students find it difficult

re 12.6   Example of an Anticipation Guide

:tions
efore you read the passage, decide whether you think each statement is true or false. Circle your choice.
s you read the passage, identify whether each statement is true or false according to what you have read.
ircle the answer and note the evidence.
√as your thinking changed or reinforced by what you read? If so, in what way?
e prepared to share your answers with the class.

•re ding	Statement	After Reading
ue lse	1. Evolution is a scientific way of explaining biological change across time. Evidence: Darwin used a lot of evidence from nature to support his theory of evolution by natural selection.	(True) False
ue Jse	2. Darwin found the source of variation to be genetics. Evidence: Darwin noted that individuals within a species show a lot of variation, but he could not explain the source of this variation.	True (False)
ue lse ?	3. In natural selection, each organism's ability to meet the challenges of survival and reproduction in the natural setting determines the mix of characteristics that will be transmitted to the next generation. Evidence: Rabbits that have the trait for thicker fur survive better in a colder climate. They pass this trait on to their babies, so the thicker-fur trait becomes more common in the next generations.	(True) False
ue ilse	4. One or two specific characteristics usually help an organism adapt in a particular environment so that it is able to survive and reproduce in the face of pressures such as competition and predation. Evidence: A mixture of many characteristics helps organisms survive and reproduce in a particular environment.	True (False)
ue ilse	5. Individual organisms do not evolve—populations evolve. Evidence: Individuals either survive or die based on their characteristics. Depending on who survives, different sets of traits are passed on to the next generations. Over time, the most common traits in a population may become very different from those that were there generations earlier. The population as a whole has evolved, but not the individuals in it.	(True) False

to think about what they would want to know about a topic, some teachers have modified this strategy to K-N-L. The "K" and "L" columns remain the same, but the "W" column is replaced with an "N," which represents "Need to know," and highlights things students should look for as they read.

Parallel note taking. Parallel note taking entails selecting a graphic organizer that is appropriate for the text structure. Text structure refers to the organizational features of text that serve as a frame or pattern (Englert and Thomas 1987) to guide and help readers identify important information and logical connections between ideas (Seidenberg 1989). Nonfiction is generally represented by one of the seven organizational patterns identified in the work of Marzano et al. (1997) and Jones et al. (1987):

- Chronological sequence
- Comparison and contrast

Figure 12.7   Example of Directed Reading/Thinking Activity (DR/TA)

What I Know I Know:
- Photosynthesis uses light for energy.

What I Think I Know:
- During photosynthesis, plants use carbon dioxide and make oxygen.
- Photosynthesis has dark and light reactions.

What I Think I'll Learn:
- I think I'll learn how photosynthesis helps plants make oxygen, and what plants do with the carbon dioxi|
- I think I'll learn what happens in the different reactions in photosynthesis.

What I Know I Learned:
- The oxygen that plants make is really a by-product that comes from water (H_2O)! During photosynthesi| light energy is used to set up a flow of electrons, which is used in an electron transport system to prod| ATP and NADPH. The electrons come from chlorophyll, the green pigment in plants. So the electrons in chlorophyll have to be replaced—and they come from splitting water molecules. When the water molecu| split, oxygen is released! So it's really the electrons that are needed for photosynthesis, and the oxyge| just a by-product (lucky for us!).
- Plants combine the carbon and oxygen from carbon dioxide with the hydrogen from water to make suga| and starch. They use energy and electrons from the ATP and NADPH that was made to do this.
- In the light (or light-dependent) reactions, water is split into hydrogen, electrons, and oxygen, and ATP and NADPH are made (first paragraph above).
- In the dark (or light-independent) reactions, sugars and starch are made (second paragraph above). The reactions don't have to be in the dark, they just need to have ATP and NADPH, so they don't require lig| directly. But because they need ATP and NADPH made in the light-dependent reactions, these reaction| can't continue for too long in the dark.

- Concept or definition
- Description
- Episode
- Generalization or principle
- Process or cause-effect

Effective readers scan the text to identify the author's organizational pattern. Is the author describing a process? Is the author plotting out a sequence across time? Is the author pulling evidence together to arrive at an explanation? Once the organizational pattern is recognized, a graphic organizer can be selected around which to take notes in a meaningful way. Examples of parallel note-taking strategies for comparison and contrast text are shown in figure 12.9, and examples for process or cause-effect text are shown in figure 12.10. Some authors make the purpose or pattern clear to the reader; such text is often referred to as "considerate text." Other text may not be well organized (inconsiderate text), so it may be more difficult to identify and apply a structure to better understand the text.

Read aloud/think aloud. The read-aloud/think-aloud strategy (Davey 1983) is a powerful strategy for developing effective readers. It provides students with the opportunity to consider processes that should be occurring in their minds as they read. You can model your thinking processes by verbalizing thoughts as you read. Students read along with you as you interact with the text. As you read aloud/think aloud with your students, look for opportunities to model strategies that do the following:

Figure 12.8 — Example of a K-W-L Chart

at I *Know*	W What I *Want* to Know	L What I *Learned*
human ulation is ving very r.	Exactly how fast is it growing? Can it continue to grow forever?	The human population is growing nearly exponentially. In 1700, the world population was under 1 billion. It took about 200 years for the population to double, reaching over 1.5 billion by 1900. It took only 65 years to double again, to 3.3 billion in 1965. Today, 45 years later, the population had doubled again, to 6.6 billion. Eventually, the population size will either level off—this is called logistic growth—or it will crash if it goes way over the carrying capacity of Earth.

Figure 12.9 — Example of Parallel Note-Taking: Comparison and Contrast Chart

Beliefs	Environmental Ethic	Human-Centered	Life-Centered
All life-forms have intrinsic value.			X
Life will flourish if humans greatly reduce their rate of population growth.			X
Earth is a collection of natural resources for humans.		X	
Earth's resources are limited.			X
Earth's resources are unlimited.		X	
Human impact must be minimalized.			X
Humans have no right to reduce the Earth's biological richness and diversity.			X
Humans should dominate the natural world.		X	
Nonhuman life-forms are commodities that have no value.		X	
People find solutions to all problems and progress continues.		X	

Figure 12.10 — Example of Parallel Note-Taking: Process or Cause-Effect Chart

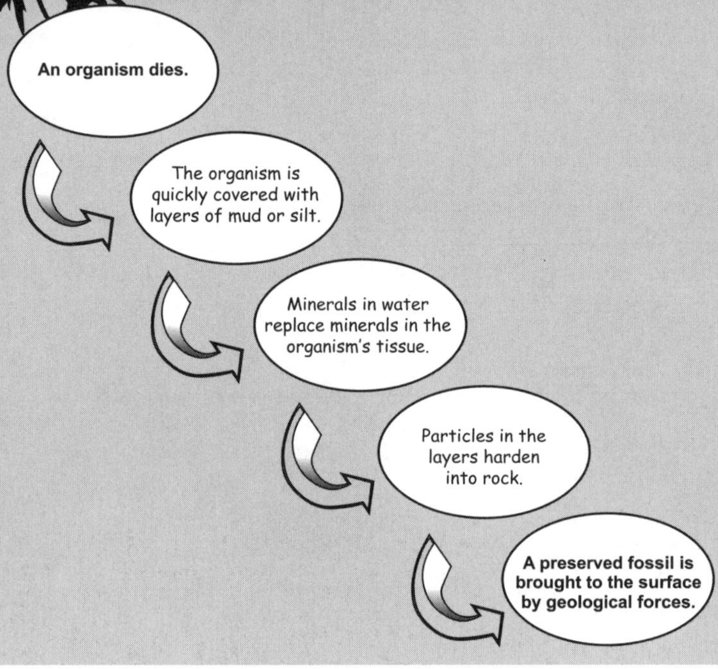

An organism dies.

The organism is quickly covered with layers of mud or silt.

Minerals in water replace minerals in the organism's tissue.

Particles in the layers harden into rock.

A preserved fossil is brought to the surface by geological forces.

- Identify a purpose for reading—"What do I hope to learn by reading this?"
- Activate prior knowledge—"According to the title, this passage must be about ...."
- Create visual images—"As I read this, I get a picture in my mind that ...."
- Make connections—"This is like the activity ...."
- Make and adjust predictions—"I thought this was going to happen, but really ...."
- Ask questions—"I wonder what the author meant by ...."
- Infer what is meant—"I think that means ...."
- Adjust the pace of reading—"This looks pretty tricky, I'd better slow down ...."
- Monitor understanding of what is being read—"I didn't get that, I'd better reread ...."
- Determine the most important ideas—"This looks important; I want to remember ...."
- Summarize—"This is what I understand ...."

This modeling helps students realize that reading is more than calling words. Reading should make sense. Effective readers monitor their comprehension and make adjustments as they read.

Reflection Strategies

Reflection deepens understanding. Reflection helps readers think about what they have read and apply it to a new situation. It can involve questioning, writing, discussing, or all of these things. We have provided six strategies for reflecting on text.

What Are the Purposes of Reflection Strategies?

Students need opportunities to reflect on what they have read. Reflection strategy instruction is designed to

- extend meaning through discussing, questioning, writing, or all of these;
- help students summarize, evaluate, and apply information; and
- develop metacognitive skills.

How Do You Select Which Reflection Strategy to Use?

Reflection strategies can be organized into three general categories: questioning, discussion, and summarizing. You can use the questioning the author (QtA) strategy to get students to think more deeply by developing questions for the author. Generating interactions between schemata and text (GIST) and read-encode-annotate-ponder (REAP) provide reflective writing opportunities in which students summarize information. Role/

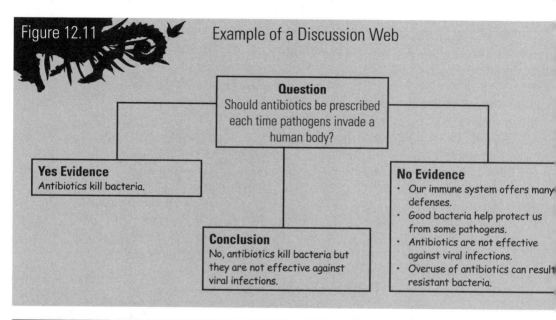

Figure 12.11

Example of a Discussion Web

Question
Should antibiotics be prescribed each time pathogens invade a human body?

Yes Evidence
Antibiotics kill bacteria.

No Evidence
- Our immune system offers many defenses.
- Good bacteria help protect us from some pathogens.
- Antibiotics are not effective against viral infections.
- Overuse of antibiotics can result resistant bacteria.

Conclusion
No, antibiotics kill bacteria but they are not effective against viral infections.

Figure 12.12

Example of the Generating Interactions Between Schemata and Text (GIST) Strategy

Directions

1. Make sure that you have read the purpose for reading. Read the first two paragraphs of the reading assignm Write a summary of the paragraphs in 15 words or less.
   Energy is required for all movement.

2. Read the next two paragraphs. Write a new summary in 15 words or less that reflects your current understand
   Muscles work in opposing groups against the skeleton to produce movement.

3. Read the next two paragraphs. Write a new summary in 15 words or less that reflects your current understand
   Different structural details allow for different kinds of movement.

4. Read the next two paragraphs. Write a new summary in 15 words or less that reflects your current understandi
   Energy enables filaments within muscle fibers to shorten the muscle and pull on bone.

5. Read the last three paragraphs. Write a new summary in 15 words or less that reflects your current understanc
   All movement requires muscles to work in opposite pairs, contracting (caused by energy) and relaxi

6. Be prepared to discuss the role that structure plays on movement.

audience/format/topic (RAFT) is a reflective writing opportunity in which students can demonstrate their understanding in a creative way. Reflecting on my understanding is a safe way for students to reflect in writing and through discussion about their current understanding of a topic. Discussion is encouraged with most of the reflection strategies; discussion webs, however, provide a protocol for discussing an issue.

Discussion Web. Discussion webs (Alvermann 1991) are designed to engage all students in a discussion. The discussion usually involves a question about a controversial issue. Students provide yes-and-no evidence based on their investigations, readings, and personal experience. First students individually complete the discussion web. Then they are asked to share their thinking with a small group of their peers. After that, each small group shares its response during a whole-group discussion. This strategy promotes time for independent thinking and small-group thinking as students look at both sides of the issue before arriving at a conclusion, which is shared with the whole class. Figure 12.11 illustrates a discussion web.

Generating Interactions Between Schemata and Text (GIST). GIST (Cunningham 1982) is an acronym for generating interactions between schemata and text. It was developed to help students learn to write organized and concise summaries of their reading. After students read a section of text, they generate one sentence (15 words or less) that summarizes the gist of the passage. Students are asked to read a second section of the text, then summarize their current understanding, again in a one-sentence summary of 15 words or less. The process continues until the reading is complete. (See the example in figure 12.12.)

Questioning the Author (QtA). QtA (Beck et al. 1998) is an acronym for questioning the author. It is designed to promote a deeper understanding of the text by focusing on a query or probing question that will prompt discussion and build understanding (figure 12.13). The question is geared toward the author of the text and encourages students to work together to understand the author's point. Some general queries may be "What is the author trying to say?" "What is the author's message?" and "What does the author mean?" "Does this make sense with what the author has said before?" This type of questioning and group discussion challenges students to grapple with and make sense of the text.

Read-Encode-Annotate-Ponder (REAP). REAP (Eanet and Manzo 1976) is a strategy for helping students read and understand text. REAP stands for read-encode-annotate-ponder. Students are asked to complete a graphic organizer as they read (figure 12.14). As they complete the graphic organizer, students (encode) convey the main ideas in their own words, (annotate) summarize important information, and (ponder) think about the text from the author's point of view.

Figure 12.13 — Example of the Questioning the Author (QtA) Strategy

Directions

1. What does the author mean by the statement "Although evolutionary history does not change, the classification schemes that scientists use to reflect that history improve with new knowledge and may change a great deal"? It might help to think about the query by asking these questions:
   - How do scientists classify organisms?
   - How has the classification system changed?

2. Be prepared to discuss the query with the class.

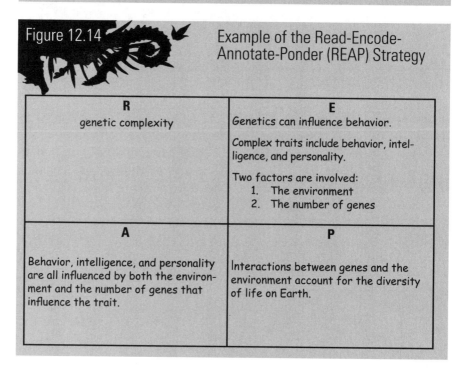

Figure 12.14 — Example of the Read-Encode-Annotate-Ponder (REAP) Strategy

R	E
genetic complexity	Genetics can influence behavior.
	Complex traits include behavior, intelligence, and personality.
	Two factors are involved: 1. The environment 2. The number of genes

A	P
Behavior, intelligence, and personality are all influenced by both the environment and the number of genes that influence the trait.	Interactions between genes and the environment account for the diversity of life on Earth.

Reflecting on My Understanding. Reflecting on my understanding is a modification of the directed reading/thinking activity—DR/TA strategy (Stauffer 1969). Reflecting on my understanding provides students with an opportunity to express what they know they know and what they think they know about a topic before they begin to read. This process activates their prior knowledge. Following the reading, they are asked to share what they know they learned and what they think they learned (figure 12.15). An important next step is providing students with an opportunity to clarify their thinking through a class discussion. Encourage students to listen to each other and ask each other questions during the discussion time. It is important that you push for accuracy (while maintaining a safe learning environment) during the discussion time. See chapter 15 for more ideas on how to create a classroom environment that encourages and is safe for student-student conversations.

Role/Audience/Format/Topic (RAFT). The RAFT strategy (Santa 1988) is a way for students to demonstrate their understanding of informational text in a nontraditional format. RAFT is an acronym for role of the writer (the role the writer will assume), audience (who will be reading the writing), format (how the writing will be presented), and topic (the subject of the writing). Students can add a creative twist as they reflect on what they know about a topic. Through the RAFT scenario, students can share their knowledge of content and their understanding of perspective. Three questions students should keep in mind as they develop their RAFT scenario are "Who am I and what are some aspects of my personality?" "What are my feelings, beliefs, ideas, and concerns about the topic?" and "What do I know that I need to share in my writing?" Each RAFT scenario allows students to describe their understanding from an unusual point of view. Creative assignments like this ask students to apply high-level thinking skills to both

Figure 12.15	Example of the Reflecting on My Understanding Strategy	
	What I Know I Know	**What I Think I Know**
Prereading	DNA contains information critical to the structure and function of body cells.	Replication of DNA allows organisms to pass a set of genetic instructions to their offspring.
	What I Know I Learned	**What I Think I Learned**
Postreading	We have 23 pairs of chromosomes. The DNA molecule serves as a template for information transfer. DNA is a double helix.	Complementary pairing explains how DNA is able to be replicated.

content and literacy. Figure 12.16 illustrates a RAFT scenario in which students can demonstrate their understanding of the immune system.

From Scaffolding to Strategic Use

Our goal is to help you provide all students with the information and tools necessary to promote scientific literacy. Strategies are designed to provide a scaffold for student understanding that supports students as they learn. You need to help students identify and clarify the purpose for reading text, you need to model the kind of thinking that goes on while you are reading scientific text, and you need to help students understand when and how to select appropriate strategies. Research results support the idea that teachers should provide explicit instruction in

- identifying and clarifying the purpose for reading;
- explaining the purpose for using a strategy;
- modeling how, when, and where to use the strategy and how to evaluate its effectiveness;
- guided and independent practice; and
- helping students transfer strategies to new text.

Figure 12.16   Example of a **R**ole/**A**udience/**F**ormat/**T**opic (RAFT) Scenario

Directions

1. Read the article to determine how vaccines provide a powerful attack against pathogens.

2. Reflect on how you can use the information that you have learned in this article, as well as your previous study, to create your own RAFT scenario. Your RAFT scenario should be based on the following.

   a. **R**ole: Police log reporter

   b. **A**udience: Police log readers

   c. **F**ormat: Police log report like one you might find in a newspaper (Make it humorous and short—one or two paragraphs)

   d. **T**opic: Description of events that occurred inside the body of a person who has been vaccinated for the flu and has recently come in contact with the flu virus.

3. Be prepared to share your RAFT scenario with the class.

Late last night, an innocent human body fell victim to a home invasion. A masked flu virus (aka the pathogen) was the nasty culprit, armed with nausea and vomiting. Luckily, the unnamed human had been vaccinated with the very same flu virus strain just weeks before the attack. The vaccine memory cells quickly jumped into action, fighting and eventually killing the intruder. The unsuspecting human survived the incident without a sniffle.

You need to model effective use of literacy strategies for students, ask students to apply strategies in guided practice, and, eventually, ask students to try out these strategies on their own with feedback from you or their peers. The read-aloud/think-aloud strategy (Davey 1983) described earlier is an effective way to introduce and model literacy strategies. Many teachers introduce a strategy to the entire class. That way they can incorporate and monitor the thinking of several students as they walk through the process.

Rather than introducing a wide variety of strategies immediately, we suggest that you begin with a limited number to develop the reading skills that you feel are most needed and most fundamental for your students. Be sure to model these strategies for your classes multiple times and to scaffold students' growing independence in applying them. For example, use the read-aloud/think-aloud strategy initially in reading entire short passages, with the whole class following along. Later, read the first paragraph with the whole class and then have students continue individually or in their teams. Finally, you can assign readings to students with the instruction to interact with the text as you have modeled and they have practiced in class. Even then, however, reinforce the strategy by occasionally reading short selections or initial paragraphs aloud as a whole class.

A focus on developing literacy skills throughout your course will pay off as students begin reading more and more for meaning. Students will become better at identifying confusing points and will be able to frame more specific questions. They will engage in richer conversations about the content with you and their peers. They will become better at making connections among what they read, what they do in activities, and what they discuss in class. Finally, students will likely find that they can apply some of the literacy strategies they have learned in their other classes.

Chapter 13

How to Help Your Students Evaluate Information*

Every day, we are bombarded with information on many issues from a wide variety of sources. Newspapers, magazines, books, television, radio, experts, friends, and, increasingly, the internet provide us with an enormous amount of sometimes conflicting information. Today's students are especially adept at accessing information through the internet. They likely are much less adept at assessing the intent, relevance, and validity of that information. How can you help your students make sense of what they access on the internet and elsewhere and develop informed opinions about the important issues of the day? This chapter suggests strategies for developing students' skills for evaluating information that they gather from a variety of sources.

Opinions Matter

Begin by helping students recognize that their opinions influence their day-to-day actions and plans for the future. An example such as the following may help them understand the impact of their opinions. Individuals' opinions about a variety of environmental issues likely will influence whether they

- buy a gasoline-powered or hybrid vehicle,
- wear sunscreen when outdoors,
- vote for candidates who spend their tax dollars on conservation programs, or
- drink bottled water purchased at the store or tap water.

Next, emphasize the importance of developing informed opinions. The goal of any scholarly debate or discussion in your class—or in your students' lives—is to discover the truth about an issue as best as possible with the information available. To discover the truth, students need to understand the issue. Informed opinions are based on deep understanding, and they result in decisions and choices that truly reflect students' values and have the best outcomes given the existing circumstances and knowledge about an issue.

Develop Class Guidelines for Analyzing Information

To develop an informed opinion about an issue, students must collect and analyze information. The first task is to collect information, but students often neglect the critical task of analyzing that information.

As a class, spend some time developing a list of critical-analysis questions, questions that students should ask themselves whenever they analyze a bit of information they have collected. The following questions are potential starting points for the list:

*Adapted from BSCS. 2003. *The Commons: An environmental dilemma.* Dubuque, IA: Kendall/Hunt.

- "Is this information relevant to the issue?"
- "Is the source of this information credible and reliable?"
- "Is this information accurate?"
- "Is this information timely or outdated?"
- "What can I infer from this information?"
- "What more do I need to know to make sense of this information?"

Practice Thinking Critically

The following example exercise provides students with practice in thinking critically. Doing this or a similar exercise early in the year can lay the groundwork for the type of thinking, analysis, and opinion forming that you expect students to apply to their work in your class. Note that the purpose of this exercise is to practice the intermediate step of analyzing the relevance and validity of the information regarding the issue; the purpose is not the initial step of gathering information or the final step of articulating an informed opinion.

Critical-Thinking Exercise

Purposes
- Practice analyzing the intent, relevance, and validity of the information collected to address an issue.
- Identify additional information needed to support an informed opinion regarding the issue.

Issue
People's access to safe drinking water

Setup
Present the following scenario to your students:

Imagine that you are working for a charitable organization that provides funds to address global issues related to human health. This organization receives many requests and must decide which requests merit its support. Recently, the organization received a request for funding to make safe drinking water available in all the countries in the world.

The director of the organization set up a task force to investigate the question: "Do the world's people have access to safe drinking water or not?" The members of the task force discovered that this issue is debated among a variety of experts. The task force collected some of the arguments and information that have fueled the debate about the world's drinking-water supply from a variety of sources, including the following books:

- *The State of Health Atlas*, J. Mackay, 1993
- *Gaia: An Atlas of Planet Management*, N. Myers, 1993
- *The Ultimate Resource 2*, J. Simon, 1996
- *Population Matters: People, Resources, Environment, and Immigration*, J. Simon, 1990

Note: You may want to provide this list to students as a handout or project it.

Next, the members of the task force began asking critical-analysis questions about the information they had gathered. At this point, you were hired by the organization and assigned to the task force to help analyze the information collected.

Task
Explain to students that they will practice analyzing information critically: Photocopy Drinking Water: Safe and Accessible or Not? and distribute it to students (a copy is located at the end of the chapter). Point out that some of the items on the handout have already been analyzed, and then look at one of the items with your students. Tell students to use the critical-analysis questions they developed as a class to analyze the other items. Give them approximately 10 minutes to do this. Then pair up the students and ask them to compare their analyses.

Wrap Up
Wrap up the exercise by asking students whether they feel they have enough information for an informed opinion. Hopefully, they will say that although they understand issues related to safe drinking water better than before they need additional information that is more current, more relevant, and from additional sources before they can make an informed opinion. (If they do not, challenge them by asking questions about the relevance, accuracy, timeliness, thoroughness, and sources of the information they have.) Working as a class, list some aspects of the issue that the additional information should address, based on students' analyses of the current information. You may also want to ask students to identify possible sources for that information.

Emphasize to students that they will apply this type of critical thinking to all of the issues they will study in your class to help them develop informed opinions.

Sample Critical-Thinking Exercise

Drinking Water: Safe and Accessible or Not?

he following statements provide some of the arguments and information that have fueled
e debate over the status of the world's supply of drinking water. The often-conflicting
formation varies greatly in quality, relevance, and timeliness. The first four statements
ive been analyzed for you. Look at them and determine how they reflect the critical-
alysis questions developed in class.

*w much more? A lot or
ittle?*

1. More than 1 billion people around the world have little or no access to safe
   drinking water.

   *This means 5 billion
   people do not have access
   to water.*

   *When was this
   true? Recently or
   in distant past?*

   *What does it mean to
   have "access"? Check
   dictionary or references.*

   *Is there any more
   recent data?*

   Find out which countries (if possible).

2. In the early 1990s, the World Health Organization reported that children under
   five years old in 20 countries around the world suffered from five or more
   episodes of diarrhea each year due primarily to drinking unclean water.

   *Find out if kids can
   die from diarrhea.*

   Such as what? Find out.

   *I guess it's not a problem in
   developed countries.*

3. At least 80 percent of the diseases that affect people in emerging countries are
   transmitted through dirty water.

   *People may not be drinking the water—they could be washing in it—so these
   data may not be important for the issue I'm researching.*

4. The percentage of people having access to safe drinking water has generally been
   increasing in both urban and rural area of the Southern Hemisphere, where most
   emerging countries are located.

   *Find out which countries are in
   the Southern Hemisphere.*

**Table 1: Percentage of People in Different Areas With
Access to Safe Drinking Water**

Year	Urban Areas	Rural Areas
1970	67%	14%
1975	77%	22%
1980	75%	29%

*Data are nearly 30
years old! Might be too
old to use. Find more
recent data.*

*Decreased from 1975 to 1980. Could
be even lower today!*

*Low! Means 71% of people don't
have access!*

*ss is
asing
s*

y low.

Now, you analyze the next four statements using the same types of questions. Write your analysis next to each statement, as shown in the example on the previous page.

5. About 93 percent of the people living in the Northern Hemisphere have access to safe drinking water. About 69 percent of the people living in the Southern Hemisphere have access to safe drinking water.

6. The World Health Organization estimated that during the 1980s an additional 225 million urban residents and 310 million rural residents in poor countries were newly supplied with safe drinking water. This increased people's access to safe water from 76 to 78 percent of the population in urban areas and brought access in rural areas up to 46 percent.

7. Despite the use of water-treatment plants in the developed world, people are increasingly distrustful of the safety of domestic drinking-water supplies. Sales of bottled and distilled water are booming, and one survey indicated that more than 25 percent of the people living in London, England, never drink water directly from the tap.

8. The percentage of water-quality monitoring sites in the United States reporting good drinking water has increased dramatically since monitoring began in 1961. The Environmental Protection Agency stopped publishing such data after 1974, apparently because the problem of drinking-water contamination had diminished significantly.

Table 2: Quality of Drinking Water in the United States
(% of monitoring sites)

Year	Good	Fair	Poor
1961	42%	28%	30%
1967	52%	32%	18%
1974	61%	31%	8%

Chapter 14

How to Help Students Construct Their Understanding of Science Concepts

Section IV

Helping students construct understanding is more time consuming, but much more rewarding, than simply providing information to students. When you focus on helping students construct their understanding of concepts, you operate as a diagnostician, a prescriber of appropriate learning activities, and a facilitator of learning. The role of students in this model switches from "passive sponge" to "active player," where they are responsible for their own learning by developing their own theories, comparing their theories with those of other classmates, and summarizing and displaying their theories.
—*Susan Loucks-Horsley,* Elementary School Science for the '90s, *1990, p. 51*

Conscientious biology teachers continually strive to improve their instructional practices to enhance student learning. At the heart of this goal is a focus on making sure that students understand the biology you are teaching. One important way to increase your focus on teaching that leads to an understanding of biology concepts is by using coordinated and coherent lesson sequences that are based on learning cycles or instructional models.

Research corroborates this idea. Reports such as *How People Learn: Brain, Mind, Experience, and School* (Bransford et al. 2000) and its companion, *How Students Learn: Science in the Classroom* (Donovan and Bransford 2005), have confirmed what educators have asserted for many years: The sustained use of an effective, research-based instructional model can help students learn fundamental concepts in science and other domains.

Since the late 1980s, BSCS has developed, used, and refined one instructional model extensively in the design of new curriculum materials and professional development experiences. You may be familiar with this model, commonly referred to as the BSCS 5E Instructional Model, or the

5Es. It consists of the following phases: *Engage, Explore, Explain, Elaborate,* and *Evaluate.* Each phase has a specific function and contributes to the teacher's coherent instruction and to the learners' formulation of a better understanding of scientific and technological concepts. The model can frame the sequence and organization of units of instruction of varying sizes. Once you internalize it, it also can inform the many instantaneous decisions that you must make in classroom situations. Chapter 14 describes the historical and intellectual roots of the BSCS 5E Instructional Model and how you can use this model to help your students achieve a conceptual understanding of biology.

The Roots of the BSCS 5E Instructional Model

In the late 1950s and early 1960s, an era of curriculum reform, instructional models were popularized by leaders of the reform movement. Robert Karplus, a theoretical physicist at the University of California–Berkeley, became interested in science education in the late 1950s. His interest led to an exploration of children's thinking and their explanations of natural phenomena. By 1961, Karplus began connecting the developmental psychology of Jean Piaget to the design of instructional materials and science teaching. At the same time, J Myron Atkin, then at the University of Illinois, shared Karplus's ideas about teaching science to young children. Eventually, they collaborated on a model of *guided discovery* in instructional materials (Atkin and Karplus 1962). Karplus continued refining his ideas and the instructional model as he tested different instructional materials and observed the responses of elementary children.

By 1967, Robert Karplus and his colleague Herbert Thier provided greater clarity and a curricular context as they described the three phases of their model for science teaching: "The plan of a unit may be seen, therefore, to consist of this sequence: preliminary exploration, invention, and discovery" (1967, 40). *Exploration* refers to relatively unstructured experiences in which students gather new information. *Invention* refers to the opportunity for students, with teacher support, to develop or "invent" a formal statement, often the definition and terms for a new concept. Following the exploration, the invention phase allows students to interpret newly acquired information through the restructuring of prior concepts. The *discovery* phase involves application of the new concept to another, novel situation. During this phase, the learner continues to develop a new level of cognitive organization and attempts to transfer what he or she has learned to new situations.

In the 1980s, Lawson (1988) and others slightly modified the terms used for the learning cycle. The modified terms are *exploration, term intro-*

duction, and *concept application.* Although the terminology changed, the conceptual foundation of the learning cycle remained essentially the same. Many researchers studied the impact of the learning cycle on student learning, and many studies found the model to be highly effective. For example, analyses of elementary programs indicate that the Science Curriculum Improvement Study (SCIS), which uses the learning cycle instructional model, was one of the most effective programs (Shymansky et al. 1983). The effectiveness of the learning cycle is also well documented in more contemporary research. Like the earlier studies, recent research studies link the use of the learning cycle to positive changes in students' mastery of subject matter, scientific reasoning, and interest and attitudes toward science. (Ates 2005; Billings 2001; Ebrahim 2004; Lord 1997). On the basis of this research, as well as on increasing understanding of human cognitive processes, using a learning cycle approach to teaching and learning continues to be supported in significant reports, such as *How People Learn* (Bransford et al. 2000).

The Birth of the BSCS 5E Instructional Model

In the mid-1980s, BSCS received a grant from IBM to conduct a design study that would produce specifications for a new science and health curriculum for elementary schools. Among the innovations that resulted from this design study was the BSCS 5E Instructional Model. The model has five phases: *Engage, Explore, Explain, Elaborate,* and *Evaluate.* When formulating the BSCS 5E Instructional Model, we began with the SCIS learning cycle. The middle three elements of the 5E instructional model are fundamentally equivalent to the three phases of the SCIS learning cycle. Table 14.1 shows the key learning focus and the essence of each phase of the 5Es. Because the focus of the BSCS 5E Instructional Model is on understanding, it is most effective for learning or teaching new concepts as opposed to acquiring new facts, skills, or behaviors.

The recommendations from the research summary *How People Learn,* though published nearly 20 years after the origin of the BSCS 5E Instructional Model, are fully supported by the 5E Instructional Model. The following quotation from *How People Learn* is a research-based recommendation for instruction that helps students construct understanding. It describes a structure and sequence of instruction that expose students to problem situations—engages their thinking—and then provides opportunities for them to explore, explain, extend, and evaluate their learning:

> An alternative to simply progressing through a series of
> exercises that derive from a scope and sequence chart is to

| Table 14.1 | | The BSCS 5E Instructional Model |

Phase	Key Learning Focus	Essence
Engage	Learners become engaged in the concept.	Brings the learners' frame of mind toward learning something new. Helps the teacher and each learner identify the learner's prior knowledge.
Explore	Learners explore the concept.	Provides or creates a common experience for all learners within which the learners compare their ideas with those of others. The teacher continues to learn about and challenge the learners' prior conceptions.
Explain	Learners develop an explanation of the concept.	Encourages the learners to construct an explanation. The teacher provides information to increase the accuracy of the explanation.
Elaborate	Learners elaborate the concept.	Builds on the learners' current understanding to increase the depth and breadth of understanding. Often incorporates a new or novel situation in which learners apply and demonstrate their understanding.
Evaluate	Learners evaluate their understanding of the concept.	Provides an opportunity for learners to assess their own understanding and be able to demonstrate the depth and breadth of that understanding to others.

expose students to the major patterns of a subject domain as they arise naturally in problem situations. Activities can be structured so that students are able to explore, explain, extend, and evaluate their progress. Ideas are best introduced when students see a need or a reason for their use—this helps them see relevant uses of the knowledge to make sense of what they are learning. (Bransford et al. 2000, 127)

An instructional model such as the 5Es can help you bridge theory, described above, and practice.

The BSCS 5E Instructional Model is grounded in sound educational theory, has a growing base of research to support its effectiveness, and has had a significant impact on science education. Due to the relative youth of the 5E Instructional Model compared with the learning cycle, there are fewer published studies that compare the BSCS 5E Instructional Model with other modes of instruction. However, the findings of these studies suggest that, like its predecessor the learning cycle, the 5E Instructional Model is effective, in some cases comparatively more effective, than alternative teaching methods in helping students reach important learning outcomes in science. For example, several comparative studies suggest that the 5E Instructional Model is more effective than alternative approaches at helping students master science subject matter (Akar 2005; Coulson 2002).

Studies of the 5E Instructional Model conducted by the internal and external evaluators of BSCS programs show positive trends for student mastery of subject matter and interest in science. The most significant finding, however, is that there is a relationship between the fidelity of use and student achievement. In other words, the BSCS 5E Instructional Model is more effective for improving student achievement when the teacher uses the instructional model within the curriculum materials in the way it was intended. Without fidelity of use, the potential results of the program are greatly diminished. For example, Coulson (2002) explored how varying levels of fidelity to the 5Es affected student learning. He found that students whose teachers taught with medium or high levels of fidelity to the BSCS 5E Instructional Model experienced learning gains that were nearly double that of students whose teachers did not use the model or used it with low levels of fidelity.

How to Use the BSCS 5E Instructional Model

To fully understand each phase of the BSCS 5E Instructional Model, it helps to think about what the teacher is doing and what the student is doing during each "E." You can learn just as much by understanding what is not appropriate during each phase. Tables 14.2 and 14.3 indicate the teaching practices that are consistent and inconsistent with each of the Es and what the learner is doing, or should not be doing, during each phase.

In addition to becoming aware of practices that are consistent or inconsistent with each phase of the BSCS 5E Instructional Model, it is helpful to be aware of critical characteristics of instruction that help students construct their understanding of science concepts. As a teacher, you must do the following:

1. Before you begin instruction, take time to understand clearly what the students are to learn during the chapter or unit and within each lesson.
2. Become familiar with what students already know or think they know about the key concepts.
3. Periodically ask students to explain the purposes of their learning experiences in their own words.
4. Encourage collaborative teamwork and the sharing of ideas.
5. Provide time frequently for students to express their thinking and to reflect on their previous ideas—orally and in writing.

e 14.2 | The BSCS 5E Instructional Model: What the Student Does

e of the ruction al el	Consistent With This Model	Inconsistent With This Model
ge	• Asks questions such as "Why did this happen?" "What do I already know about this?" "What can I find out about this?" • Shows interest in the topic	• Asks for the "right" answer • Offers the "right" answer • Insists on answers or explanations • Seeks one solution
ɔre	• Thinks freely, but within the limits of the activity • Tests predictions and hypotheses • Forms new predictions and hypotheses • Tries alternatives and discusses them with others • Records observations and ideas • Suspends judgment	• Lets others do the thinking and exploring (passive involvement) • Works quietly with little or no interaction with others (only appropriate when exploring ideas or feelings) • "Plays around" indiscriminately with no goal in mind • Stops with one solution
ain	• Explains possible solutions or answers to others • Listens critically to others' explanations • Questions others' explanations • Listens to and tries to comprehend explanations that the teacher offers • Refers to previous activities • Uses recorded observations in explanations	• Proposes explanations from thin air that have no relationship to previous experiences • Brings up irrelevant experiences and examples • Accepts explanations without justification • Does not attend to other plausible explanations
orate	• Applies new labels, definitions, explanations, and skills in new but similar situations • Uses previous information to ask questions, propose solutions, make decisions, and design experiments • Draws reasonable conclusions from evidence • Records observations and explanations • Checks for understanding among peers	• "Plays around" with no goal in mind • Ignores previous information or evidence • Draws conclusions from thin air • In discussion, uses only those labels that the teacher provided
uate	• Answers open-ended questions by using observations, evidence, and previously accepted explanations • Demonstrates an understanding or knowledge of the concept or skill • Evaluates his or her own progress and knowledge • Asks related questions that would encourage future investigations	• Draws conclusions, not using evidence or previously accepted explanations • Offers only yes-or-no answers and memorized definitions or explanations as answers • Fails to express satisfactory explanations in his or her own words • Introduces new, irrelevant topics

Table 14.3  The BSCS 5E Instructional Model: What the Teacher Do

Stage of the Instructional Model	Consistent With This Model	Inconsistent With This Mode
Engage	• Creates interest • Generates curiosity • Raises questions • Elicits responses that uncover what the students know or think about the concept or topic	• Explains concepts • Provides definitions and answ • States conclusions • Provides closure • Lectures
Explore	• Encourages the students to work together without direct instruction from the teacher • Observes and listens to the students as they interact • Asks probing questions to redirect the students' investigations when necessary • Provides time for the students to puzzle through problems • Acts as a consultant for the students	• Provides answers • Tells or explains how to wor through the problem • Provides closure • Tells the students that they a wrong • Gives information or facts th solve the problem • Leads the students step-by-st to a solution
Explain	• Encourages the students to explain concepts and definitions in their own words • Asks for justification (evidence) and clarification from the students • Formally provides definitions, explanations, and new labels • Uses students' previous experiences as the basis for explaining concepts	• Accepts explanations that hav justification • Neglects to solicit the stude explanations • Introduces unrelated concep skills
Elaborate	• Expects the students to use formal labels, definitions, and explanations provided previously • Encourages the students to apply or extend the concepts and skills in new situations • Reminds the students of alternative explanations • Refers the students to existing data and evidence and asks, "What do you already know?" "Why do you think …?" (Strategies from Explore apply here also.)	• Provides definitive answers • Tells the students that they a wrong • Lectures • Leads students step-by-step solution • Explains how to work throug the problem
Evaluate	• Observes the students as they apply new concepts and skills. • Assesses students' knowledge, skills, or both • Looks for evidence that the students have changed their thinking or behaviors • Allows the students to assess their own learning and group-process skills • Asks open-ended questions such as, "Why do you think …?" "What evidence do you have?" "What do you know about X?" "How would you explain X?"	• Tests vocabulary words, terr and isolated facts • Introduces new ideas or conce • Creates ambiguity • Promotes open-ended discus sion unrelated to the concep skill

6. Reflect on the 5Es and how the model promotes conceptual development within the chapter or unit and within each lesson.

The five phases of the 5E Instructional Model are designed to facilitate the process of conceptual change. Using it brings coherence to different teaching strategies, provides connections among educational activities, and helps science teachers make decisions about interactions with students. The example that follows details what instruction looks like for curriculum materials that incorporate this model. You also can use the model with other curriculum materials. To do this, identify the major concepts you want your students to learn and sequence activities and lessons in a way that helps students construct their understanding as modeled in the example.

An Example: Using the BSCS 5E Instructional Model in an Ecology Chapter

This example describes how a fictional high school biology teacher, Ms. A, planned and taught a series of lessons for chapter 9, "The Cycling of Matter and the Flow of Energy in Communities" from *BSCS Biology: A Human Approach* (BSCS 2003). This program uses the BSCS 5E Instructional Model to structure each chapter.

To begin her preparation for this chapter, Ms. A first identifies three critical ideas in the ecology chapter that she wants her students to understand:

1. Organisms within a community interact with each other and are interdependent.
2. Both biotic and abiotic matter cycles within communities.
3. Energy flows through a community, with less and less energy available to organisms at the higher tropic levels.

Next, Ms. A examines the questions in the Evaluate section of the chapter and identifies two sets of questions related to these critical ideas that she will emphasize for evaluating student understanding. The program's resources include a rubric she will use for scoring students' responses. She chooses questions that she feels students should be able to answer successfully at the end of the chapter if she achieves her instructional goals. She feels these questions would be interesting to her students and useful for herself and the students in assessing their understanding.

- *Question set 1.* A natural disaster occurs in which volcanoes around the world erupt simultaneously. The resulting ash and debris block 75% of the sunlight reaching Earth's surface. What is the effect of the blocked sunlight on the following organisms: an earthworm, a shark, a maple tree, a saguaro cactus, and a teenager? What effect does the reduction of sunlight have on the cycling of matter through a community?

- *Question set 2.* Suppose you were snowed in for the winter in a remote mountain cabin, isolated from the outside world. The only food sources you have available are 20 cans of peaches, 2 100-pound sacks of wheat, and 8 hens. Discuss the advantages and disadvantages of each of the following survival strategies: (a) feed the wheat to the hens, eat their eggs until the wheat is gone, then kill and eat the hens; (b) kill the hens first and freeze their carcasses in the snow, then live on wheat porridge and chicken; (c) eat a mixture of wheat porridge, eggs, and 1 hen per week, feeding the hens enough wheat to keep the eggs coming until they are all gone.

Now that Ms. A has her instructional goals and final assessment strategies firmly in mind, she feels she is ready to examine the flow of instruction in the chapter and how it will help her students achieve these goals. The chapter begins with an activity that will allow her to assess students' current level of understanding with regard to the three critical ideas (the Engage phase). Next, students spend several class periods studying how matter cycles in simple communities (the Explore phase). Ms. A reminds herself that it is for this phase of the instructional model that students set up and began observing earthworm habitats several weeks ago. Then, as students describe the cycling of matter that they have observed, they will be challenged to add ideas about energy flow through the communities as well (the Explain phase). In the Elaborate phase, students will have an opportunity to apply their understanding of the concepts that matter cycles and energy flows through communities by developing and testing compost recipes. Ms. A believes these activities, related reading assignments, and small-group and class discussions will enable students to answer successfully the assessment questions in the Evaluate phase.

ENGAGE

Ms. A greets her 10th-grade biology students at the door of the classroom and hands each student a clear, sealed bag of trash. She instructs students to examine their bags of trash carefully (without opening them). Students are intrigued and a little amused to be studying trash. Next, she asks students to open their science notebooks and construct a data table with four columns. In the first column, they are to list the individual items they can see in the trash. As soon as students finish the first task, Ms. A gives them instructions for the remaining three columns of the data table: In the second column, list the origin of each trash item (for example, newspaper comes from trees); in the third column, answer yes or no whether they could find each item in their own household trash; and, in the last column, list at least two possible fates for each item (for example, the trash ends up in a landfill or as food for another animal). Conversations are lively as students complete this task. Ms. A moves from student to student, asking questions, probing for their ideas about the fates and origins of trash, and listening to their conversations with each other. Finally, Ms. A asks students to answer, in their science notebooks, questions about how waste from one organism might be useful to another, what this means about how organisms in communities might depend on one another for matter and energy, and how different types of matter cycle in different communities.

At the end of the class period, students have completed their data tables, articulated some of their ideas about "trash," and begun to relate their current understanding to ideas about matter and energy that they learned earlier in their biology course. No overt instruction has occurred during this session; instead, Ms. A has spent most of the class period listening to her students and making notes about what she hears. Although the questions she asks help students express accurate understandings they already hold, they also reveal students' understandings that are inaccurate, incomplete, or less solid.

Ms. A now has many insights about her students' understanding of the cycling of matter and the flow of energy in communities. She notes that all of her students have a general understanding that at least some matter—such as food refuse—can recycle, but they are less clear about how it happens. She makes a note to emphasize the role of decomposers in communities. Ms. A also notices that only two students listed compost as a possible fate for some trash items and she recognizes that most are unfamiliar with this idea—an important insight because, later in the chapter, students will be constructing compost columns. Although her students seem to understand that organisms can use wastes from other organisms, indicating that organisms in a community depend on each other, students expressed this only after Ms. A probed their understanding with several focused questions. Ms. A concludes that the concept of interdependence is one that she should reinforce and further develop throughout the chapter. Finally, Ms. A notices that quite a few of her students still seem to hold the idea that energy from food and other items is lost after the item is discarded. That is another idea she will need to challenge as the chapter moves forward.

EXPLORE

When students arrive for the next class period, Ms. A directs them to make final observations of the earthworm habitats that they set up several weeks ago. She then convenes a whole-class discussion in which students use the observations they have recorded in their science notebooks to describe the differences in habitats with and without earthworms, and with and without added organic matter. Ms. A's questions focus students' attention on the ways in which the earthworms modified their environment. She notes that this line of questioning helps students develop a clearer understanding of the ways in which organisms within a community depend upon and interact with each other. Next, Ms. A and the class read together an essay that gives more information about how earthworms affect topsoil. Together, they relate the concepts and information in the essay to the observations they made of their earthworm habitats.

Ms. A prompts students with questions such as "What happens when earthworms eat organic matter?" and "What happens to the waste products they eliminate?" Students' responses assure her that her students are more confident in their understanding that organisms in a community interact with and depend on each other. Next, she gives students a challenge: They are to design an experiment that will provide evidence that matter cycles in a community. She will provide them with snails, *Anacharis* (a water plant), and materials and equipment to support these organisms, as well as a system for indicating carbon dioxide (CO_2) and oxygen (O_2) levels (the matter) in the water. Students spend the next several class periods designing and conducting their experiments. Ms. A moves among student groups, asking questions that help students focus their ideas and offering advice when asked. Some groups plan outlandish experiments, suggesting that they might add soda or other beverages to their experimental systems to "see what happens." Ms. A refocuses them on the objective of the experiment, asking them to explain how this design will help them collect evidence that matter cycles in a community. The students revise their initial plans.

At the end of this phase of the instructional model (Explore), students prepare lab reports and present their findings to one another. Ms. A asks each group to describe the evidence it collected that the organisms in the environment interact with each other and that matter (CO_2 and O_2) cycled in the system. Students are beginning to construct explanations about the interactions of organisms in communities, leading to the next phase of the instructional model.

EXPLAIN

Based on the evidence that her students provided when they presented the results of their experiments to each other, Ms. A believes they now have a solid understanding of the cycling of matter in communities. Consequently, she believes students are ready to add the concept of energy flow to their understanding of the interactions among organisms in a community.

Ms. A begins the class session by reminding her students that in a previous chapter they studied how energy is stored in matter. She relates this to the matter that they observed cycling in their experiments and in the essays they read. Next, she asks students to write in their science notebooks their ideal menu for one day. This leads to a lively discussion among students, even though they are each writing individual menus. For example, two of Ms. A's students are vegetarians and the other students are interested to see the differences between those students' menus and their own.

Once students have completed their menus, Ms. A challenges them to list the ingredients in each of the foods they have listed, pointing out that foods such as "cake" actually contain a variety of ingredients, such as oil, eggs, flour, and sugar. Then, Ms. A asks students to list the source of each of the ingredients they have listed. For example, flour comes from wheat, sugar from sugar cane, and eggs from chickens. For some ingredients, students have no problem completing the task, but for others they struggle. Finally, Ms. A tells students to focus on the animals they have listed and to list several foods that each of these animals eats. The students are amazed at the complexity of the foods and the sources of the foods that they eat. Finally, Ms. A shows students a sheet of paper that she has divided into five sections. The four bottom sections are labeled "producers," "herbivores," "omnivores," and "carnivores," and the top section is left blank. Ms. A challenges her students to sort the organisms from their lists into those categories on their own papers. Finally, Ms. A tells students to draw arrows from organisms that provide energy to organisms that receive energy from them, thus creating food webs.

Although students complete these tasks individually, Ms. A encourages them to discuss their dilemmas and decisions with each other. Much conversation ensues. She moves among the students, offering guidance where requested, confirming students' accurate explanations, and, where their explanations are inaccurate, asking probing questions that help them construct accurate understanding of the relationships and the energy flow among organisms. For example, some students are unsure where to place the plants on their lists. Rather than simply telling the students where to place the plants on their lists, Ms. A convenes a brief, whole-class discussion to talk about this critical idea. She begins with the question, "In which category did you place the plants?" Several students answer, "The producer category," and Ms. A asks them to explain why. Although most of the students are certain their placement is correct, they struggle with the rationale. Ms. A guides them with a question that focuses their attention on energy: "What is the difference between the way plants obtain energy for growth and activities and the way animals do?" Students recall previous lessons in which they studied how plants capture energy from sunlight to create their own "food," or energy for growth and other activity. Ms. A continues with more questions: "And where do animals get their energy?" "Where does their food come from?" She sees several "ahas" on students' faces, and one says, "Oh! We can trace all the energy that animals get from food back to some plant that captured energy from the Sun. So, I guess the plants kind of 'produce' energy for the rest of the organisms in the community!" Ms. A smiles as she observes that students are developing their own, accurate, explanations of energy flow in a community. These explanations are reinforced in the reading assignment Ms. A gives the students as homework.

Ms. A begins the next class session with a discussion of the reading. She connects it to the food webs students developed the previous day by asking them to describe how energy flows through the community they depicted. Then she asks, "Where is the most energy available in your food web?" Because students appear a bit confused by this question, she follows up with questions such as, "How does the number of organisms in each section of your chart compare?" and "Why do you think there are so many more producers and herbivores than carnivores in your food webs?" Students offer their ideas, such as the relative sizes of the organisms. Ms. A focuses students' attention on energy by connecting this to what students learned previously about photosynthesis. She asks students if plants capture all of the energy available in sunlight. She hears several students say, "Oh, yeah!" and asks them to explain to others in the class what they just realized. These students point out that they learned previously that plants only transform a small amount of the energy from sunlight into energy in the biomolecules in plants. Then, Ms. A asks students, "Is all of the energy in plants available to the organisms that eat them?" Her students begin to realize that smaller and smaller portions of the energy originally captured from sunlight are available as they move further away from the producers on the food web. They correctly answer Ms. A's original question: Most of the energy in the food webs they have drawn is at the producer level. Some students express this by saying, "Energy is lost as you move up the food chain." Ms. A asks, "Can energy be lost? Can you destroy it?" She asks them to think about this question and bring their ideas to the next class session. Her question addresses one of the misunderstandings she heard among students during the Engage phase (the idea that energy is lost) and leads into the Elaborate phase of the instructional model.

ELABORATE

When students arrive in Ms. A's class the next day, they see the word *compost* written on the board. It is clear that some (but not all) students are puzzled by the word. Ms. A begins class by reading a short story about a boy who abbreviates his Saturday chore of cutting the grass by piling the grass clippings in a corner of the yard on some newly turned soil, instead of bagging them. He promptly forgets about returning to complete the job until another week has passed. When he finally gets back to the job, it is a cool morning and he notices steam rising from the middle of the clippings.

Ms. A asks the students, "What is happening to the clippings?" Students have general ideas: The clippings are rotting; they're decomposing. With some prompting, they become more specific: There are earthworms and other organisms such as bacteria in the pile that are using the matter from the clippings for their own life processes. Several students say, "Matter in the pile is cycling through the organisms that live there!" Ms. A confirms these responses and congratulates students for using what they learned about matter cycling in communities in their explanations. She points out that the earthworms and bacteria in the pile of grass clippings and soil are decomposers, an important component of food webs that they did not include in the diagrams they prepared earlier. She asks them to label the fifth section of their food webs "decomposers" and to add several examples of this type of organism to that section.

Then Ms. A probes further to encourage students to add their understanding of energy flow in communities to their explanation of the phenomenon in the story she read: "Why is the pile hot?" Students have to think a little harder about this question. Ms. A asks students, "What is heat?" Students respond, "a type of energy." She then asks them to explain where that energy came from, because energy cannot be created. Ms. A sees some glimmers of understanding on students' faces, so she reminds them of the question that ended the last class session, "Can energy be lost? Can you destroy it?" She sees more glimmers of understanding, and then students explain that energy is not lost, but converted into heat and then it is no longer available to organisms at higher levels in the food chain. Some students insist that this is the same as losing energy, but Ms. A persists: "Has the energy been destroyed?" A lively discussion follows, and finally students agree to the explanation: "As you move to higher levels in a food chain, some of the energy in lower levels is lost (i.e., not useful) to the organisms in the higher levels, not because it is destroyed but because it is converted to heat." Ms. A drives the point home by asking if energy cycles in communities just as matter does. Her students explain that energy does not cycle, but has a one-way flow through communities.

Then, Ms. A challenges students to provide evidence for their explanation of energy flow through communities by demonstrating that some of the energy is converted to heat. She explains that they will do this by designing compost systems. Many students appear confused by the word *compost,* so Ms. A asks students to review the tables they made for the possible fates of different kinds of trash from the beginning of the chapter. A few students had listed compost on their tables. Ms. A asks them to explain what composting means. Following a discussion of composting, she presents the materials that students have available for constructing their own compost systems. Ms. A organizes students into teams and challenges them to see who can come up with the best compost recipe as determined by the amount of heat produced. The next three class sessions are devoted to constructing the compost systems and measuring and recording the temperatures. At the end, students present their recipes, graphs of their data, and explanations of how their system demonstrated both matter cycling and energy flow through the communities.

EVALUATE

Ms. A begins the last class session for the chapter by asking students to review what they have written in their science notebooks for this chapter: responses to questions, data and conclusions from their experiments, the class presentations they have made. She invites them to share with their group members what they think are the "big ideas" from the chapter. The groups have a whole-class discussion so that there is some consensus about the big ideas. Ms. A notes whether students are expressing the three critical ideas she identified in her initial planning before beginning the chapter. She asks questions, as needed, to make sure she and the students hear the three critical ideas.

To further assess student understanding of the critical ideas of this chapter, Ms. A describes the two scenarios she decided to use for evaluation when she began planning for this chapter: (1) consequences of volcanic ash and debris blocking sunlight and (2) survival based on limited resources. She tells students they are to write explanations individually for the questions related to each scenario, as a way to check their understanding of the chapter concepts about matter and energy in communities. She encourages them to use their science notebooks and textbooks as they develop answers to these two open-ended questions. Ms. A distributes the scenarios and questions to students, along with the rubric that tells students how she will evaluate their responses.

A Challenge: Analyze the Instructional Strategies in the BSCS 5E Instructional Model

To help you get the most out of this example, we challenge you to analyze the scenario. Review Ms. A's instruction for the ecology chapter. Answer the following questions:

- What did Ms. A do in the Engage phase? What did her students do?
- What did Ms. A do in the Explore phase? What did her students do?
- What did Ms. A do in the Explain phase? What did her students do?
- What did Ms. A do in the Elaborate phase? What did her students do?
- What did Ms. A do in the Evaluate phase? What did her students do?
- Compare your analyses for the above questions to the characteristics listed in tables 14.2 and 14.3.
- What strategies did Ms. A use to create a student-centered classroom?
- Where might Ms. A have missed a learning opportunity?
- When might Ms. A have shared information or ideas with her students to help them further develop their understanding?
- What strategies did Ms. A use to assess student understanding? (Include formative assessment strategies—and see chapter 16 for more formative assessment strategies.)
- In which phases of the instructional model did Ms. A use the above assessment strategies?

We end by asking you to read again the quote that began this chapter. It was written by the late Susan Loucks-Horsley, a leader in transformative professional development for science education. Return to this quote, and ponder it periodically as you transform your teaching practices into those that help students construct their own understanding. What does she say that rings true with you? In what ways are you becoming a diagnostician, prescriber, and facilitator of student learning? How are your students' behaviors changing? We hope you will find that you agree with Loucks-Horsley, that helping your students construct their understanding is far more rewarding than simply providing information for them.

Chapter 15

How to Promote Scientific Conversations Among Your Students*

Science often is a collaborative endeavor, and all science depends on the ultimate sharing and debating of ideas. When carefully guided by teachers to ensure full participation by all, interactions among individuals and groups in the classroom can be vital in deepening the understanding of scientific concepts and the nature of scientific endeavors.
—*National Research Council,* National Science Education Standards, *1996, pp. 31–32*

The *National Science Education Standards* (NRC 1996), quoted above, emphasizes the importance of student inquiry and discourse for constructing an understanding of science concepts. Helping students develop skills for scientific conversation has many benefits. Engaging in scientific conversation accomplishes the following:

- *Elicits students' prior knowledge.* When students talk about scientific phenomena, you gain insight into what they already know, what they do not understand, and what is confusing to them. This valuable information helps guide your planning and teaching.
- *Enables students to construct their understanding of science concepts.* When students converse with each other and you, they begin to make meaning of their observations and investigations. They share thoughts and ideas, reflect, compare, connect, test, modify, and maybe even abandon pre-existing ideas for new ones that more accurately represent phenomena. As students express their understanding of concepts, they clarify their own thinking and help others see concepts from a different point of view.
- *Encourages all students to participate in science.* Creating a classroom culture in which conversations among students, not just between one or a few students and the teacher, is one way for you to emphasize that

---

*Adapted from BSCS. 2006. Promoting scientific conversation. In *BSCS science tracks handbook*, 169–174. Dubuque, IA: Kendall/Hunt; and Blosser, P. E. 2000. *How to ask the right questions.* Arlington, VA: National Science Teachers Association.

science is for all. When all students are engaged in the conversation, they all experience how collaboration enriches the theories they are building. They become more confident about their contributions and abilities in science.

• *Reflects the nature of science.* Sharing ideas and exposing them to examination is part of the scientific enterprise. When students critique their own and others' ideas, they are engaging in one aspect of science. When students hear others' ideas and insist that their colleagues provide evidence that supports their ideas, students develop scientific attitudes described in the *NSES*: being skeptical, relying on data, accepting ambiguity, respecting reason, being honest, and being willing to modify explanations.

How, then, can you promote scientific conversation among your students? Your questioning practices are a primary means of stimulating discussion among students; however, lesson structure, classroom norms, and even classroom arrangement can encourage—or discourage—this type of discourse. Chapter 15 begins with strategies for organizing your classroom and conducting your lessons that support scientific conversation, and then highlights questioning practices that enhance the level of discourse in your classroom.

Classroom Arrangement

The layout of your classroom and your position in it have an impact on the quantity and quality of student discussion in your class. The following paragraphs suggest ways to adjust these things to create a culture that encourages conversation.

Organize seating to accommodate conversation. The arrangement of desks and tables in a classroom can influence the level of conversation. If they are arranged so that students have to talk to the back of each other's heads, then conversation will be physically difficult. Consider how you can move the desks or chairs so that students can see each other while they are talking. Some teachers modify their room arrangement frequently to support the type of activity that will occur in class on a particular day. On days when students are expected to share and compare results, desks are arranged so that everyone can see each other. This change signals to students as they arrive in class that they will be engaging in conversation, helping establish a culture of discourse.

If the tables and desks in your classroom are fixed in place, you will have to be more inventive in creating physical arrangements that support conversation. Perhaps you can arrange chairs around the outside of desks or tables, facing into the room. You may have to limit most conversations to small groups around one or two tables, instead of whole-class discussions.

Consider your physical position. Whether and where the teacher sits or stands during conversations is a subtle factor that can also influence the nature of conversations. If you stand above students, they will tend to look to you as the final authority, checking their responses and questions by looking at you even when their comments are directed to other students. Encourage students to converse with one another by sitting down beside students in small groups or in the classroom with the whole group.

Lesson Structure

Review the structure of your lessons. Are they organized in ways that make students comfortable engaging in conversation? Consider the following suggestions for lesson structures that encourage high-quality discussions.

Provide opportunities for students to talk in small groups first. The structure of a lesson or activity can encourage scientific conversation and develop students' confidence in engaging in these conversations. If students work initially in small, collaborative teams, they can interact with each other more easily. When they work together over an extended period of time, they become more comfortable expressing their ideas to each other and are more willing to listen to others because they know that they, too, will have opportunities to talk. Creating an accountability structure in which students are responsible for the learning of their team members also encourages meaningful conversation. See chapter 10 in this volume for more information about how to organize and structure teams in your classroom.

Follow up on team investigations or activities by asking each team to compare its findings and ideas with those of one or more teams, with the whole class, or with both. Sharing their team's ideas may particularly help students who are nervous about talking in front of the class, because they have the encouragement of their fellow team members.

Classroom Norms

Students will not engage in scientific conversation if they fear they will be put down. Institute and enforce the following classroom norms to create a safe environment for students to share ideas.

Reinforce the role of team messenger or communicator by assigning a team member who goes to and asks for advice from you or another team (or, for students who are experienced and effective in collaborative learning groups, asking them to designate a team member to be the communicator). Some teachers regularly suggest that teams designate one member to go out and scout other teams and then bring new ideas back to the team.

Emphasize that students are to critique ideas, not people. Do not allow students to make fun of their classmates' responses or to mutter derogatory comments, such as "That's so lame." Students will not participate in discussions if they feel disrespected or unsafe. Challenge incorrect or inadequate ideas tactfully. Model the following strategies, and insist that students follow this model in their interactions with each other:

- Encourage students to confer with their teammates if they seem unsure of the answer. It is less intimidating for students to share ideas if they feel the support of their team members.
- Provide respectful mechanisms for students to use in responding to each other's comments. For example, when students disagree, tell them to give their reasons for disagreeing. Similarly, when they agree with an idea, tell them to give reasons for agreeing.
- Encourage students to ask each other to justify their responses with questions such as "Why do you think so?" and "What evidence makes you think that?" rather than immediately rejecting another's idea. You may want to post these or similar questions in the classroom to keep discussions focused on ideas and evidence.

Questioning Practices

Questioning practices are at the heart of much of teaching. The suggestions in this section will help you develop and strengthen question practices that elicit higher levels of scientific discourse among students in your class.

Assess your questioning behaviors. To help promote scientific conversation in your classroom, it is important to analyze the kinds of questions you commonly ask and your purpose for asking them. Blosser (1973) described four major types of questions used by teachers: managerial ("Who needs more time?"), rhetorical ("Producers are eaten by primary consumers, right?"), closed ("What are the subunits for proteins?"), and open ("What could you do to help reduce environmental waste?"). All of these types of questions play important roles in the classroom: Managerial questions help keep things running smoothly, rhetorical questions emphasize a point, and closed questions help teachers check the retention of information learned previously. But open questions, which have a wide range of acceptable responses, are the most helpful for stimulating conversation and learning. Monitor the types of questions you ask in class and strive to increase the proportion of open questions.

Wait three to five seconds after asking an open question before you call on someone to answer. This provides time for students to think about the question and devise a response. Wait again after a student responds. This encourages the responding student to elaborate or modify his or her response; it also provides an opportunity for other students to react to this response and add their own ideas. Research by Mary Budd Rowe (1973; 1987) identified a number of benefits of increasing these wait times:

- The length and number of responses increase.
- More students participate in the discussion.
- More student-student comparisons of results and discussions of alternative interpretations take place.
- Students recognize the connection between evidence and inference more often.
- The number of questions and related investigations proposed by students increases.
- There is more student-student interaction.
- The need for disciplinary actions decreases.

Avoid the teacher-student, question-and-response pattern of dialogue. This pattern discourages student-student interaction. The second wait time, described above, is one way to increase the amount of conversation among students. Table 15.1 lists questions and statements you can use to encourage students to question and respond to other students.

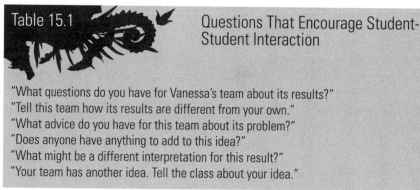

Table 15.1   Questions That Encourage Student-Student Interaction

"What questions do you have for Vanessa's team about its results?"
"Tell this team how its results are different from your own."
"What advice do you have for this team about its problem?"
"Does anyone have anything to add to this idea?"
"What might be a different interpretation for this result?"
"Your team has another idea. Tell the class about your idea."

Do not repeat student responses. If you repeat their responses, students are encouraged to listen only to you and not to each other. They develop sloppy listening habits, and true group discussion is inhibited. Instead of repeating a response, follow it with one of the questions in table 15.1 or say, "Some of your classmates didn't hear what you said, Ashley. Could you repeat it, please?" This will encourage students to listen attentively to each other.

Develop a set of noncommittal responses that encourage further student conversation. By simply nodding or smiling, you can affirm students' input without setting yourself up as the ultimate authority. Noncommittal verbal responses include comments such as "That's interesting," "Thank you," "I see," "That's a possibility," and "Show us."

Develop a repertoire of productive questions. Productive questions promote interest, reflection, reasoning, discussion, and activity. Table 15.2 lists a variety of questions that can help you create a culture of scientific conversation in your classroom. You may find it helpful to write directly into your lesson plans two or three possible questions to use at various points in a lesson. As you continue using these and similar questions in your teaching, they will become a natural part of your instructional style. Your students' experience in your classroom will be exemplified by scientific conversation and enhanced learning stimulated by these conversations.

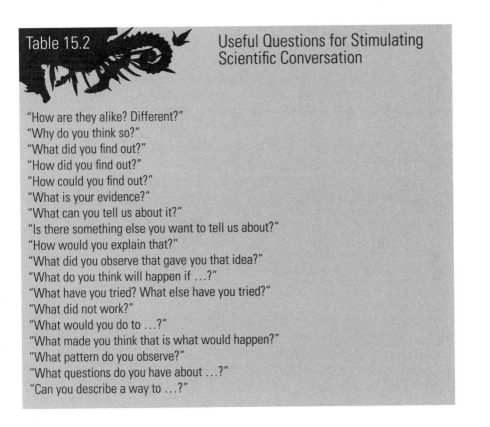

Table 15.2   Useful Questions for Stimulating Scientific Conversation

"How are they alike? Different?"
"Why do you think so?"
"What did you find out?"
"How did you find out?"
"How could you find out?"
"What is your evidence?"
"What can you tell us about it?"
"Is there something else you want to tell us about?"
"How would you explain that?"
"What did you observe that gave you that idea?"
"What do you think will happen if …?"
"What have you tried? What else have you tried?"
"What did not work?"
"What would you do to …?"
"What made you think that is what would happen?"
"What pattern do you observe?"
"What questions do you have about …?"
"Can you describe a way to …?"

Chapter 16

How to Use Assessments to Improve Student Learning*

Teachers need to have strong ideas about what will serve as evidence of students' understanding of biology, or any other content, before beginning teaching (Wiggins and McTighe 2005). Once you know what will serve as evidence for understanding, then sequencing effective learning experiences is likely to be targeted and more clearly focused. Surely summative tests such as end-of-unit or semester examinations represent one important way to assess student knowledge. But formative assessments (sometimes called ongoing assessments) such as monitoring students' small-group conversations or evaluating students' science notebooks are another. When you assess students' ongoing learning, you gather information that can direct your teaching decisions in the moment. These in-the-moment assessments are the focus of chapter 16.

Goals for Meaningful Assessment of Biology Learning

What are your goals for assessing students' understanding of and abilities in biology? Your overarching goal should be that assessments align with

Table 16.1 	Connections Between the Key Findings About Learning the Assessment of Biology Skills and Concepts

Key Finding from *How People Learn**	What That Means for Assessing Biology Skills and Concepts
1. Learners come to the classroom with current conceptions about the world around them.	• Assessments should provide opportunities for students to demonstrate what th know and what they do not know about asking scientifically testable questions designing investigations, using evidence to develop explanations, and commun cating findings to others.
2. Learners need a deep foundation of conceptual knowledge upon which to build improved understandings.	• Assessments need to be conceptually coherent and connected to students' cur foundation of the understanding and abilities in biology. • Assessments need to be ongoing to continually add layers to the foundation of knowledge and abilities related to biology. • Assessments need to be balanced to provide a complete picture of what students kn
3. Learners need opportunities to monitor their own learning.	• Assessments need to provide students with opportunities to assess themselves ways that help them monitor how strong their understanding is and at what po it begins to break down. • Assessments need to be relevant and compelling so that students will see the value in monitoring their understanding.

* Bransford, J. D., A. L. Brown, and R. R. Cocking. 2000. *How people learn: Brain, mind, experience, and school.* Washington, National Academy Press.

*Adapted from Van Scotter, P., and D. Pinkerton. 2008. Assessing Science as Inquiry in the Classroom. In *Science as Inquiry in the Secondary Setting,* eds., J. Luft, R. L. Bell, and J. Gess-Newsome, 107–119. Arlington, VA: National Science Teachers Association.

instruction and with the current findings about how students learn, since assessment is a key component of the learning process. Table 16.1 shows how the findings from research on learning can match with the key features of biology skills and concepts assessment. Note that the biology skills include science as inquiry.

Within this big-picture framework of recommendations for assessing biology skills and concepts, a second goal emerges: Assessments in our biology classes should be balanced and authentic. By balanced, we mean that we want to assess the many ways and the many points at which students represent what they know or are in the process of learning about science as inquiry. By authentic, we mean that we want the assessments to reflect the nature of science and the way it is practiced in scientists' endeavors. Let's consider these two features of assessment in more depth so that we can place formative assessments in their proper context.

Balanced Assessments Include a Range of Types

The first step is to consider the types of assessments that, taken together, will compose a balanced approach. Using the principles of backward design (Wiggins and McTighe 2005), these assessment types follow from the outcomes of inquiry that we are after (NRC 1996), as shown in table 16.2.

Table 16.2 Outcomes of Learning Biology Skills and Concepts Lead to a Range of Assessment Types

Targeted Outcome of Biology Skills and Concepts	Assessment Type	How Outcome Aligns With Assessment Type
Attaining knowledge about biology	Endpoint (summative, point-in-time, static, delayed feedback)	Biology is a body of knowledge that can be tested objectively after instruction.
Ability to perform biology investigations using scientific inquiry	Dynamic (formative, ongoing feedback, "in the moment")	Biology involves a process that can be monitored and evaluated as students perform it.
Conceptual understanding of biology	Conceptual framework (cognitive associations, mental structures, conceptual connections)	Biology learning produces changes in students' conceptual framework, moving them toward expertlike thinking.

Endpoint assessments evaluate what our students know in a single point in time, usually after instruction. For example, tests and quizzes give teachers information on how students respond to classroom activities. Typically, endpoint assessments require students to interact with nonchanging (static) prompts such as multiple-choice or free-response questions. Feedback from the teacher to the student is delayed. Endpoint assessments make it difficult for teachers to know exactly what students were thinking, especially when written responses are sparse or difficult to interpret, but they do provide important objective documentation of a student's abilities at a moment in time.

Dynamic assessments determine how students respond to changing (dynamic) prompts. For example, teachers use questions in conversations with students to pinpoint what they can answer on their own and what they need help to answer. The fluid nature of teacher–student, real-time feedback provides information for ongoing learning (Vygotsky 1962). The same type of back-and-forth interaction occurs among students during investigations (Hake 1992). This is especially true when teachers orchestrate conversational prompts to probe students' prior conceptions, to link evidence and interpretation, or to construct meaning through argumentation and inference. Students' science notebooks also provide a record of these in-the-moment interactions. You can use the notebooks to assess the ongoing aspects of student learning (BSCS 1994). (See chapter 11 for more ideas about how to use science notebooks to assess student learning.)

Conceptual framework assessments give teachers insight to the way students store, retrieve, and associate knowledge. The association and hierarchy of concepts form the basis of mental structures that students use to do well in school. Cognitive framework assessments inform teachers about the effect their teaching has on those structures. For example, the concept maps and graphic organizers of experts in a field are consistently different from novices (Novak 1990).

Designing Balanced Assessments

One way to ensure a balanced approach to assessment is to design a scoring scheme or rubric that reflects the desired balance among endpoint, dynamic, and conceptual framework assessments. This way, you have data to triangulate effectively what students know and can do. As a result, you can improve your ability to individualize instruction, a key feature of effective formative assessments.

As an example, imagine a unit on designing, conducting, and communicating the results of a scientific investigation in biology. How do you construct a balanced rubric for this? Naturally, assessing biology skills and concepts works best and most efficiently within a context, namely, specific biology content. For this example on assessing inquiry, consider the following focus question posed to students: "What affects the rate of diffusion through a semipermeable membrane?"

Note that a full inquiry would stage the activity so that students formulate their own questions, but in many school circumstances, time does not allow full inquiry in every activity. Nonetheless, each aspect of inquiry can be assessed, documented, and used to guide instruction. (See section II for detailed discussion about the value of using different levels of inquiry in the classroom.)

Before students begin their investigation, communicate all assessment criteria in the form of a scoring rubric. The rubric tells students ahead of time what is important and what a high-quality performance looks like. Rubrics accomplish this, in part, by reflecting the intended balance of assessment types. The balance structured into the rubric sends a clear message to students about what is essential for them to learn. If balance is important, then it should be assessed in student performance.

A rubric design matrix can help ensure a balanced assessment. Think of a design matrix as systematic brainstorming. That is, you generate ideas for assessments by thinking of examples from specific categories of assessment. In the design matrix, you list the concrete tasks to be assessed in the "task" column. Generally, only one task for each category of assessment is necessary.

Next, you form questions that a specific assessment type would tend to answer. Note that students will not have to answer all questions from each category of assessment. At this stage you should generate as many questions per category as possible as you would in a brainstorming activity. Eventually, convert some of these questions into concrete performance-level indicators associated with specific tasks. These performance criteria show up in the final rubric.

Because the assessment categories represent a balanced assessment, the final rubric should also be balanced. When the rubric is balanced and students use the rubric to guide their work, then the work students do should also be balanced. Table 16.3 is a completed rubric design matrix for the diffusion activity.

After filling each cell in the design matrix, use the completed matrix to decide the best match between task and assessment type. For example, in table 16.3, the individual multiple-choice test best aligns with endpoint assessments. Eventually, each task is assessed by one type of assessment. Of course, there is overlap, but your teacher judgment decides the final

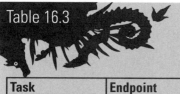

Table 16.3		Sample Design Matrix to Help Ensure a Balanced Assessment for a Task	
Task	**Endpoint**	**Dynamic**	**Conceptual Framework**
Generate, complete, and evaluate the results of a systematic procedure to answer the focus question.	• Does the student produce a procedure? • Does the student carry out the procedure? • Does the student evaluate the results?	• Are there various drafts of the procedure in the student's notebooks? • Are there notes from discussions during design iterations? • Do you see evidence of ongoing adjustments to the design, based on feedback from others? From the phenomenon? • Is there evidence of an emerging conclusion based on ongoing evaluation?	• Does the student use the language of biological inq properly? • Does the student use the focus question to make decisions about steps in th design? • Does the student construc conclusions based on evidence? Are they logical ar consistent?
Take individual multiple-choice test regarding essential understanding about diffusion through a semipermeable membrane.	• What is the raw percentage of correct answers?	• How much time was required? • Did the student request clarification or elaboration during the test? • What appears on the scratch paper?	• What type of questions w missed most often (concep tual, algorithmic, or recall • How does the student's distribution of missed iten compare with the highest-performing students' distribution?
Review and analyze a research article about the essential understanding of diffusion through semipermeable membranes.	• Are there notes in science notebook? • Did the student list key words in the notebook? • Can the student write an effective summary paragraph analyzing the research and the findings?	• Does the student use literacy strategies during reading? • Does the student debrief with peers about the article? • Are there notes from peer debriefings that indicate thoughtful discussion?	• Can the student generate concept map by using the essential terms of the arti • Does the concept map der strate coherent principles conceptual connections? • Are the extent and sense relatedness among concep similar to those of teacher experts'?

division. A balanced assessment results from spreading the types of assessment among the tasks on the rubric and giving significant weight to each assessment type in scoring. Finally, you write performance-level indicators for each task and decide how to weight each task for scoring purposes. The rubric in table 16.4 results from the design matrix just discussed.

e 16.4 Balanced Scoring Rubric That Weights Each Task Sufficiently to Communicate the Importance of All Outcomes to Students

er Levels of Performance

ight	Task	3	2	1
	Design, conduct, and evaluate the results of an investigation to answer the focus question.	Exhibits detailed ongoing progress in the science notebook of the design process by documenting the development of procedures, the responses to peer feedback, and the generation of conclusions.	Documents and exhibits an understanding of the final design only, not ideas and drafts of ongoing design development.	Records data from the investigation with little reference to ongoing procedural adjustments and developing interpretations of data.
	Take individual multiple-choice test regarding essential understanding about diffusion through semipermeable membranes.	Selects between 81% and 100% of the multiple-choice answers correctly.	Selects between 61% and 80% of the multiple-choice answers correctly.	Selects between 0% and 60% of the multiple-choice answers correctly.
	Create a concept map, demonstrating a rigorous review and analysis of an article about the essential understanding of diffusion through semipermeable membranes.	Designs, generates, and explains a concept map containing key ideas related to an understanding of diffusion, which reflect the article's conceptual hierarchy, connectedness, and application.	Constructs a concept map with key concept terms but does not show and explain the hierarchy, connectedness, or application among those terms from the article.	Produces a physical arrangement of terms from the article that has little discernible rationale, reflection of hierarchy, connectedness, or application of the key understanding of diffusion.

In this balanced rubric, you use the concept map task to assess conceptual framework knowledge, the multiple-choice test as an endpoint assessment, and documentation in students' science notebooks (along with real-time teacher observations during lab) to focus on dynamic assessment. Two of the three assessment types, the concept map and the investigation design, are mostly formative assessments. Thus, formative assessments represent the majority of how you effectively assess student learning. The end product is a balanced assessment from which teachers produce a balanced learning environment—one most capable of enhancing achievement for a broad diversity of learners.

The Influence of Instructional Models on Formative Assessments

Constructivist instructional models represent a family of instructional models that, among other things, foster balanced and authentic assessment. Such models orchestrate learning for students in a way that supports enduring understanding and provides a framework for constructing knowledge about scientific inquiry (Bybee 1997). Specific examples can help demonstrate the ways in which stages of an instructional model are linked to different types of assessment. The examples also illustrate how these assessments are learning opportunities for students.

In the invitation or engagement phase of an instructional model as well as during the discovery or exploration phase, opportunities exist for dynamic assessments of abilities and understandings of inquiry. For example, let's imagine a teacher named Ms. Washington who assigned to her class the diffusion investigation mentioned earlier. Because Ms. Washington assigned her investigation design task as part of ongoing class activities, she could become part of the assessment through dialogue, especially in the form of questions. She could monitor the design process with observations of student interactions, by reviewing student science notebooks, and by evaluating the activity results. As part of monitoring the design process, she would involve herself in informal feedback sessions with students. Then she would use the trajectory of these interactions to assess the dynamic (ongoing) growth in a student's abilities of inquiry. Examine the following dynamic assessment version of Ms. Washington's design task and look for evidence of in-the-moment learning.

Student: Ms. Washington, what do we do next? You didn't give us a worksheet with the steps.

Teacher: Does the focus question give you any ideas?

Student: It just asks what affects the rate of diffusion through a semipermeable membrane. It doesn't say what to do.

Teacher: Well, I see you have two beakers, a graduated cylinder, and some sodium chloride at your lab station. How did you know to use those materials? The focus question didn't have that in there.

Student: How else are we supposed to make the concentration do something?

Teacher: Good thinking, Eddie, you have to have different concentrations. Write down how you're going to do that in steps that other students could follow.

Student: Is that all we have to do?

Teacher: Well, what else have you done when you have design investigations in class?

Student: Let's see. We've been careful to change the thing we want to study and keep the other things the same.

Teacher: OK, now you're putting some good ideas together. Try putting those ideas in your design. Then call me over and we'll talk some more.

Ms. Washington didn't accept Eddie's initial knowledge position as an accurate reflection of his true ability. So she thought of questions to probe Eddie's deeper understanding. In Eddie's first response, she noticed how he had inferred the need for different concentrations from the focus question. Then she prompted specific actions (writing a design and procedure) that caused Eddie to formalize and record his thinking. Finally, she foreshadowed the need for continued feedback as she and Eddie work toward a finished design.

Application and evaluate-type lessons can be used to assess changes in students' conceptual frameworks. This is a critical first step in learning (Bransford et al. 2000). For example, to engage students' prior knowledge about using evidence to develop explanations of diffusion, you might ask students to construct a concept map, using their current understanding of the importance of evidence. After progressing through conceptually coherent, carefully sequenced activities, you would ask students to construct another concept map from the same concept words. By comparing the before and after maps with an expert map, you can validly assess changes in the conceptual frameworks of the students (Pinkerton 1998). Other forms of assessing aspects of changes in students' conceptual frameworks include performance on conceptually oriented tests, generation of graphic organizers that convey a conceptual hierarchy and connectivity, and the solving of open-ended problems, such as those typically found in authentic assessments.

Student Self-Assessment: When Inquiry Becomes Personal

Balanced and authentic approaches to assessing inquiry teach students about multiple sources of feedback, not just feedback from the teacher. Among the most important sources of feedback is the one students receive from monitoring their own thinking—metacognition (Bransford et al. 2000). This monitoring reflects the important goals for assessment outlined in table 16.1 that link assessment to what we know about learning. Self-assessment involves an ongoing and iterative interaction with the prompt at hand, be it a reading, an investigation, or an open-ended project. Students use the information they obtain from self-monitoring to assess their understanding and adjust their learning paths. Rubrics such as the ones in tables 16.3 and 16.4 are useful tools for students in this process. In many ways, the active meta-"dialogue" necessary for student self-assessment is at the heart of effective inquiry.

Using formative assessment methods such as dynamic and conceptual framework assessments in addition to endpoint assessments teaches students self-assessment skills by example. For example, consider what it takes to teach students how to learn from mistakes. It requires explicit instruction on how to pinpoint, articulate, and remedy mistakes on content-related activities. In effect, students who learn from mistakes learn to monitor their ongoing thinking and use it to plan actions and solve problems. Used with unit tests, learning from mistakes through self-assessment and peer dialogue shifts endpoint assessments toward dynamic assessments and fosters greater balance and higher achievement (Pinkerton 2005).

When students learn and practice self-assessment skills, they move toward greater intellectual independence. They tend not to require as much external feedback from teachers and can chart their own way through an investigation. In turn, teachers can allot more of their time to those students who still are struggling, thus spending time where it is most needed. In effect, teaching self-assessment skills shrinks the effective class size by increasing the number of students who can apply the outcomes of inquiry to doing the business of school.

Conclusion

The message is clear—the ability of students to "do" biology and to understand biology concepts is essential. Developing biology lessons and assessing for an understanding of biology skills and concepts go hand in hand. In fact, well-designed biology lessons result from well-designed assessments—ones focused on the important key understandings in biology. This backward design approach begins with the end (the assessment), which, in turn, provides a specific target for the learning sequence that builds toward the assessment task. That is, the process begins with what is important for students to know (the essential skills and understandings of inquiry) and ends up with an effective learning environment (the day-to-day experiences that shape what students know and understand).

Assessments in biology classrooms should align with what we know about learning and should be balanced and authentic. That is, they should include all the important core concepts in biology for the grade level you teach, not just those that are easy to assess. This approach helps ensure that all students acquire the knowledge and skills that we consider important about scientific inquiry in biology. In turn, this foundation of knowledge should help all students participate more effectively in an increasingly complex world.

Chapter 17

How to Select Programs for Your Inquiry Classroom

Besides teachers and students, the most consistent presence in school science is the instructional materials. Because of the central and ubiquitous role instructional materials play in learning and teaching science, teachers owe students and themselves the best possible materials.

BSCS asserts that identifying and implementing instructional materials that are consistent with an inquiry approach to instruction require more than examining the table of contents of a textbook and attending an orientation workshop on the materials. In collaboration with the K–12 Alliance of WestEd, we have developed a process and set of tools to help teams of science teachers from a school or district analyze instructional materials for their compatibility with an inquiry-oriented approach to teaching science. Completing this process, known as Analyzing Instructional Materials, or AIM, can help you in the selection and subsequent implementation of instructional materials. Although developed for selecting curriculum materials, the AIM process has also proved valuable for analyzing and supporting the use of a program that has already been selected.

Selecting and implementing new instructional materials tends to be a relatively massive undertaking that involves significant resources of energy, money, and time to support people through the process. AIM does not decrease the need for resources. It does, however, create tremendous opportunities for professional learning. As an evidence-based process that promotes true collaboration—learning together, not just working together—it contributes to the development of a professional learning community. Given the significant district investment in instructional materials, their longevity and presence in the system, and their potential impact on teacher practice and student learning, the up-front investment in the selection process is worthwhile.

AIM is an inquiry-based approach to examining instructional materials, and it supports the user's construction of knowledge. The AIM process appeals to science teachers because of its use of evidence to surface ideas and guide discussion. A well-facilitated experience with AIM creates a structure that compares teachers' existing ideas with ideas from the research. It also offers opportunities for teachers to feel dissonance and be reflective about their practice. AIM becomes a transformative professional development experience because it can lead to a change in beliefs about the nature of science, teaching, learning, and the usefulness of well-designed instructional materials.

The following questions are examples of those that you and your team could answer through the use of the AIM process and tools:

1. What are the characteristics of high-quality instructional materials?
2. How can we select a new set of instructional materials?

3. How can we inform the future use of instructional materials?
4. How can we determine where new or existing instructional materials are aligned with standards?
5. How can we determine whether new or existing instructional materials support students' inquiry-based learning?
6. How can we determine where new or existing instructional materials are rigorous and have a rich array of assessments?
7. How can we inform the design of professional development to support the implementation of instructional materials?

In this chapter, we introduce the philosophy and process of using AIM. To realize its full benefits, it should be conducted in your district by a trained facilitator. If your school district is interested in learning more about AIM and using it in your curriculum selection process or as professional development around curriculum materials, visit the BSCS website at *www.bscs.org* or contact BSCS at *pdcenter@bscs.org*.

Analyzing Instructional Materials (AIM) Process and Tools

A systematic approach for examining instructional materials can support you and your colleagues in developing a common understanding of the research about instructional materials and how it is executed in the materials. What are the characteristics of high-quality instructional materials, and how can you understand and identify them? Based on characteristics proposed by the American Association for the Advancement Science in its 1997 *Resources for Science Literacy*, F. James Rutherford (BSCS 2000) describes the properties of science courses and, by association, the instructional materials used in them:

> The content of science courses [and instructional materials] should have four properties. First, it should be *significant*. It is not reasonable to expect students to learn all of the facts, concepts, and principles in the world of science or to become knowledgeable about all of the topics to which science relates. Choices have to be made, and those choices should favor the content that will best serve students for a lifetime in the real world of ideas and action. And of course, the content should be *accurate*. Errors of fact and wrong or misleading presentations of laws, principles, and concepts have no place in science courses—though leavened, of course, by the realization

that the expression of content needs to be age appropriate. Third, content should be *aligned* with desired or declared learning goals. Developers often claim this for their products these days, but actually honor it more in rhetoric than in practice. And then there is *coherence*. (24–25)

According to the *National Science Education Standards* (NRC 1996), a program of study should be developmentally appropriate and relevant to students' lives as well as emphasize student understanding through inquiry-based learning experiences. Materials should support engaging and assessing students' prior knowledge. They should help students develop metacognitive skills to reflect on what and how they learned (NRC 1999). Materials should embed a variety of assessment resources that measure student understanding and inform instruction (NRC 2001). They should be designed to support teachers by providing background on teaching and learning strategies and information on the use of teacher support materials.

AIM is both a systematic process and a collection of tools that helps you and your colleagues recognize these qualities in instructional materials. AIM can help you develop an operational definition of the research on teaching and learning as it applies to instructional materials. Teacher teams use the tools to help them gather and analyze evidence of these qualities from the instructional materials. The AIM process uses the evidence to develop a common understanding of the nature of the materials. By using the process, you and your colleagues build consensus in the selection of instructional materials or develop a deeper understanding of how your existing materials relate to the characteristics of high-quality instructional materials. Regardless of the focus, AIM is fundamentally a professional development strategy that supports the implementation of high-quality materials to create a coherent science program—biology or otherwise.

Before beginning the AIM process, you and your colleagues first identify the criteria for high-quality instructional materials that support both student learning and teacher practice and that are based on your district's science program. The criteria include goals, standards, and the curriculum framework. The AIM process has five basic components (see figure 17.1):

1. *Prescreen materials* as needed to reduce the number of programs that undergo full analysis.
2. *Complete a "paper screen"* on the materials to examine them based on the identified criteria.
3. *Pilot test the materials* in the classroom to gather evidence based on the use of the materials by both teachers and students.

4. *Select the instructional materials* based on the evidence gathered and the consensus built through the process.
5. *Scale up for full implementation* of the materials.

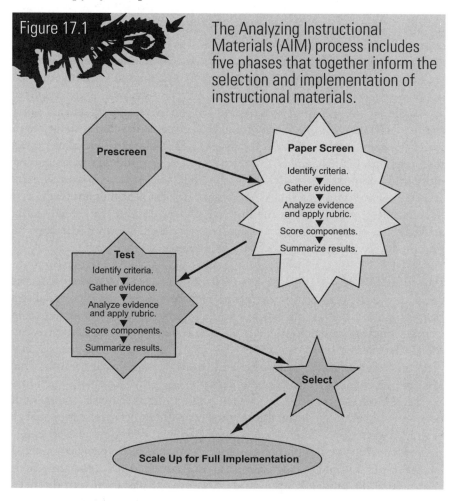

Figure 17.1

The Analyzing Instructional Materials (AIM) process includes five phases that together inform the selection and implementation of instructional materials.

Identifying Criteria

The first step in a selection process is to identify the criteria upon which you will base your decision about instructional materials. You should ask yourself questions such as "How are instructional materials important to students?" and "How are instructional materials important to teachers?" This helps set the stage for thinking, guided by the AIM tools. In doing so, you likely will think about the content required by your district or state standards and how well the materials, including the ancillary materials available to teachers, are aligned with those standards.

To emphasize the important role of instructional materials in student learning, it is essential that you and your colleagues work together to identify specific criteria for the materials in addition to alignment with district or state standards before opening the first book. You might want to think about how the instructional materials help students make the conceptual connections that are critical in learning for understanding. How are students involved in designing and conducting scientific investigations? How accessible are the learning experiences? Do the materials situate the learning in a relevant context, provide multiple entry points for students with various learning styles, and adequately assess student learning? How do the materials support teachers? Are they part of a research-based instructional model that helps teachers identify and address students' preconceptions?

After learning to use the AIM Process and Tools, you and your district or school leaders can determine how closely the criteria embedded in the AIM rubrics match local student and teacher needs. The tools can then be modified to better reflect your district's needs.

AIM Prescreen Process and Tools

You can expect to receive as many as 25 programs from publishers at the beginning of a biology adoption cycle. A prescreen helps you limit the number of programs that undergo the more in-depth paper screen to only those that meet a limited number of must-have criteria. The criteria that guide the AIM Prescreen Process and Tools are often a subset of those identified in the first stage of the process.

In the AIM prescreen, the teacher and student materials from each program are carefully checked for evidence of these necessary criteria. For example, your district may decide that evidence of inquiry-based experiences is essential along with support for teachers in terms of content background, examples of common student preconceptions, and the use of an instructional model. If a program does not incorporate these must-have criteria, then you would not consider those materials for further review.

Completing the AIM Paper Screen

Following the prescreen, the remaining materials undergo a more in-depth analysis, called the AIM Paper Screen Process and Tools. The paper screen is an iterative process during which instructional materials are analyzed based on four major criteria: science content, student learning experiences, assessment, and support for teachers. To find evidence of these criteria, you and your team use tools that include four rubrics titled Science Content Rubric,

Work Students Do Rubric, Assessment Rubric, and Work Teachers Do Rubric (visit the BSCS website at *www.bscs.org* or contact BSCS at *pdcenter@bscs.org* for information). Each rubric includes specific components that come from the research base about learning and instructional materials. For example, the rubric on science content includes rows to rate characteristics of the materials such as standards alignment, concept development, and the context in which the concepts are developed. This rubric incorporates key findings from *How People Learn* (Bransford et al. 2000; also see chapter 1 for discussion of these findings) and provides an opportunity to assess instructional materials based on these findings. Similarly, two of the components on the Work Students Do Rubric are the understandings about scientific inquiry and abilities necessary to do scientific inquiry that come from the *National Science Education Standards* (NRC 1996).

For each rubric, you gather evidence from the instructional materials, analyze the evidence using the rubric, and give a quantitative score to each of the components (see figure 17.2). You also use the rubrics to gather qualitative evidence to identify the strengths and limitations of the program. You can use this information to inform future professional development on the program, should it be selected. You may also use the limitations to identify gaps in the program related to specific student or teacher needs.

Each program receives a score for each rubric. The total score becomes the basis for comparing programs. Thus, we recommend choosing similar representative units or chapters from each program. For example, you could gather evidence from the section that focuses on ecosystems in all the biology programs under consideration.

Throughout the process, evidence is used as the focus of discussions and to promote consensus building. The evidence collected from the instructional materials is represented visually when you and your team collaboratively construct a conceptual flow graphic (CFG; see figure 17.3). The CFG includes the concepts addressed by the instructional materials, arranged logically and connected by arrows that represent the strength of connections among the concepts. You place icons on the CFG to indicate that specific components of the materials meet the criteria on the various rubrics. Additional information from each rubric is added to the CFG as you and your team discuss the evidence collected from the materials.

For example, the CFG shown in figure 17.3 indicates that one overarching concept and six major supporting concepts were identified from one chapter in the unit under consideration. (Several of the major supporting concepts had subconcepts, which is why there are 12 notes instead of 6.) The bold arrows indicate strong connections, and the other arrows represent connections of medium strength between concepts. Of the six

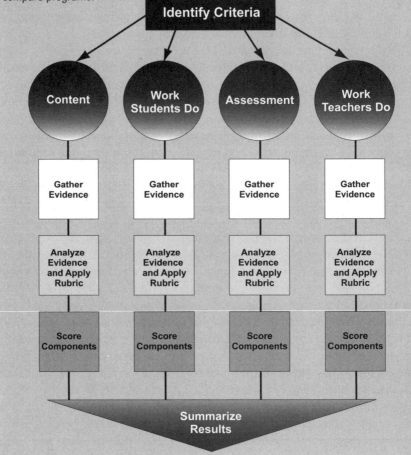

Figure 17.2 — The AIM Paper Screen Process and Tools

The AIM Paper Screen Process and Tools is an iterative process that includes tools such as rubrics, evidence-gathering charts, and a score sheet. For each of the four rubrics, teachers gather evidence based on the components, analyze and apply the rubric, and score each criterion. The scores are summarized and the results are used to compare programs.

re 17.3 — Conceptual Flow Graphic (CFG)

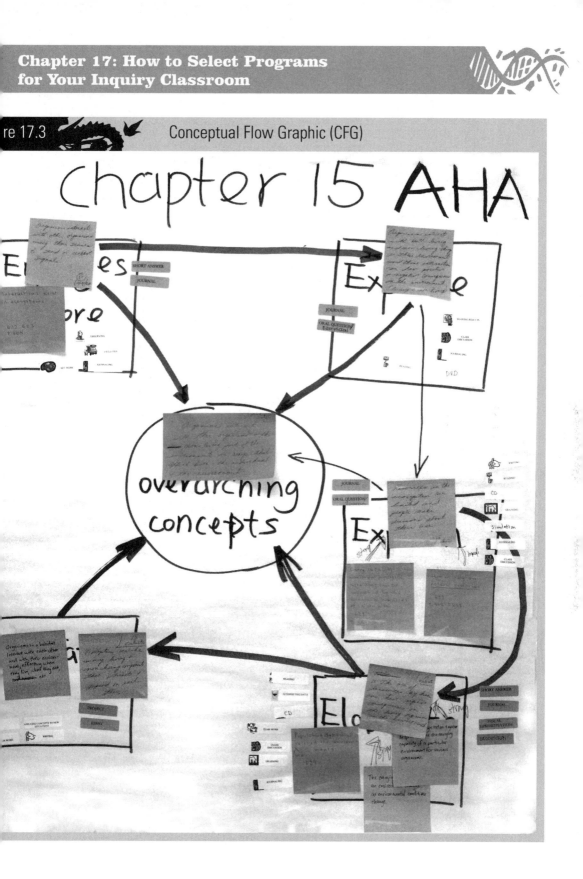

supporting concepts, most were strongly connected to the overarching concept, as represented by the bold arrows. The general direction of the arrows indicates that the learning experiences are well sequenced. Icons are used as visual evidence of the presence of specific criteria found on the AIM rubrics. The icons associated with each concept on the CFG shown in figure 17.3 indicate that the materials embed powerful learning experiences, provide many assessment opportunities, and include support for teachers. Although we were not privy to the authors' dialogue and did not score these materials, based on a scan of the CFG, it is likely that the materials scored well on the criteria defined by the rubrics.

Engaging in the AIM process and using the tools can be a transformative professional development experience. It will challenge you and your colleagues to think about the science concepts addressed in the materials from the learner's perspective. This focus on concepts and how they are connected in the materials can deepen your understanding of science content. By examining materials for quality student learning experiences, you develop an operational definition of what inquiry looks like in instructional materials and how the materials support the assessment of student learning. By using common criteria that promote consensus building, you consider how accessible the materials are for students and how usable the materials are for teachers:

> Coming to consensus about scoring the materials has been a learning experience for all of us in [the school district]. In the past, everyone got a voice by voting. Through AIM, you really have to provide evidence to help others see what you see. This has changed the types of conversations between teachers during the process. Learning how to use AIM was not a "sit and get" experience. Teachers were developing their learning and new understandings about inquiry-based instructional materials. By using AIM, teachers were working to put their evidence and where they found it down on paper. They were doing the learning.
>
> —Curriculum Specialist, Large Midwestern Public School District (BSCS personal communication, 2007)

After applying the rubrics to the evidence collected during the paper screen process, you can compare programs based on their scores. Then you evaluate the top one or two programs that emerge based on their use in the classroom and compare them using the AIM Implementation Process and Tools.

AIM Implementation Process and Tools

The AIM Implementation Process and Tools can be used to test materials in the classroom. Whether the test is considered a field test, a pilot, or a classroom trial, the AIM Implementation Process and Tools is designed to go beyond considering what's on paper and move to a consideration of how the materials work with students and for teachers in the classroom.

Once the structural aspects of the test have been negotiated—such as which chapters or units you will test, which teachers will try out the materials, and in which classes or sections—your team undergoes a three-phase process:

1. Planning for the implementation of the chapter or unit
2. Trying the materials out in the classroom
3. Compiling the evidence collected, summarizing the results, and reflecting on the process

The implementation process embeds the same iterative steps experienced during the paper screen (see figure 17.4). During the planning phase, your team works together to identify criteria and clarify the evidence that will be collected from students and related to your own experience using the materials. You will gather evidence related to student understanding and teacher implementation during the implementation phase. The evidence includes student work, student reflections, and teacher reflections. For example, students are asked to reflect on their learning from the lessons by responding to questions such as the following:

- What did you learn?
- What do you still need to know?
- How hard did you work?
- What was most helpful for your learning?
- What was least helpful for your learning?

During the reflection phase, teachers analyze the evidence and score the criteria using rubrics for assessing student understanding and teacher implementation. They summarize the results, which then contribute to the decision on the selection of instructional materials. The results also inform professional development for the program selected.

Making a Selection

At the conclusion of the paper screen and implementation, you will have analyzed various programs at face value and compared them in the classroom. The results from each process yield qualitative and quantitative

Figure 17.4 — The AIM Implementation Process and Tools

The AIM Implementation Process and Tools involves identifying criteria and gathering evidence related to the *Student Understanding Rubric* and the *Teacher Implementation Rubric*.

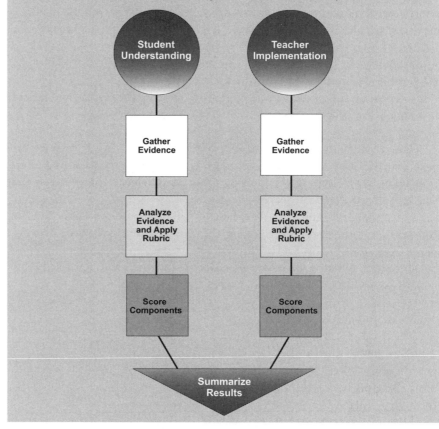

evidence that you can summarize to make a case for recommending a program that supports a high-quality biology program.

AIM as Professional Development

AIM is flexible in its application and can be used for a variety of purposes from the selection of instructional materials to developing a deeper understanding of existing instructional materials. Thus, AIM is also a professional development strategy. As an evidence-based process that promotes collaboration, it provides a rich resource to support a professional learning community. The process provides a common learning experience for you and your colleagues that focuses on instructional materials.

Through the AIM process, you learn more about existing instructional materials, how those materials are aligned with your district's standards, and how they develop science concepts. You make connections between the standards and how the content is addressed (or not) in the instructional materials.

In a different way, through the development of the CFG, you build an operational definition of concept development and therefore a deeper understanding of how students learn science through their instructional materials. An outgrowth of the work is a clearer picture of how each student learning experience contributes to his or her understanding of the science concepts addressed in the materials. This focus on student learning is another characteristic of a professional learning community among teachers.

You also learn how your instructional materials embed (or don't embed) activities that build students' abilities to do inquiry and to develop understandings about inquiry. In addition, you learn how your instructional materials incorporate other powerful learning strategies, what types of assessments are included and how the materials promote their use to inform instruction, and how accessible the learning experiences are to students. Any of these topics could reveal areas of focus for future professional development. For example, you and your colleagues might identify a need to understand more about differentiation or the use of formative assessments as part of your school's or district's efforts in improving the use of your instructional materials.

Although the AIM Paper Screen Process and Tools helps you learn more about the content of your instructional materials and how they are put together, the AIM Implementation Process and Tools provides you with an opportunity to consider the materials' use with students—again through a collaborative, evidence-based process.

Whether used for selection or for professional development, AIM can transform the ways in which you and your fellow teachers view and use instructional materials in the classroom. Through becoming more clear about the connections among ideas, you are more prepared to support students in making conceptual connections. You and your colleagues also become more clear about the design of the program and the purposes of student learning experiences. With AIM as a foundation and with ongoing professional development, you and your colleagues will be more likely to make instructional choices that are more consistent with the overall design of the program. The result is a more coherent learning experience for students.

SECTION IV REFERENCES

Akar, E. 2005. Effectiveness of 5E learning cycle model on students' understanding of acid-base concepts. *http://edu.lib.metu.edu/tr/upload/12605747/index.pdf.*

Alvermann, D. E. 1991. The discussion web: A graphic aid for learning across the curriculum. *The Reading Teacher* 45 (2): 92–99.

American Association for the Advancement of Science (AAAS). 1997. *Resources for science literacy: Professional development.* New York: Oxford University Press.

Ates, S. 2005. The effectiveness of the learning-cycle method on teaching DC circuits to prospective female and male science teachers. *Research in Science and Technological Education* 23 (2): 213–27.

Atkin, J. M., and R. Karplus. 1962. Discovery of invention? *Science Teacher* 29 (5): 45.

Beck, I. L., M. G. McKeown, R. L. Hamilton, and L. Kucan. 1998. Getting at the meaning: How to help students unpack difficult text. *American Educator* 85 (Spring–Summer): 66–71.

Billings, R. L. 2001. Assessment of the learning cycle and inquiry-based learning in high school physics education. Abstract in *Masters Abstracts International* 40 (4): 840.

Biological Sciences Curriculum Study (BSCS). 1994. *BSCS middle school science and technology teacher's guide.* Dubuque, IA: Kendall/Hunt.

———. 2000. *Making sense of integrated science: A guide for high schools.* 1st ed. Colorado Springs, CO: BSCS.

———. 2003. *BSCS biology: A human approach.* Dubuque, IA: Kendall/Hunt.

———. 2003. *The commons: An environmental dilemma.* Dubuque, IA: Kendall/Hunt.

———. 2006. *BSCS Biology: A human approach assessment DVD.* Dubuque, IA: Kendall/Hunt.

———. 2006. *BSCS biology: A human approach* teacher resource CD. Dubuque, IA: Kendall/Hunt.

———. 2006. Promoting scientific conversation. In *BSCS science tracks handbook,* 169–174. Dubuque, IA: Kendall/Hunt.

Blosser, P. E. 1973. *Handbook of effective questioning techniques.* Worthington, OH: Education Associates.

———. 2000. *How to ask the right questions.* Arlington, VA: National Science Teachers Association.

Bransford, J. D., A. L. Brown, and R. R. Cocking. 2000. *How people learn: Brain, mind, experience, and school.* Washington, DC: National Academy Press.

Bybee, R. W. 1997. *Achieving scientific literacy: From purposes to practices.* Portsmouth, NH: Heinemann.

Coulson, D. 2002. *BSCS science: An inquiry approach—2002 evaluation findings.* Arnold, MD: PS International.

Cunningham, J. 1982. Generating Interactions between Schemata and Text. In *New inquiries in reading research and instruction*, eds. J. Niles, and L. Harris, 42–47. Thirty-first Yearbook of the National Reading Conference. Washington, DC: National Reading Conference.

Davey, B. 1983. Think aloud: Modeling the cognitive processes of reading comprehension. *Journal of Reading* 27 (1): 44–47.

Donovan, M. S., and J. D. Bransford. 2005. *How students learn: Science in the classroom.* Washington, DC: National Academy Press.

Eanet, M., and A. Manzo. 1976. R.E.A.P—a strategy for improving reading/writing study skills. *Journal of Reading* 19: 647–652.

Ebrahim, A. 2004. The effects of traditional learning and a learning cycle inquiry learning strategy on students' science achievement and attitudes toward elementary science. PhD diss., Ohio Univ., Athens. Abstract in *Dissertation Abstracts International,* DAI-A 65/04 (Oct. 2004): 1232.

Eeds, M., and W. A. Cockrum. 1985. Teaching word meanings by extending schemata vs. dictionary work vs. reading in context. *Notebook of Reading* 28 (6): 492–497.

Englert, C. S., and C. C. Thomas. 1987. Sensitivity to text structure in reading and writing: A comparison between learning disabled and non-learning disabled students. *Learning Disability Quarterly* 10: 93–105.

Frayer, D. A., W. C. Frederick, and H. J. Klausmeier. 1969. A schema for testing the level of concept mastery. Technical Report No. 16. Madison, WI: University of Wisconsin, Research and Development Center for Cognitive Learning.

Gillett, J. W., and C. Temple. 1983. *Understanding reading problems: Assessment and instruction.* Boston: Little, Brown.

Hake, R. 1992. Socratic pedagogy in the introductory physics laboratory. *The Physics Teacher* 30 (9): 546–552.

Herber, H. 1978. *Teaching reading in content areas.* 2nd ed. Englewood Cliffs, NJ: Prentice Hall.

Johnson, D. D., and P. D. Pearson. 1984. *Teaching reading vocabulary.* 2nd ed. New York: Holt, Rinehart and Winston.

Jones, B. F., A. S. Palincsar, D. S. Ogle, and E. G. Carr. 1987. *Strategic teaching and learning: Cognitive instruction in the content areas.* Alexandria, VA; Elmhurst, IL: Association for Supervision and Curriculum Development/North Central Regional Educational Laboratory.

Karplus, R., and H. D. Thier. 1967. *A new look at elementary school science.* Chicago: Rand McNally.

Lawson, A. E. 1988. A better way to teach biology. *American Biology Teacher* 50 (5): 266–78.

Lord, T. R. 1997. A comparison between traditional and constructivist teaching in college biology. *Innovative Higher Education* 21 (3): 1127–47.

Loucks-Horsley, S., R. Kapitan, M. Carlson, P. Kuerbis, R. Clark, G. Melle, T. Sachse, and E. Walton. 1990. *Elementary school science for the '90s.* Andover, MA: The Network.

Mackay, J. 1993. *The state of health atlas.* New York: Simon & Schuster.

Marzano, R. J., and D. J. Pickering. With D. E. Arredondo, G. J. Blackburn, R. S. Brandt, C. A. Moffett, D. E. Paynter, and J. S. Whisler. 1997. *Dimensions of learning.* 2nd ed. Alexandria, VA: Association for Supervision and Curriculum Development.

Myers, N., ed. 1993. *Gaia: An atlas of planet management.* New York: Anchor Books.

National Research Council (NRC). 1996. *National Science Education Standards.* Washington, DC: National Academy Press.

———. 1999. *Selecting instructional materials: A guide for K–12 science.* Washington, DC: National Academy Press.

———. 2001. *Classroom assessment and the national science education standards.* Washington, DC: National Academy Press.

Novak, J. 1990. Concept maps and vee diagrams: Two metacognitive tools to facilitate meaningful learning. *Instructional Science* 19 (1): 29–52.

Ogle, D. 1986. The K-W-L: A teaching model that develops active reading of expository text. *The Reading Teacher* 39 (February): 564–570.

———. 1989. The know, want to know, learning strategy. In *Children's comprehension of text*, ed. K. D. Muth, 205–223. Newark, DE: International Reading Association.

Pinkerton, K. D. 1998. Network similarity (NETSIM) as a method of assessing structural knowledge for large groups. *Journal of Interactive Learning Research* 9 (3/4): 249–270.

———. 2005. Learning from mistakes. *The Physics Teacher* 43 (8): 510–513.

Readence, J. E., T. W. Bean, and R. S. Baldwin. 2004. *Content area literacy: An integrated approach.* 8th ed. Dubuque, IA: Kendall/Hunt.

Rowe, M. B. 1973. *Teaching science as continuous inquiry.* New York: McGraw-Hill.

———. 1987. Using wait time to stimulate inquiry. In *Questions, questioning techniques, and effective teaching*, ed. W. W. Wilen, 95–106. Washington, DC: National Education Association.

Santa, C. M. 1988. *Content reading including study systems*. Dubuque, IA: Kendall/Hunt.

Santa, C. M., L. T. Havens, and S. Harrison. 1996. Teaching secondary science through reading, writing, studying, and problem solving. In *Content area reading and learning: Instructional strategies*, eds. D. Lapp, J. Flood, and N. Farnan, 165–180. Needham Heights, MA: Allyn & Bacon.

Schwartz, R. 1988. Learning to learn vocabulary in content area textbooks. *Journal of Reading* 32 (November): 108–117.

Seidenberg, P. L. 1989. Relating text-processing research to reading and writing instruction for learning disabled students. *Learning Disabilities Focus* 5 (1): 4–12.

Shymansky, J. A., W. C. Kyle, and J. M. Alport. 1983. The effects of new science curricula on student performance. *Journal of Research in Science Teaching* 20: 387–404.

Simon, J. 1990. *Population matters: People, resources, environment, and immigration*. New Brunswick, NJ: Transaction Publishers.

Simon, J. 1996. *The ultimate resource 2*. Princeton: Princeton University Press.

Stauffer, R. G. 1969. *Developing reading maturity as a cognitive process*. New York: Harper & Row.

Tovani, C. 2005. The power of purposeful reading. *Educational Leadership* 63 (2): 48–51.

Van Scotter, P., and D. Pinkerton. 2008. Assessing science as inquiry in the classroom. In *Science as Inquiry in the secondary setting*, eds., J. Luft, R. L. Bell, and J. Gess-Newsome, 107–119. Arlington, VA: National Science Teachers Association.

Vygotsky, L. 1962. *Thought and language*. Cambridge, MA: Harvard University Press.

Wiggins, G., and J. McTighe. 2005. *Understanding by design*. 2nd ed. Alexandria, VA: Association for Supervision and Curriculum Development.

Section V

Introduction

BSCS and Biology Education

An understanding of where we have been and where we are going is helpful for professionals in any discipline. By the end of the 19th century, science had been established as a critical part of the high school curriculum. Fewer than 10% of people attended high school, however, and most of these students continued their studies into college. Secondary school enrollments increased substantially during the next few decades and included students who went directly to the workforce following graduation. By the end of the first decade of the 20th century, the assumption that the same curriculum served equally well students who would go on to colleges and universities and those who would go on to vocations immediately following high school was vigorously questioned. Thus, precollege education from the 1920s to the 1950s became more student centered and the application of science concepts to everyday life was highlighted. There was also a growing belief that education should accommodate the different needs of vocational- and college-oriented students.

Science textbooks tended to mirror these ideas about precollege science education. The textbook was the first basic component of American secondary education. The conventional science textbook came to be in the period from 1890 to 1929. It served as a curriculum guide for the relatively small, homogeneous schools of that period. The college-bound students in schools of the time were very much alike, not only in scholastic aptitude but also in educational and career objectives; thus, the high school curriculum during these years consisted of the prerequisite courses for college.

The earliest high school biology textbooks were written by working scientists who knew the discipline. They contained a mass of disconnected facts and elementary generalizations that were presented almost entirely as description. The lack of synthesis and breadth in these biology textbooks, however, accurately represented the state of the discipline at that time.

As student enrollment in high school increased during the period from 1929 to about 1956, concern for the increasingly diverse abilities, interests, backgrounds, and intentions of high school students brought about modifications of the conventional science textbook. One result was that the relationship between secondary science textbooks, including biology textbooks, and the working scientist was lost. There was no longer an emphasis on biology content and the knowledge necessary for college work. Biology and other science disciplines were somewhat distorted by attempts to adapt them to the needs and interests of the various social classes within the community.

By the late 1940s and early 1950s, dissatisfaction with American education in general and secondary school science education in particular was being expressed by parents, teachers, and school administrators. But, in the case of science, the greatest objections were voiced by scientists working at the collegiate level. Knowledgeable teachers, too, understood the gap between what was occurring in the research laboratory and what was being taught in the schools. The exciting recent advances in disciplines such as genetics were nowhere to be found in secondary school biology books. Biology, as practiced by biologists, was moving into the areas of molecular biology, cellular biology, biochemistry, molecular genetics, ultrastructure, and dozens of other new fields, while American secondary biology books were still emphasizing morphology and systematics.

Teachers and students felt that somehow the exciting discoveries they were reading about in newspapers or hearing about over the radio were unrelated to the morphology and systematics they were studying in the classroom. There was a strong feeling that the textbook should enrich the curriculum. Before 1929, the secondary school biology textbooks and curriculum were primarily of a college-preparatory nature. The pendulum had swung from college-preparatory work to a curriculum that failed to reflect the discipline.

Thus, the appearance of Sputnik in 1957 did not initiate concern about improving the teaching of science in American secondary schools, as is often related. Rather, it propelled the already growing concerns that something should be done to improve the quality of science instruction, and soon. In 1957, the National Science Foundation funded the Physical Science Study Committee, which began work on a secondary course to present physics as a unified and integrated process that would help high school students understand their physical world. Other science curriculum studies, including the Biological Sciences Curriculum Study (BSCS), followed.

In section V, we provide a brief look at the history of BSCS, an organization established some 50 years ago to develop state-of-the-art biology textbooks to counter the "fact-packed, conceptless" textbooks that were standard at that time. Chapter 18 focuses on the first 50 years of BSCS and how its initial mission expanded over those years. Chapter 19 offers BSCS's perspective on contemporary biology education.

Chapter 18

BSCS's Influence in Biology Education

This chapter describes the dominating concerns in science education over the past 50 years. It also discusses the way BSCS has addressed those concerns through curriculum and professional development and through research and evaluation. It is a brief overview of secondary biology education from the 1960s to the present day, organized into six time periods. Statements from the six directors who led BSCS during those years capture the theme and educational climate of each time period.

BSCS Begins: "A Novel Force in American Education"

Along with other curriculum studies, the BSCS represents a novel force in American education. A curriculum study of this kind is a new arrival on the American educational scene and for this reason deserves close scrutiny. The ... reason for writing this book is to indicate the value to our modern society of a curriculum study as an important educational institution. What, then, is a curriculum study? A curriculum study consists of a relatively autonomous group of scholars and teachers in a particular discipline who contribute systematically to curriculum improvement in that discipline.

—Arnold B. Grobman, BSCS Director, 1958–1965
The Changing Classroom: The Role of the Biological Sciences Curriculum Study, 1969, 2

In 1958, the National Science Foundation (NSF) awarded a grant to the American Institute of Biological Sciences (AIBS) for the establishment of the Biological Sciences Curriculum Study (BSCS). BSCS was to review the current status of biology textbooks and produce new, updated curriculum materials. To achieve this goal, the project team convened meetings among teachers from high schools, educators from colleges and universities, and scientists from their laboratories, none of whom had previously

been in contact with each other. After some study and discussion, these individuals recommended that BSCS concentrate initially on preparing a 10th-grade textbook that would present "the most modern content scientists could bring to bear, in the most effective pedagogical matrix that educators could devise, and in the most teachable form that teachers could contrive" (Mayer 1978, 6–7). The 10th grade was selected as the target primarily because most American high school students first encounter biology as a discrete discipline at that time.

Surveys of high school teachers about their classroom instruction at the time indicated that the textbook was the single most-important classroom aid. Teachers derived their curriculum from existing textbooks, and thus there was a tendency for one to reinforce the other—textbooks dictated what was taught and curriculum guides were prepared from text material. The aim of the BSCS was to improve biological education, not to reinforce the status quo. Thus, the project team devoted itself to considering how to update the content and introduce new classroom and laboratory strategies without eliminating so much of the existing textbook approaches and teaching practices that teachers would reject new ones as too radical to implement. After extensive conversations regarding what topics should be investigated, what major generalizations and conceptual schemes should represent biology in the book, and what modes of investigation should be selected, it was decided that the best mechanism for arranging the content was in levels of biological organization. This was a novel approach, as biology textbooks of the time were organized essentially on two levels: the whole organism and its organs and tissues.

Two of the levels—the organism and organ-and-tissue levels—are intrinsic to a study of systematics and morphology, and although those levels characterized biological studies by scientists when the earliest biology textbooks were written, this was no longer the case. Historically, the earliest biologists, limited by both equipment and techniques, could extend their investigations only as far as gross anatomy. As biology developed as a science, however, the functions of the organs revealed by anatomy were investigated and physiology was born. This study of the functions of organs and tissues led to greater interest in the cell itself and ultimately to the molecular functioning of the cell. In the opposite direction, biology moved beyond the organism as an individual to a study of populations, communities, and the world biome. Because modern biological investigations considered different levels of organization, the project team believed textbooks should introduce those levels to the beginning student. This called for less emphasis on classical morphology and the systematics approach. BSCS identified seven levels of biological organization as those to which all students should be exposed: the molecular level; the cellular level; the organ-and-tissue level; the organismic level; the population level; the community level; and the world biome level. The early BSCS leaders asserted that a biology textbook could emphasize any given level, provided that the other levels were also included in the program.

The BSCS team agreed that one of the textbooks being prepared would emphasize the molecular level of biology, using it as a springboard to study the broad spectrum of levels (this became the BSCS Blue Version). A second textbook would focus on the cellular level, using the cell as the basis for understanding the other levels (the BSCS Yellow Version), and a third would emphasize the community and world biome levels, focusing on the content of biology at these levels of organization (the BSCS Green Version).[1]

The BSCS project directors used a novel approach for developing the textbooks, an approach that has remained a hallmark of BSCS curriculum development. A writing conference was convened in the summer of 1960, and textbook chapters were written, reviewed, and revised by teams of university biologists and practicing teachers. This ensured that the content was both current and teachable. The first, experimental textbooks were then field-tested with more than 100 teachers and 14,000 students across the country. Teachers and students of the experimental materials provided voluminous feedback to the writers, who incorporated this feedback as they revised the materials in a second writing conference the following summer. The revised materials were field-tested again the next year, and final revisions based on the second round of field testing occurred before the three versions were released commercially in 1963. By this time, 1,000 teachers and 165,000 students in 47 states had participated in field-testing the programs. Grobman (BSCS 2001, 5) observed, "That three-year testing program probably constituted American education's largest experimental use of text material prior to general distribution to schools."

In addition to the three high school biology textbooks, BSCS in its early years produced a set of open-ended investigative lab exercises (*Laboratory Blocks*) that could be used at appropriate points in any of the three textbooks. The organization also prepared biology programs for special groups of students: gifted high school students, students who were unsuccessful learners, and mentally challenged children.

During this first period in BSCS's history, it is fair to say that the organization reintroduced the concepts of evolution, human reproduction,

---

[1]The Blue [*BSCS Biology: A Molecular Approach*] and Green [*BSCS Biology: An Ecological Approach*] versions are still available, now in their 9th and 10th editions, respectively. The Yellow Version [*BSCS Biology: An Inquiry into Life*] was retired after its 4th edition.

and scientific inquiry into the biology curriculum. In subsequent years, the books of major publishers would follow suit, but until the early 1960s when the BSCS programs entered the market, evolution and human reproduction were missing or vastly diluted in existing textbooks. The BSCS textbooks also placed biology in the context of inquiry, replacing the fact-based, cut-and-dried approach of earlier textbooks with actual investigative experiences in which students were stimulated to develop the techniques and thinking processes that lead to scientific discovery.

BSCS Matures: "Materials Alone Were Not Sufficient"

It became apparent early in the program of the BSCS that materials alone were not sufficient to change either methodology or content of biology courses substantially. Problems arose during trial use of the materials that required changes in them. Questions needed to be answered, teachers needed to be reoriented, administrators needed to be informed, and the forward motion needed to be sustained.

—William V. Mayer, BSCS Director, 1965–1982
BSCS Progress Report, 1969 (BSCS 2001, 33)

During the 1960s and 1970s, it became clear that BSCS would continue to be a key player in science curriculum improvement, which is integral to the fabric of biology education. BSCS completed revisions of the original three programs and expanded its curricular offerings to include a second course in high school biology (Biological Science: Interaction of Experiments and Ideas), a middle school program (Human Sciences), an elementary science program, curriculum materials for environmental studies, and several films and filmstrips for use in classrooms. In addition, the organization placed increasing emphasis on efforts to support biology teachers as they implemented new curriculum materials.

The science curriculum reform movement initiated by NSF in the late 1950s made it necessary for most science teachers to be updated in both science content and teaching pedagogy to maximize the potential of the new curriculum materials. In particular, teachers needed to understand inquiry-based instructional strategies so that their students could experience and learn scientific inquiry themselves. More and more feedback accumulated from teachers, students, educators, and scientists that demonstrated to BSCS that curriculum development per se was not sufficient to bring about the changes required to affect the secondary school curriculum in biology. Bill Mayer (Mayer 1978, 23), second director of BSCS, explained: "The concept of curriculum development without accompanying implementation could be compared to having a child and then leaving it on someone else's doorstep to rear. Although the child would have the necessary hereditary factors, the influence of the environment might diminish an excellence in heredity."

During a 15-year period following the funding of the curriculum studies, NSF established a variety of inservice science teacher education programs, of which the summer institutes were the most popular. BSCS worked with directors of these institutes to acquaint them with the goals of the BSCS programs, in particular the teaching strategies that would convey the inquiry design and spirit. In some cases, experienced teachers of BSCS materials were members of the institute instructional teams. In addition to the summer institutes, professional development at this time included the availability of area consultants for teachers who used BSCS materials in their classes. Each consultant was selected on the basis of his or her experience as a BSCS teacher or college biologist who had worked closely with BSCS. Although it was an informal organization of volunteers willing to help their fellow teachers, the area consultants program was sizable. Each state had at least one consultant. Dick Smith, an area consultant for eastern Pennsylvania, described how important the consultant program was: "People were calling all the time. They had no concept of what the word *inquiry* meant. Working with the great minds of science education totally changed my philosophy of teaching science" (BSCS 2001, 32).

During this time, BSCS also produced the first edition of *The Biology Teacher's Handbook*. Initially, the handbook featured a number of "Invitations to Enquiry," (see chapters 6 and 7 of this edition of the handbook) as well as discussions of material related to biology (for example, physics and biochemistry), the teaching of biology in high school classrooms, and the theoretical and practical aspects of the art of teaching. Grobman (1969, 265) reported that the handbook "has been found to be of unusual value by many teachers."

Although BSCS was founded as a project of AIBS, its original leaders and staff members recognized that it should be an ongoing organization to continue curriculum development for target groups beyond the average 10th-grade student and, especially, to continue the professional development necessary to implement BSCS programs for maximum impact. Thus, BSCS left the auspices of AIBS to become a center of the University of

Colorado in 1968. In 1971, BSCS was re-created as an independent, non-profit educational corporation.

BSCS Faces Challenges: "But Our Mission ... Remains the Same"

BSCS has a new address and several new people have joined the staff, but our mission—the development and testing of curriculum materials for the purpose of advancing scientific literacy and improving education in the sciences—remains the same as it has for more than a quarter of a century. Today, we continue to conduct basic research in the development of curriculum materials in various science areas and to produce model materials that will aid teachers in preparing students to live more productive and satisfying lives in the years to come.

—Jack Carter, BSCS Director, 1982–1985
BSCS Newsletter, October 1983 (Carter 1983)

In the early 1980s, the emphasis in science education moved from the strong discipline-based perspective of the curriculum reform movement to a perspective with greater emphasis on the connections between science and society. The publication of *A Nation at Risk* (NCEE 1983) reignited a mood of crisis regarding U.S. education. This report identified mathematics and science education as areas especially at risk. There was general support among science educators for continuing an inquiry approach to teaching science that emphasized the process of doing science alongside the products of science. But they also advocated greater emphasis on scientific literacy: the applications of science concepts in the daily lives of students who would be nonscientist citizens in the 21st century.

The 1980s, however, also signaled the gravest period in BSCS history. NSF's budget was cut dramatically with the result that NSF-sponsored education programs, including BSCS's, were left with one-third of the financing previously proposed. BSCS reduced its staff dramatically and moved its headquarters from Boulder, Colorado, to the campus of Colorado College in Colorado Springs. Despite this discouraging turn of events, the organization immediately began rebuilding itself and, by the late 1980s, had produced new programs to accommodate modern changes in the educational landscape and the findings of current scientific research. Such programs included ENLIST Micros for the use of computers in science education, three new programs in genetics (Basic Genetics: A Human Approach; Living with Cystic Fibrosis; and Genes and Surroundings), five modules for a program titled Innovations: The Social Consequences of Science and Technology, and an elementary curriculum called Science for Life and Living: Integrating Science Technology and Health.

BSCS also entered more formally into the arena of science education policy at this time. The organization hosted the annual meeting of the Commission for Biological Education of the International Union of Biological Sciences, a subgroup of the International Council of Scientific Unions that was concerned with research, development, and promotion of biology education. Biology educators from 15 countries, as well as science faculty from colleges and universities in Colorado, spent a week discussing mutual interests and common problems in science education. This meeting demonstrated BSCS's prestigious role in both the national and international scientific community.

BSCS Perseveres: "Education Done Well"

I often say that our role in science education is to make people uncomfortable with stasis. I want us to push people. … Science content will change, educational technology will change, and even the structure of schools may change. None of that, however, will change the fact that education done well can nurture a simple question germinating in the mind of a curious student until the question blossoms into an idea of sufficient substance to keep that student company for a lifetime.

—Joseph D. McInerney, BSCS Director, 1985–1999
BSCS 40th Anniversary Address, 1998 (BSCS 2001)

The "standards" era that began during the last decade of the 20th century was ushered in with the publication of *Science for All Americans* (Rutherford and Ahlgren 1990). The opening sentence of the book set the stage: "*Science for All Americans* consists of a set of recommendations on what understandings and ways of thinking are essential for all citizens in a world shaped by science and technology." This statement made it clear that science educators believed that an emphasis on society should remain in science curricula. Schools were slowly integrating computers into instruction, though the level of technology varied widely from school to school and the best use of this technology for learning was unclear. The Human Genome Project, initiated in 1990, was in full force and the speed and dramatic results of that project presaged dramatic impact on medicine, forensics, and ethics. It was clear that the students of the day must be armed with a fundamental, accurate understanding of biology (and other science) concepts as they moved into the 21st century. In the midst of these changes, BSCS remained steadfast in its vision of "education done well."

The authors of *Science for All Americans* also contended that some content and concepts are more critical than others, and that science educators needed to reach some consensus on what essential science knowledge is (Rutherford and Ahlgren 1990). During the 1990s, two groups developed sets of guidelines for the content that should be included in science courses. The American Association for the Advancement of Science (1993) published *Benchmarks for Science Literacy* and the National Research Council (1996) published the *National Science Education Standards*. Both organizations worked with large groups of scientists and science teachers. In a comparison of the two publications, Bybee (1997) estimated that there is about a 90% overlap between the two sets of recommendations. This remarkable consensus underscores the significance of the work of these publications. Their impact on science education initiatives at the end of the 20th century cannot be overemphasized, and they continue to influence science education today.

Beginning in the 1990s, all BSCS precollege curriculum materials were based on the national standards. In addition to reflecting national content standards, the organization's materials incorporated pedagogical strategies based on insights about learning that were emerging from the growing body of research in human cognition. BSCS conceived and designed the BSCS 5E Instructional Model under the leadership of Rodger W. Bybee, who was the associate director of BSCS at the time (Bybee et al. 2008). This instructional model was developed as an expansion of the Atkin and Karplus learning cycle (1962) and applied understanding about how people learn to instructional materials and practices. The BSCS 5E

Instructional Model calls for instruction that first *engages* students' interest and elicits their prior conceptions about the relevant concept. Students then *explore* the phenomenon through experiential activities such as laboratory or field investigations, readings, or modeling, and use those experiences to *explain* the phenomenon. Further experiential activities allow students to *elaborate* on their initial understanding and explanations, either by applying them to new contexts or extending and modifying their ideas. Finally, students *evaluate* their own understanding in a final project or experience. The model has proved to be amazingly robust and represents a major contribution of BSCS to science education. Writing in 2008, Bybee says, "One innovation that has been more successful than I ever could have imagined is the BSCS 5E Instructional Model. BSCS originally developed this instructional model in the late 1980s for use in its elementary science program Science for Life and Living and have included it in most programs since that time. However, the dissemination and success of the model far exceeds the development of BSCS programs or implementation in professional development institutes. The BSCS 5E Instructional Model is known internationally, is now included in state frameworks for science and other disciplines, has been adapted by other science programs, and is widely used in classroom practices." (6)

During the latter part of the 20th century, BSCS established a new practice for considering the launch of a new curriculum project. This practice was called a design study. A design study is a rigorous process of investigating the current status of an educational issue through a review of the literature and through primary research such as surveys and interviews.

BSCS conducted design studies for elementary science (New Designs for Elementary School Science and Health 1989), middle school science, and high school and introductory college biology (Developing Biological Literacy 1993), and produced full programs for each of these levels. Science for Life and Living, mentioned previously, was developed for elementary science and published in 1992; Middle School Science and Technology was published in 1994 for that level; *BSCS Biology: A Human Approach* was published in 1997 for the high school level; and *Biological Perspectives* was published in 1999 for introductory biology courses at the college level.[2]

BSCS continued leading the profession by introducing innovative topics into the high school science curriculum, such as a unit on genetic technology and a multimedia program to remedy inadequacies of high school earth science and biology instructional materials in the area of evolution.

---

[2] *Science for Life and Living* has been re-created as modular programs titled *BSCS Science TRACKS.* *BSCS Middle School Science and Technology* is now published as *BSCS Science and Technology.* All of the programs listed here are currently available in their third editions.

The organization also produced several modules based on the technologies and findings of the Human Genome Project.

BSCS continued its influence on science education policy. In 1988, the organization conducted a symposium called Curriculum Development for the Year 2000. Topics included a wider recognition of demographic changes entering the 21st century, the selection of content, contemporary research on teaching and learning, and educational technology. BSCS also began work on a series of policy statements on curriculum, in cooperation with the Network, Inc., a nonprofit organization in Massachusetts. This work assessed what is taught in elementary, middle, and high school science and made policy recommendations for improving the science curriculum. In 1989, BSCS entered into a collaboration with the Social Science Education Consortium to produce a policy-oriented document to develop a curriculum framework for integrating the history and nature of science and technology in school science and social studies programs.

In 1993, BSCS moved from the Colorado College campus to a new building in Colorado Springs, where it remains today. Innovation in the 1980s and 1990s had taken new forms, most notably in the direction of educational technology, genetics, policy formation, and an emphasis on creating a K–13 approach to scientific literacy in an increasingly complex world.

BSCS Shows the Way: "The Capacity for Leadership"

With more thorough analysis of BSCS' fifty-year history, other insights important for science education emerge. The success of organizations with guiding principles and the capacity for leadership in curriculum, professional development, and research and evaluation is evident in the leadership BSCS provides in science education. This type of leadership is very different and more fundamental than measuring the success through textbooks or workshops.

—Rodger W. Bybee, BSCS Director, 1999–2007
Measuring Our Success (BSCS 2008, 11)

If the end of the 20th century can be characterized as the "era of standards," the beginning of the 21st century marks the beginning of the "era of accountability." The No Child Left Behind Act (NCLB), signed into law on January 8, 2002, is the 21st-century iteration of the Elementary and Secondary Education Act of 1965 (U.S. Department of Education 2003). It represented an unprecedented increase in the level of federal involvement in education. Compliance with the law is mandatory for states to continue receiving federal funds for education. The NCLB legislation specifies that improvement in education for all students will occur by ensuring that every classroom teacher is highly qualified, by holding schools accountable for helping students meet achievement standards, and by requiring every school district to make adequate yearly progress in meeting achievement goals. Even while schools and states debate the criteria for "highly qualified" and "adequate yearly progress," the call for curriculum materials and instructional strategies of proven effectiveness, based on research evidence, goes out. As a curriculum study, BSCS was well placed to answer this call as it continued to study curriculum and develop materials and professional development that responded to the findings of its studies.

To emphasize the multiple roles that BSCS fulfills in leading biology education, in 2002 three centers were established within the organization: the Center for Curriculum Development, the Center for Professional Development, and the Center for Research and Evaluation. BSCS is clear that the centers do not represent a splintering of the organization's goals, but instead are an efficient mechanism for achieving BSCS's vision to (BSCS 2002, 5) "improve all students' understanding of science and technology by developing exemplary curricular materials, supporting their widespread and effective use, providing professional development, and conducting research and evaluation studies." Indeed, staff members move freely from one center to another and frequently serve in more than one center at a time.

In the curriculum development sphere, BSCS conducted two more design studies for high school science in the early 2000s: *Making Sense of Integrated Science* (BSCS 2000) for integrated and multidisciplinary science, and *The Cornerstone-to-Capstone Approach* (BSCS 2006) for the physics-chemistry-biology sequence for high school science. The former design study led to BSCS's most recent full program, *BSCS Science: An Inquiry Approach* (2008).

BSCS's Center for Professional Development developed, tested, and implemented the National Academy for Curriculum Leadership (NACL), beginning in 2000. The NACL focuses on preparing district-level science leaders to help science teachers identify the research-based curriculum materials that best accommodate their district's educational goals and to support district teachers in the inquiry approaches needed to implement these programs effectively (Bintz and Martin 2007).

The Center for Research and Evaluation continued evaluating field-test versions of BSCS materials and expanded its evaluation work by contracting with external, like-minded groups to conduct evaluation studies of their projects. BSCS also began two multiyear research studies in the early 2000s, to study the effectiveness of curriculum-based professional development and to examine the impact of fidelity of implementation on student achievement. The results of these studies are just beginning to emerge. They promise to contribute generally to the body of knowledge about the role of curriculum materials and professional development in teaching and student learning and specifically to the development of more-effective curriculum materials and teaching institutes.

BSCS Endures: "To Improve the Learning of Science for All Students"

Most people recognize the first half of our name, "biological sciences," and have some working idea of what this might be. The second half of our name, "curriculum study," is less often recognized. … A curriculum study studies the role of curriculum in schools. To study the role of curriculum, one must think about programs and instructional materials, professional development, research, and evaluation in an effort to improve the learning of science for all students. This is what BSCS has done for more than 50 years.

—Janet Carlson Powell, BSCS Director, 2007–present
Measuring Our Success (BSCS 2008)

At the present time, BSCS's emphasis on evidence-based curriculum materials and instructional practices continues, as does the focus on science for learners of all racial and ethnic backgrounds, socioeconomic groups, genders, and ability levels. International comparisons reveal the relatively poor state of U.S. students' science knowledge, and the cry is to increase the focus, rigor, and coherence of U.S. science education.

It is in this climate that BSCS endures, continuing to study the role of curriculum in teaching and learning, identifying the characteristics of the most effective curriculum materials and professional development, infusing those characteristics into the programs BSCS develops, and supporting teachers as they enhance science learning for all students.

Chapter 19

A BSCS Perspective on Contemporary Biology Education

Biology teachers have many and varied issues to attend to in their class-rooms. For example, high school students will hear about such issues as obesity, human reproduction, stem cell research, climate change, resource management, and environmental problems. How should biology teachers respond to concerns about these issues? On the perennial issue of biological evolution, some groups, unfortunately, will continue fighting for includ-ing nonscientific views in biological perspectives. Many biology teachers understand that teaching about evolution and other scientific issues is a professional obligation.

We also have to ask, "Are students ready to study such issues?" Do they understand the basic concepts of biology and the fundamental processes of science well enough to engage in these and other biology-related issues? We think the answer to these questions is *no*! Our view sets the stage for the organization and the discussion in chapter 19.[1]

This chapter arises from an opportunity to pause and reflect on biology education in the past (Hurd et al. 1980; Mayer 1986; Rosenthal and Bybee 1987) and what it will be in the immediate future. In the 20th century, progress in biology far surpassed our capacity to reform biology education. This disparity stands as a remarkable contrast. When we began thinking about this chapter, our first inclination was to establish themes such as revolutions in biology and education, the frontier of biology and biology education, or biology in the 21st century and the implications for educa-tion. We decided against such themes. Rather, we selected themes that seemed basic to biology education. In the following sections, we address four themes: (1) implementation of fundamental biological ideas, (2) basic scientific thinking, (3) social contexts for biology and teaching, and (4) biology education and the scientifically literate citizen.

Fundamental Ideas for Biology Education

If we examine only the scientific advances of the past 100 years, we get a sense of several major ideas that help us explain the natural world. One example is discovering the *structure of DNA*. In other cases, we see an understanding of major ideas, such as the *germ theory of disease* applied to a contemporary problem, such as the *discovery of penicillin* or the *identifica-tion of the virus that causes AIDS*. It is tempting to begin any discussion of contemporary biology education with recent advances in the life and health sciences. What domains of research are at the frontiers of biology? Such a question has a ring of relevance and reasonableness. Shouldn't students understand recent scientific advances? The answer is a qualified yes. But

---

[1]Portions of chapter 19 are adapted from an earlier essay: Bybee, R. W. 2002. Biology education in the United States: The unfinished century. *Bioscience* 52 (7) (July): 560–567.

research on student understanding and learning counsels us toward developing in students a deep conceptual framework for the discipline before teaching the complex, and often abstract, knowledge needed to understand the frontiers of a science discipline such as biology.

Contemporary biology consists of a vast body of knowledge ranging from an understanding of molecules to an understanding of the biosphere. The details of any scientific discipline sometimes stagger the minds of scientists, not to mention students. Thus, a first step in teaching the basic biological ideas in a school curriculum is to acknowledge the fact that educators do not have to include all biological knowledge. A second step is to recognize that school science does not have to address the frontiers or cutting-edge advances in science. Frontiers and advances, after all, are based on and are elaborations of major scientific ideas that guide inquiry. If students do not understand the basic ideas, they may, at best, memorize the knowledge associated with frontiers but it will have little or no meaning. The third step is to teach the biology content you select with an enthusiasm that you communicate to your students. Students who understand why biology is worth becoming excited about are more likely to follow the advances in the discipline as they appear in the popular media. The fourth step is to accept that, regardless of what is suggested as basic ideas for the school science curriculum, there will be criticism for not including other ideas.

Capturing the basic spirit of biology requires educators to provide students with opportunities to learn a set of major ideas. These ideas, in turn, will help students learn to explain the natural world. Proposing that the school curriculum emphasize major scientific ideas is not new or unique (NSTA 1964; Rutherford and Ahlgren 1989; DeBoer 1991). Table 19.1 reviews biological ideas in the *National Science Education Standards* (NRC 1996), *Benchmarks for Science Literacy* (AAAS 1993), and *Developing Biological Literacy* (BSCS 1993).

Two other works that have influenced our thinking at BSCS include *Fulfilling the Promise: Biology Education in the Nation's Schools* (NRC 1990) and John A. Moore's great contributions to our understanding of major ideas in biology through his series *Science as a Way of Knowing* (Moore 1983, 1984, 1985, 1986, 1987, 1988).

Basic Scientific Thinking

A contemporary perspective on biology education includes the procedures and processes of science that represent basic scientific thinking, usually referred to as scientific inquiry. Including scientific inquiry in biology education helps young people develop the abilities of inquiry as well as

Table 19.1		Major Ideas for the Biology Curriculum
National Science Education Standards (NRC 1996) Life Science, Grades 9–12	**Benchmarks for Science Literacy (AAAS 1993) The Living Environment The Human Organisms**	**Developing Biological Literacy (BSCS 1993)**
The Cell	Cells (The Living Environment)	Energy, Matter, and Organization
Molecular Basis of Heredity	Heredity (The Living Environment)	Genetic Continuity and Reproduction
Matter, Energy, and Organization in Living Systems	Flow of Matter and Energy (The Living Environment)	Energy, Matter, and Organization
Behavior of Organisms	Learning (The Human Organism)	Maintenance of a Dynamic Equilibrium
Biological Evolution	Evolution of Life (The Living Environment) Diversity of Life (The Living Environment)	Evolution: Patterns and Products of Change
Interdependence of Organisms	Interdependence of Life (The Living Environment)	Interaction and Interdependence
The Cell	Human Development (The Human Organism)	Growth, Development, and Differentiation

Sources: National Research Council. 1996. *National Science Education Standards*. Washington, DC: National Academy Press; American Association for the Advancement of Science (AAAS). 1993. *Benchmarks for science literacy*. Washington, DC: AAAS; Biological Sciences Curriculum Study. 1993. *Developing biological literacy: A guide to developing secondary and post-secondary biology education*. Dubuque, IA: Kendall/Hunt.

understandings about inquiry. Based on their investigations, students can develop the thinking and reasoning abilities that characterize the process by which biologists' claims result in new knowledge. Classroom experiences with scientific inquiry provide insights into science, help students differentiate science from other ways of knowing, and reinforce practical abilities, such as critical thinking and communicating.

Table 19.2 summarizes the abilities that define scientific inquiry, and table 19.3 summarizes the understandings of scientific inquiry for grades

9 through 12 from the *National Science Education Standards* (NRC 1996). These Standards and their implications are elaborated on in the volume *Inquiry and the National Science Education Standards: A Guide for Teaching and Learning* (NRC 2000). Helping students form these abilities and understandings should be based on a variety of laboratories, investigations, and field experiences that are a part of biology education. With inquiry-based activities, students can develop an appreciation for the difficulties of designing an investigation; the hurdles of obtaining accurate, valid, and reliable data; the challenges of establishing cause-and-effect relationships; and the intellectual struggles of using evidence to form explanations.

Table 19.2	Abilities of Inquiry, Grades 9–12

- Identify questions and concepts that guide scientific investigations.
- Design and conduct scientific investigations.
- Use technology … to improve investigations and communications.
- Formulate and revise scientific explanations and models using logic and evidence.
- Recognize and analyze alternative explanations and models.
- Communicate and defend a scientific argument.

Source: National Research Council. 1996. *National Science Education Standards.* Washington, DC: National Academy Press.

Table 19.3	Understandings of Inquiry, Grades 9–12

- Scientists usually inquire how physical, living, or designed systems function.
- Scientists conduct investigations for a wide variety of reasons.
- Scientists rely on technology to enhance the gathering and manipulation of data.
- Mathematics is essential in scientific inquiry.
- Scientific explanations must adhere to criteria such as: a proposed explanation must be logically consistent; it must abide by the rules of evidence; it must be open to questions and possible modification; and it must be based on historical and current scientific knowledge.
- Results of scientific inquiry—new knowledge and methods—emerge from different types of investigations and public communication among scientists.

Source: National Research Council. 1996. *National Science Education Standards.* Washington, DC: National Academy Press.

Hands-on activities are an essential strategy for helping your students develop the abilities and understandings of scientific inquiry, but other approaches may be required for them to develop a full appreciation of inquiry. Historical case studies and contemporary examples of some of the basic scientific ideas can point out the subtle variety and challenges of scientific inquiry. Excellent examples and cases include narrative stories about the discovery of DNA structure, Alexander Fleming's discovery of penicillin, the cloning of Dolly, the effectiveness of Jonas Salk's polio vaccine, the dynamics of epidemics, and the health hazards of smoking. The Beyond Discovery series produced by the National Academy of Sciences (NAS 2003) is a collection of articles, each with a story line that shows how basic scientific research can lead to human benefits that were not anticipated when the research was conducted. The series includes titles such as "Human Gene Testing," "Disarming a Deadly Virus: Proteases and Their Inhibitors," and "Designer Seeds." They are available on the NAS website *(www.beyonddiscovery.org)*. Such stories present the human dimensions of scientific inquiry; the role of technology; and the ethical, legal, and social implications of discovery that students may not gain in other classroom activities.

Social Contexts for Biology and Teaching

Many news stories show the generally positive effects of science on society, especially in terms of biology and health issues. For example, one news event in the 20th century symbolizes society's initial awareness of environmental problems and the human influence on those problems. That is Rachel Carson's *Silent Spring* (1962), a book that stirred a controversy at the time. From the longer view of history, its basic argument about our environment has been sustained.

There stands a great paradox in this story of science and technology as the means of nurturing greater cultural harmony. On the one hand, science and technology contribute to human understanding and adaptation and to increased social harmony. On the other hand, there are science- and technology-related problems that could result in irreversible damage to the environment, depletion of natural resources, and unthinkable destruction to human populations. The threats associated with changes in Earth systems require an understanding of science and technology and the global issues common to all people, in both developing and developed nations.

Even though newsworthy items with negative implications, such as problems with DDT, ozone depletion, changes in rates of species extinction, or global climate change, are balanced by items with positive implications, such as better understanding of the human genome and advances in health sciences, the public perception of science and technology remains mixed. In addition, the level of scientific literacy is lower than needed for democratic participation (Miller 1983, 1996, 1997, 2000). Given the prominence of science and technology in today's world, sustaining a democracy requires a public that has some understanding of science and technology in personal and social contexts.

The national standards (NRC 1996) include a framework for considering how to incorporate current issues into the biology curriculum in a manner that creates coherence. The standards suggest organizing specific issues into these categories: health; population growth; natural resources; environmental quality; natural and human-induced hazards; and science and technology in local, national, and global perspectives.

If the past century provides any indication of what we will confront in the 21st century, science and society issues will continue to be in the headlines and very likely more often. Individuals and societies will have to decide on many issues involving scientific research and technological innovations. These decisions will not be easy. They clearly involve basic scientific and technological concepts, but such concepts are often presented in contexts in which the issues, much less the solutions, are not clear. Often, individuals harbor the misconception that science can tell us what should happen. A basic education in biology must extend beyond the introduction of concepts and help students realize the limits of science and technology in interpreting global issues. Decisions about major issues, such as global climate change, infectious diseases, extinction of species, or bioterrorism, involve the assessment of alternatives, risks, costs, and benefits. Further, and very important, students should have the experience of considering who benefits and who suffers, who pays and who gains, and what the perceived and actual risks are and who will bear those risks. In reviewing any science issue relevant to the subjects of health, population, resources, environments, and hazards, students will benefit from asking and answering a number of basic questions. What is the evidence? How reliable is the information? Based on the information, what are the predictions about what might happen? What are the odds of it happening? How do scientists and engineers know what will happen?

Biology Education and the Scientifically Literate Citizen

Science classrooms can be instrumental in shaping future citizens' understanding of the role of civil discourse in the United States. The context of science provides the opportunity to model the essential place of facts, data, and evidence in scientific arguments. One basic connection between science and civil discourse centers on the importance of facts and evidence—rather than personal opinions or political authority—in dialogue, debate, and publications. Personal opinions provide the basis of many debates, which some authors now have labeled as the *argument culture* and the *culture of complaint* (Hughes 1993). These social critics wrote that, in many instances, the United States has gone too far. More than 15 years ago, the late Arthur Schlesinger (1992) pointed out that we have gone to the point of "disuniting our society." For too many, the basis for debate is the expression and unconditional acceptance of one view and the declaration that any other view is, by definition, unacceptable. This perspective of only one view, only one truth, based on political power rather than facts, data, and evidence runs counter to a free society in which scientific findings have a role in putting opinions to rest. For biology teachers, this is best exemplified in the continuing conflicts that center on teaching about biological evolution.

A vibrant and productive society requires disagreement and resolution of those disagreements through deliberation and attention to scientific evidence that has met the rigor of the peer-review process. Individuals and our legislators must debate to decide, and they must decide to form public policy. Civil dialogue assumes that individuals know and appeal to facts as opposed to opinions. In biology, there may be several alternative explanations for a particular phenomenon, but the explanation with several independent lines of research and the most supporting evidence should carry the day. Through their experiences in an inquiry-oriented biology program, students should begin to develop the skills and abilities required for civil discourse on the scientific dimensions of global issues, in a process that provides them with valuable experiences that can support the ideals upon which the United States is based.

An education in biology also must recognize the values and ideals that underlie the scientific enterprise. Advances of scientific knowledge are guided by values, such as respect for evidence, openness to skeptical review, and public disclosure of research methods and procedures. Values such as these make the enterprise work; they are values that most biologists have internalized as part of the process of doing science. In *Science and Human Values*, Jacob Bronowski (1965, 68) expressed this view when he wrote:

> The society of scientists is simple because it has a directing purpose: to explore the truth. Nevertheless, it has to solve the problem of every society, which is to find a compromise between [the individual and the masses]. It must encourage the single scientists to be independent,

and the body of scientists to be tolerant. From these
basic conditions, which form the prime values, there
follows step by step a range of values: dissent, freedom of
thought and speech, justice, honor, human dignity, and
self-respect. Science has humanized our values. [People]
have asked for freedom, justice, and respect precisely as
the scientific spirit has spread among them.

For biology teachers, their teaching of the basics of biology also
should introduce students to the tolerance and empiricism of science as
they engage in debates and dialogue about societal issues that include
scientific evidence. In the midst of these debates, biology teachers can
introduce the scientific spirit of skeptical review, always with an appeal
to evidence that will temper the two sides and focus the discussion on
constructive resolutions.

A leading news story of the 20th century, the U.S. use of nuclear weap-
ons, provided the context for Jacob Bronowski's insights about science and
human values. Bronowski struggled with questions engaged by reviewing
the ruins of Nagasaki: "Has science left society with a means of destruction
that it can neither undo nor master?" "Has science numbed our sense of
values?" He concluded that science has not left society with values that are
at odds with the survival values of humankind. In fact, it is the opposite. In
light of the aforementioned culture of argument and complaint and concerns about the environment, natural resources, and human populations,
this great scientist and philosopher noted:

> The dilemma of today is not that the human values
> cannot control a mechanical science. It is the other
> way about: the scientific spirit is more human than the
> machinery of governments. We have not let either the
> tolerance or empiricism of science enter the parochial
> rules by which we still try to prescribe the behavior
> of nations. Our conduct as states clings to a code of
> self-interest which science, like humanity, has long left
> behind. (Bronowski 1965, 70)

Conclusion

In this chapter, we developed themes addressing the topic of biology education in the United States. We advocate that you express the nature of
science in terms of scientific inquiry, keep inquiry central to your classroom, and use a curriculum framework based on key biological concepts to

incorporate current issues into your teaching. Doing all of this will provide a classroom culture that encourages all students to learn and allows you to promote civil discourse and a free society.

RESOURCES

In addition to the literature cited in the references, we recommend the following resources:

Bloom, M. 2001. Molecular biology and technology. *The American Biology Teacher* 63 (8): 557–560.

Bransford, J., A. Brown, and R. Cocking. 1999. *How people learn: Brain, mind, experience, and school.* Washington, DC: National Academy Press.

Bybee, R. W., et al. 1990. *Science and technology education for the middle years: Frameworks for curriculum and instruction.* Washington, DC: National Center for Improving Science Education.

Duschl. R., H. Schweingruber, and A. Shouse, eds. 2007. *Taking science to school: Learning and teaching science in grades K–8.* Washington, DC: National Academy Press.

Fensham, P. J. 1992. Science and technology. In *Handbook of research on curriculum,* ed. P. W. Jackson, 789–829. New York: Macmillan.

International Technology Education Association (ITEA). 2002. *Gallup report.* Blacksburg, VA: ITEA.

Michaels, S., A. Shouse, and H. Schweingruber. 2008. *Ready, set, science! Putting research to work in K–8 science classrooms.* Washington, DC: National Academy Press.

Tannen, D. 1998. *The argument culture: Moving from debate to dialogue.* New York: Random House.

Uno, G. E., and R. W. Bybee. 1994. Understanding the dimensions of biological literacy. *BioScience* 44 (8): 553–557.

SECTION V REFERENCES

American Association for the Advancement of Science (AAAS). 1993. *Benchmarks for science literacy.* Washington, DC: AAAS.

Atkin, J. M., and R. Karplus. 1962. Discovery of invention? *Science Teacher* 29 (5): 45.

Bintz, J., and G. Martin. 2007. The BSCS national academy for curriculum leadership. *The Natural Selection* (Spring): 13–23.

Bronowski, J. 1965. *Science and human values.* New York: Harper and Row.

BSCS. 1993. *Developing biological literacy: A guide to developing secondary and post-secondary biology education.* Dubuque, IA: Kendall/Hunt.

———. 1999. *Biological perspectives.* Dubuque, IA: Kendall/Hunt.

———. 2000. *Making sense of integrated science: A guide for high schools.* Colorado Springs, CO: BSCS.

———. 2001. *The BSCS story: A history of the Biological Sciences Curriculum Study.* Colorado Springs, CO: BSCS.

———. 2002. *BSCS 2008.* Colorado Springs, CO: BSCS.

———. 2006. *BSCS biology: An ecological approach,* 10th ed. Dubuque, IA: Kendall/Hunt.

———. 2006. *BSCS biology: A human approach,* 3rd ed. Dubuque, IA: Kendall/Hunt.

———. 2006. *BSCS science: An inquiry approach.* Dubuque, IA: Kendall/Hunt.

———. 2006. *BSCS biology: A molecular approach,* 9th ed. New York: Glencoe/McGraw–Hill.

———. 2006. *The cornerstone-to-capstone approach: Creating coherence in high school science.* Colorado Springs, CO: BSCS.

Bybee, R. W. 1997. *Achieving scientific literacy: From purposes to practices.* Portsmouth, NH: Heinemann.

———. 2002. Biology education in the United States: The unfinished century. *Bioscience* 52 (7): 560–567.

———. 2008. Measuring our success: An introduction. In *Measuring our success: The first 50 years of BSCS,* BSCS, 1–11. Dubuque, IA: Kendall/Hunt.

Bybee, R. W., J. A. Taylor, A. L. Gardner, P. Van Scotter, J. C. Powell, A. Westbrook, and N. Landes. 2008. The BSCS 5E instructional model: Origins and effectiveness. In *Measuring our success: The first 50 years of BSCS,* BSCS, 113–83. Dubuque, IA: Kendall/Hunt.

Carson, R. 1962. *Silent spring.* Boston: Houghton-Mifflin.

Carter, J. L. 1983. BSCS today. *BSCS* 83 (October): 1.

DeBoer, G. 1991. *A history of ideas in science education.* New York: Teachers College Press.

Grobman, A. B. 1969. *The changing classroom: The role of the Biological Sciences Curriculum Study.* Garden City, NY: Doubleday.

Hughes, R. 1993. *Culture of complaint: The fraying of America.* New York: Oxford University Press.

Hurd, P. D., R. W. Bybee, J. Kahle, and R. Yager. 1980. Biology education in secondary schools of the United States. *American Biology Teacher* 42: 388–410.

Mayer, W. V. 1986. Biology education in the United States during the twentieth century. *Quarterly Review of Biology* 61: 481–507.

Mayer, W. V., ed. 1978. *BSCS biology teachers handbook.* New York: John Wiley and Sons.

Miller, J. D. 1983. *The American people and science policy: The role of public attitudes in the policy process.* New York: Pergamon.

———. 1996. Scientific literacy for effective citizenship. In *Science, technology and society as reform in science education,* ed. R. E. Yager, 185–204. New York: State University of New York Press.

———. 1997. Civic scientific literacy in the United States: A developmental analysis from middle-school through adulthood. In *Scientific literacy*, eds. W. Graber and C. Bolte. Kiel, Germany: University of Kiel, Institute for Science Education.

———. 2000. The development of civic scientific literacy in the United States. In *Science, technology, and society: A sourcebook on research and practice*, eds. D. D. Kumar and D. Chubin, 21–48. New York: Kluwer Academic / Plenum.

Moore, J. A. 1983. *Evolutionary biology*. Vol. 1 of *Science as a way of knowing*. Baltimore: American Society of Zoologists.

———. 1984. *Human ecology*. Vol. 2 of *Science as a way of knowing*. Baltimore: American Society of Zoologists.

———. 1985. *Genetics*. Vol. 3 of *Science as a way of knowing*. Baltimore: American Society of Zoologists.

———. 1986. *Developmental biology*. Vol. 4 of *Science as a way of knowing*. Baltimore: American Society of Zoologists.

———. 1987. *Form and function*. Vol. 5 of *Science as a way of knowing*. Baltimore: American Society of Zoologists.

———. 1988. *Cell and molecular biology*. Vol. 6 of *Science as a way of knowing*. Baltimore: American Society of Zoologists.

National Academy of Sciences (NAS). 2003. Beyond discovery: The path from research to human benefit. *www.beyonddiscovery.org*.

National Commission on Excellence in Education (NCEE). 1983. *A nation at risk: The Imperative for Educational Reform*. Washington, DC: U.S. Department of Education.

National Research Council (NRC). 1990. *Fulfilling the promise: Biology education in the nation's schools*. Washington, DC: National Academy Press.

———. 1996. *National Science Education Standards*. Washington, DC: National Academy Press.

———. 2000. *Inquiry and the National Science Education Standards: A guide for teaching and learning*. Washington, DC: National Academy Press.

National Science Teachers Association (NSTA). 1964. *Theory into action*. Washington, DC: NSTA.

Rosenthal, D. B., and R. W. Bybee. 1987. Emergence of the biology curriculum: A science of life or a science of living? In *The formation of the school subjects: The struggle for creating an American institution*, ed. T. S. Popkewitz, 123–144. London: Falmer Press.

Rutherford, F. J., and A. Ahlgren. 1989. *Science for all Americans: A Project 2061 report*. Washington, DC: American Association for the Advancement of Science.

———. 1990. *Science for all Americans*. New York: Oxford University Press.

Schlesinger, A. M. 1992. *The disuniting of America*. New York: W.W. Norton.

U.S. Department of Education, Office of Vocational and Adult Education. 2003. *The high school leadership summit*. Washington, DC: U.S. Department of Education.

Appendixes

313

Appendix A: National Science Education Standards for 9–12 Life Science

The *National Science Education Standards* presents a vision for scientifically literate citizens. It outlines standards for science teaching, professional development for teachers of science, assessment in science education, science content, science education programs, and science education systems. In appendix A, we list the science content standards most relevant for the high school biology course: the grades 9–12 standards for science as inquiry, life science, and history and nature of science. For full elaboration of these content standards, as well as additional content standards and standards for teaching, professional development, assessment, and science education programs and systems, see National Research Council. 1996. *National science education standards.* Washington, DC: National Academy Press.

Standard A: Science as Inquiry

Abilities Necessary to Do Scientific Inquiry
- Identify questions and concepts that guide scientific investigations.
- Design and conduct scientific investigations.
- Use technology and mathematics to improve investigations and communications.
- Formulate and revise scientific explanations and models using logic and evidence.
- Recognize and analyze alternative explanations and models.
- Communicate and defend a scientific argument.

Understandings About Scientific Inquiry
- Scientists usually inquire about how physical, living, or designed systems function.
- Scientists conduct investigations for a wide variety of reasons.
- Scientists rely on technology to enhance the gathering and manipulations of data.
- Mathematics is essential in scientific inquiry.
- Scientific explanations must adhere to criteria such as: a proposed

explanation must be logically consistent; it must abide by the rules of evidence; it must be open to questions and possible modification; and it must be based on historical and current scientific knowledge.

- Results of scientific inquiry—knowledge and methods—emerge from different types of investigations and public communication among scientists.

Standard C: Life Science

The Cell
- Cells have particular structures that underlie their functions.
- Most cell functions involve chemical reactions.
- Cells store and use information to guide their functions.
- Cell functions are regulated.
- Plant cells contain chloroplasts, the site of photosynthesis.
- Cells can differentiate, and complex multicellular organisms are formed as a highly organized arrangement of differentiated cells.

The Molecular Basis of Heredity
- In all organisms, the instructions for specifying the characteristics of the organism are carried in DNA.
- Most of the cells in a human contain two copies of each of 22 different chromosomes. In addition, there is a pair of chromosomes that determines sex: [XX (female) and XY (male)].
- Changes in DNA (mutations) occur spontaneously at low rates.

Biological Evolution
- Species evolve over time.
- The great diversity of organisms is the result of more than 3.5 billion years of evolution that has filled every available niche with life forms.
- Natural selection and its evolutionary consequences provide a scientific explanation for the fossil record of ancient life forms, as well as for the striking molecular similarities observed among the diverse species of living organisms.
- The millions of different species of plants, animals, and microorganisms that live on earth today are related by descent from common ancestors.
- Biological classifications are based on how organisms are related.

The Interdependence of Organisms

- The atoms and molecules on the earth cycle among the living and nonliving components of the biosphere.
- Energy flows through ecosystems in one direction, from photosynthetic organisms to herbivores to carnivores and decomposers.
- Organisms both cooperate and compete in ecosystems. Interrelationships and interdependencies of these organisms may generate ecosystems that are stable for hundreds or thousands of years.
- Living organisms have the capacity to produce populations of infinite size, but environments and resources are finite.
- Human beings live within the world's ecosystems [and modify them] as a result of population growth, technology, and consumption.

Matter, Energy, and Organization in Living Systems

- [Because] all matter tends toward more disorganized states, living systems require a continuous input of energy to maintain their chemical and physical organizations.
- The energy for life primarily derives from the Sun [plants capture the Sun's energy and use it to form covalent bonds between the atoms of organic molecules].
- The chemical bonds of food molecules contain energy.
- The complexity and organization of organisms accommodate the need for obtaining, transforming, transporting, releasing, and eliminating the matter and energy used to sustain the organism.
- The distribution and abundance of organisms and populations in ecosystems are limited by the availability of matter and energy and the ability of the ecosystem to recycle materials.
- As matter and energy flows through different levels of organization of living systems—cells, organs, organisms, communities—and between living systems and the physical environment, chemical elements are recombined in different ways [resulting] in storage and dissipation of energy into the environment as heat.

The Behavior of Organisms

- Multicellular animals have nervous systems that generate behavior.
- Organisms have behavioral responses to internal changes and to external stimuli.
- Like other aspects of an organism's biology, behaviors have evolved through natural selection.
- Behavioral biology has implications for humans, as it provides links to psychology, sociology, and anthropology.

Standard G: History and Nature of Science

Science as a Human Endeavor
- Individuals and teams have contributed and will continue to contribute to the scientific enterprise.
- Scientists have ethical traditions [demonstrated by the value they place on] peer review, truthful reporting about the methods and outcomes of investigations, and making public the results of work.
- Scientists are influenced by societal, cultural, and personal beliefs and ways of viewing the world.

Nature of Scientific Knowledge
- Science distinguishes itself from other ways of knowing and from other bodies of knowledge through the use of empirical standards, logical arguments, and skepticism.
- Scientific explanations must meet certain criteria [such as they must be consistent with experimental and observational evidence about nature, make accurate predictions about systems being studied], be logical, respect the rules of evidence, be open to criticism, report methods and procedures, and make knowledge public.
- Because all scientific ideas depend on experimental and observational confirmation, all scientific knowledge is … subject to change as new evidence becomes available.

Historical Perspectives
- In history, diverse cultures have contributed scientific knowledge and technologic inventions.
- Usually, changes in science occur as small modifications in extant knowledge.
- Occasionally, there are advances in science and technology that have important and long-lasting effects on science and society. Examples relevant to biology include … biological evolution; germ theory; … molecular biology; … medical and health technology.
- The historical perspective of scientific explanations demonstrates how scientific knowledge changes by evolving over time, almost always building on earlier knowledge.

Appendix B: Common Solutions for the High School Biology Laboratory

Solutions and Media

Agar, Plain

Purchase ready made or

1. Add 15 g agar (nonnutrient) to enough distilled water to make 1 L solution.
2. Mix and autoclave or pressure-cook at 15 psi for 15 minutes.
3. Cool to 60°C before pouring; allow 20–25 mL per plate.

Agar, Nutrient

Purchase ready made or

1. Dissolve 23 g nutrient agar in 1 L warm water.
2. Autoclave or pressure-cook at 15 psi for 15 minutes.
3. Cool to 60°C before pouring; allow 20–25 mL per plate.

Agar, Phenolphthalein

Purchase ready made or

1. Mix 30 g plain agar per liter distilled water and bring to a boil while stirring constantly.
2. Let the mixture cool, but before it solidifies stir in 1 g phenolphthalein powder per liter water used.
3. If the mixture is pink, add a few drops of dilute (0.1 M) hydrochloric acid (HCl) until the pink disappears.
4. Pour mixture into a flat-bottomed pan to a depth of a little over 3 cm.
5. When the agar has solidified, cut into blocks 3 × 3 × 6 cm.

Agar, Starch

Purchase ready made or

1. Add 15 g plain agar and 10 g soluble starch to enough distilled water to make 1 L solution.
2. Mix and autoclave or pressure-cook at 15 psi for 15 minutes.
3. Cool to 60°C before pouring; allow 20–25 mL per plate.

Agar, Yeast Growth Medium (YED)

Purchase ready made or
1. In a dry, 1 L flask, combine 5 g Difco bacto-yeast extract, 10 g anhydrous dextrose (glucose), and 10 g Difco bacto-agar.
2. Measure 500 mL distilled water.
3. Pour about one-fourth of the measured water into the dry ingredients and swirl briskly to moisten.
4. Add the rest of the water by pouring it against the inside of the container to wash down any ingredients stuck to the sides.
5. Cover loosely with a beaker or foil.
6. Autoclave or pressure-cook at 15 psi for 15 minutes.
7. When the pressure returns to normal, remove the flasks and immediately swirl vigorously to mix.
8. Cool to 60°C before pouring (about 30 minutes).
9. Allow 20–25 mL per plate.

Benedict's Solution

Purchase ready made or
1. Dissolve 173 g sodium citrate and 100 g anhydrous sodium carbonate (Na_2CO_3) in 800 mL distilled water.
2. Filter and dilute to 850 mL.
3. Dissolve 17.3 g crystalline copper sulfate ($CuSO_4$) in 100 mL distilled water.
4. Pour the $CuSO_4$ solution into the carbonate citrate solution, stir, and add enough water to make 1 L.

Biuret Solution

Purchase ready made or
1. Dissolve 3 g copper sulfate ($CuSO_4$) in 100 mL distilled water.
2. Slowly add 25 mL of this 3% solution to 1,000 mL 10% sodium hydroxide (NaOH) solution, while stirring constantly.
3. Label "CAUTION: Irritant."

Bromothymol Blue

Purchase ready made or
1. Prepare a 0.1% stock solution by dissolving 0.5 g bromothymol blue in 500 mL distilled water.
2. Add a trace of ammonium hydroxide (NH_4OH) to turn the solution a deep blue.
3. Test the solution by breathing through a soda straw into a test tube containing a small quantity of solution, until a yellow floor is produced.
4. If it is too alkaline, add a drop of extremely dilute hydrochloric acid (HCl).

Buffer Solution, pH 5, 6, 7, and 8

1. Dissolve 17.96 g sodium phosphate dibasic ($Na_2HPO_4 \cdot 7H_2O$) in distilled water in a volumetric flask and fill to the 1,000 mL mark.
2. Dissolve 9.07 monopotassium phosphate (KH_2PO_4) in distilled water in a volumetric flask and fill to the 1,000 mL mark.
3. Combine these solutions as shown in table B.1.

Table B.1   Preparation of Buffer Solutions

pH of Solution	mL of $Na_2HPO_4 \cdot 7H_2O$	mL KH_2PO_4
5	1	99
6	20	80
7	60	40
8	95	5

Catalase Solution (Homogenates)

In a household blender, blend 10 g liver or potato in 100 mL distilled water.

Gelatin, Suspension—2% and 10%

2%

1. Mix 2 g dry gelatin in enough distilled water to make 100 mL.
2. Heat to suspend; do not boil.
3. Store in refrigerator if it is to be kept more than a few hours.

10%

1. Mix 1 g dry gelatin in 10 mL distilled water.
2. Heat to suspend; do not boil.
3. Store in refrigerator if it is to be kept more than a few hours.

Hydrogen Peroxide

Purchase % needed, ready made.
   Must be fresh.

Lugol's Iodine Solution

Purchase ready made or

1. Dissolve 10 g potassium iodine (KI) in 100 mL distilled water.

2. To this solution, add 5 g iodine crystals.
3. Dilute 1:5 with distilled water.
4. Label "WARNING: Poison if ingested; irritant."

pH Solutions

PH 7
Use distilled water that has been boiled to drive off the carbon dioxide.

PH 6
1. Start with 1,500 mL distilled water.
2. Add small amounts of dilute hydrochloric acid (HCl; 0.2 M) to the water, checking the pH (with a pH meter or narrow-range pH paper) until a pH of 6 is reached.
3. Pour off 300 mL for the pH 6 solution.

PH 5
1. Continue to add dilute HCl until a pH of 5 is reached.
2. Pour off 300 mL for the pH 5 solution.
3. Continue to do this until you have reached the pH 2 solution.
4. Keep tightly stoppered.
5. Label "CAUTION: Irritant."

Potassium Hydroxide Solution, 10%
1. Place 100 g potassium hydroxide (KOH) pellets in a 1 L flask and slowly add 500 mL distilled water, constantly swirling until dissolved.
2. Add enough distilled water to bring the volume to 1,000 mL.
3. Label "WARNING: Corrosive liquid."

Salt Solutions

1%
Dissolve 1 g sodium chloride (NaCl) in enough distilled water to make 100 mL solution.

2%
Dissolve 2 g NaCl in enough distilled water to make 100 mL solution.

3%
Dissolve 3 g NaCl in enough distilled water to make 100 mL solution.

5%
Dissolve 5 g NaCl in enough distilled water to make 100 mL solution.

Silver Nitrate Solution, 1%

Purchase ready made or
1. Dissolve 1 g silver nitrate ($AgNO_3$) in enough distilled water to make 100 mL solution.
2. Label "CAUTION: Irritant."

Sodium Bicarbonate Solution

To prepare 1 M solution used to neutralize hydrochloric acid (HCl) solutions, dissolve 84 g sodium bicarbonate ($NaHCO_3$) in 500 mL distilled water in a volumetric flask and fill to the 1,000 mL mark.

Sodium Hydroxide Solution, 0.1 M

Purchase ready made or
1. Place 4 g sodium hydroxide (NaOH) pellets in a 1 L flask and slowly add 500 mL distilled water, constantly swirling until dissolved.
2. Add enough distilled water to bring the volume to 1,000 mL.

Starch Suspension—5% and 10%

5%

Dissolve 5 g soluble starch in enough distilled water to make 100 mL solution.

10%
1. Dissolve 10 g soluble starch in enough distilled water to make 100 mL solution. Laundry starch or cornstarch may be substituted.
2. Filter through cloth and then through filter paper.

Or use liquid laundry starch.
Consider it as 100%.
For 5%, add 5 mL starch to 95 mL distilled water, and so on.

Sugar Solution (Sucrose)—10%, 15%, and 20%

10%

Dissolve 10 g sucrose in enough distilled water to make 100 mL solution.

15%

Dissolve 15 g sucrose in enough distilled water to make 100 mL solution.

20%

Dissolve 20 g sucrose in enough distilled water to make 100 mL solution.

Preparation of Stock Solutions

Percentage by Volume

In diluting concentrations of solutions that are measured by volume, use a starting solution of any percentage greater than what your need. Measure a volume in milliliters numerically equal to the percentage of concentration desired. Then add sufficient distilled water to bring the volume to the numerical value of the concentration of the starting solution.

For example

- If you have on hand 95% alcohol and wish to prepare a 50% alcohol solution, measure 50 mL of the 95% alcohol and add sufficient distilled water to bring the volume to the numerical percentage of the original solution—in this case, 95 mL.

Percentage by Mass

To prepare solutions by mass, place the specified number of grams of the material in a beaker and add sufficient solvent (usually distilled water) to make a total of 100 g.

For example

- To prepare a 5% (by mass) solution of a salt, dissolve 5 g salt in 95 g distilled water.
- Often, biological solutions are specified in terms of mass and volume. In this case, the specified number of grams of the material is placed in a graduated cylinder, and sufficient water (or other solvent) is added to make a total volume of 100 mL.
- To prepare a 5% solution (by mass volume) of salt, put 5 g salt in a graduated cylinder and dilute to 100 mL with distilled water.

Molar Solutions

To prepare a molar solution, dissolve the number of grams equal to the molecular mass of the substance in distilled water (or other solvent) and dilute to 1 L.
For example

- The molecular mass of sodium chloride (NaCl) is 58.45, therefore, 58.45 g NaCl is dissolved in enough distilled water to make 1 L solution. The solution is written 1 M NaCl.
- Fractional molar solutions are prepared in the same way.
- A 0.4 M solution of NaCl contains 0.4 × 58.45 (grams equal to the molecular mass of the substance), or 23.38 NaCl per liter of solution.
- Usually, a volumetric flask is used to prepare molar solutions; when filled to the etched mark on the neck, such a flask holds exactly 1 L solution.

Appendix C: Safety Issues for the Biology Classroom*

The following lists of safety practices are excerpts from the chapters in *Investigating Safely* that are most relevant to the biology course. This 2004 book by the National Science Teachers Association is a highly readable and valuable resource for teachers of all areas of science. See the book for detailed elaboration on each issue.

Educate Everyone for Safety (From Chapter 1, "Setting the Scene")
- Rather than confining safety issues to an introductory unit, introduce safe procedures with each exploration and repeat relevant safety instructions with each subsequent activity.
- Model the safe behaviors you expect your students to practice.
- Have students share responsibility for monitoring safe procedures so that safe work habits become second nature.
- Make administrators and facilities staff part of your safety team. Educate them about the conditions and facilities needed to teach science safely.
- Modify your curriculum to conform to the conditions of your facilities and the nature of your students and classes.

The Science Laboratory (From Chapter 3, "Where Science Happens")
- Conduct science activities in facilities that provide adequate space and ventilation for safety.
- Check for appropriate utilities and safety equipment for all laboratory activities. If items or conditions are not adequate, modify your curriculum to ensure that the only activities you conduct are activities than can be done safely.
- Select furniture that is stable but easily rearranged, and provide unobstructed flat work surfaces.
- Ensure that safety equipment such as fire extinguishers, fire blankets, safety showers, and eyewashes are operational and accessible.

---

*Adapted from Texley, J., T. Kwan, and J. Summers. 2004. *Investigating Safely: A Guide for High School Teachers*. Arlington, VA: NSTA Press.

- Check that electrical service and wiring to your room are well maintained, provide adequate amperage, and include appropriate ground-fault interrupter (GFI) protection.

Storage of Supplies, Equipment, and Chemicals (From Chapter 4, "Finders Keepers")

- Use well-organized and clearly marked open shelves to store supplies and equipment that students are to obtain and return on their own. Arrange the material so that a missing item is easily spotted without counting individual items.
- Include enough locked storage, inaccessible to students, for valuable and fragile supplies and equipment as well as materials too hazardous for direct student access.
- Store all chemical stocks in locked cabinets and locked chemical storerooms appropriately equipped and off-limits to students.
- Keep incompatible chemicals separated—arrange storage by chemical properties, not by alphabetical order.
- Maintain accurate, up-to-date, and regularly reviewed chemical inventories.
- Maintain materials safety data sheets (MSDS) for every product—one set in the office and one set at the storage-and-use location.
- Prepare materials and supplies for science activities in an adequate, ventilated, well-lit preparation space away from student and other traffic.
- Clear out excess supplies, equipment, and furniture regularly as a vital part of safe practice.

Living Cultures and Organisms in the Classroom (From Chapter 5, "Lively Science")

- Maintain living cultures to provide students with opportunities for activities involving observation and care of living organisms and biological systems.
- Choose organisms appropriate for the space and time available. Ensure that adequate safety and security are available and that you can maintain the organism in a healthy environment over weekends and extended vacation periods.
- Begin with simple organisms—plants and invertebrates—before trying to maintain more complex and difficult ones.
- Do not bring wild or feral animals, dead or alive, into the classroom.
- Avoid organisms that are toxic, highly allergenic, or temperamental.
- Inform students, parents, and colleagues who share facilities of your

cultures and be aware of unusual allergies.

- In shared spaces, ensure that all users agree to provide appropriate safety and security before introducing a living organism.
- Do not release, introduce, or plant non-native species in the open environment. Avoid the use of exotic species if at all possible.

Use of Biological Chemicals (From Chapter 6, "Modern Alchemy")

- Emphasize careful scientific process skills over drama.
- Where possible, use microscale experiments for safety and to encourage careful observation.
- Choose less toxic and less hazardous options over traditional labs now known to be dangerous.
- Maintain a minimal quantity and variety of chemicals—less is better.
- Require the use of appropriate safety equipment by all persons—students and adults—at all times.
- Consider the problems and costs of disposal before purchasing any chemical reagent.
- Use professional hazardous waste removal services as appropriate.

Outdoor Field Trips (From Chapter 9, "The Great Outdoors")

- Link field trips and field studies to curriculum goals.
- Preview the site and abutting properties before planning your field study.
- Determine proper clothing and footwear for the site and activities planned.
- Meet with cooperating resource people to plan activities.
- Orient and train all chaperones in your planned activities and in safety precautions.
- Plan appropriate accommodations for special needs and physically disabled students.

Index

Note: Page numbers in italics refer to tables or figures.

Index

Controversial topics (in biology
education), 127–129, 133–135, *134*
animal use in classrooms, 141
BSCS textbooks and, 133
class discussion guidelines, 146–147
classroom handling of, 144
evolutionary theory, 132
genetically modified organisms
(GMOs), 142
Human Genome Project, 142
human reproduction, 132–133, 138
knowledge versus application, 128,
133, 146
letters to parents, 145
NSES Life Science content standards,
147–149, *148–149*
recombinant DNA technology, 142–143
stem cell research, 146
support resources for, 145
See also Biology; Evolutionary theory;
Human reproduction; Science
education
The Cornerstone-to-Capstone Approach
(curriculum), 298
Critical thinking, 227
drinking water exercise in, 227–230,
229, 230
Cultural differences, 25–26, 52
Curricula, 7, 38–39
20 major concepts of biology, 38–39,
39
by BSCS, 291–292, 296
controversial topics in, 145
fundamental principles versus biology
topics, 30
inquiry-oriented, mental models of
science and, 44
NSF reform movement, 291–292
white-male interests' emphasis in, 23–24
*See also BSCS Biology: A Human
Approach*; Instructional materials;

Science teaching; *specific curricula by
name*

D
Darwin, Charles, 128
Data analysis, 124
Developing Biological Literacy (BSCS), 296
Dewey, John, 64
DNA, 33–34, 51
recombinant technology, 142–143
Dobzhansky, Theodosius, 136
Drinking water exercise, 227–230, *229,
230*
Dynamic equilibrium, 36–38
prior conceptions about, 53–54
teaching suggestions, 54

E
Ecology, 32–33
Ecosystems, 48
resilience/recovery of, 49
Energy sources (of organisms), 36
Environment, 32–33
Environmental issues
NABT position statement, 139
NTSA position statement, 139–140
Equity, definitions, 16
Evaluating information. *See* Information
evaluation
Evolution, 31–32
genetics and, 31–32
Lamarkism, 47
natural selection, 32, 47, 128, 144
origin of life and, 47
prior conceptions about, 46–48
time expanse difficulties, 48
Evolutionary theory, 132, 145
biology textbooks and, 132
Scopes monkey trial, 132
students' beliefs and, 48
See also Controversial topics

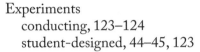

Index

letters to parents about, 145
NSTA position statement preamble, 138
See also Controversial topics; Reproduction

I

Independence of life, 48–49
Information analysis, class guidelines for, 226–227
Information evaluation, 220
critical thinking, 227
critical thinking exercise, 227–230, *229, 230*
students' opinions, 226
Information gathering, sources' credibility, 122–123
Information resources, 310
on drinking water, 228
See also Websites
Inherit the Wind (film), 132
Inquiry. *See* Scientific inquiry
Inquiry and the National Science Education Standards (National Research Council), 65, 70
Inquiry-based teaching, 18–19, 68–69
essential features, 70–71, *72*
full versus partial inquiry, 71
hands-on activities and, 74
implementation difficulties, 74–75
misconceptions about, 66, 71–75
open-ended inquiry, 73
process versus substance in, 73
professional development and, 75–76, *75*
scientific method and, 73
universal applicability of, 73–74
See also Full inquiry experiments; Invitations to inquiry; Science teaching; Scientific inquiry
Instruction. *See* Inquiry-based teaching; Learning process; Science teaching

Instructional materials
ideal properties of, 269–270
laboratory exercises, 290
standards-based, 9, 11
textbooks, 289–290
See also AIM; Curricula
International Covenant on Economic, Social, and Cultural Rights, 16–17
Investigating Safely (NSTA), 118, 324–326
Invitations to inquiry, 72
cell nucleus inquiry, 102–107, *103, 106*
difficulty of, 79
guidelines for using, 79
light and plant movement inquiry, 97–101
methods for using, 79
natural selection inquiry, 84–89
place and time of use, 79
predator-prey and natural populations inquiry, 90–95, *94, 96*
seed germination inquiry, 80–83
thyroid action inquiry, 108–114
See also Full inquiry experiments; Inquiry-based teaching; Scientific inquiry

J

Jegede, O. J., 25, 26
Johnson, D. W., 23

K

K-12 Alliance of WestEd, 268
K-W-L charts, 212–214, *215*
Karplus, Robert, 233, 295
Keller, E. F., 24
Kurth, L. A., 21

L

Laboratory instruction
breakage policies, 162

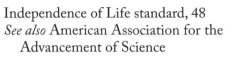

Index

individual accountability, 171
knowledge sharing, 189
leadership distribution, 188–189
modified heterogeneous teams, 170, 175–176, 185–186
neighbor interaction, 189
noncooperation, strategies for dealing with, 176–178, 186
note writing, 189
positive interdependence, 187–188
reward opportunities for, 186–187
scientific conversation in, 252–253
team self-assessment, 171
uncooperative members, 176, 187
working-relationship skills, 171, 173–175, *174*, 187
See also Collaborative learning
Terminology. *See* Scientific language
Thier, Herbert, 233
Thyroid action inquiry, 108–114
Trefil, James, 128
Trends in International Mathematics and Science Study (TIMMS project), 7

U

Unifying principles of biology, 30–31, *122*
energy, matter and organization, 35–36
evolution (patterns & products of change), 31–32
full inquiry experiments and, 121
genetic continuity and reproduction, 33–34
growth, development and differentiation, 34–35
interaction and interdependence, 32–33

maintenance of dynamic equilibrium, 36–38
See also Biology
United Nations, International Covenant on Economic, Social, and Cultural Rights, 16–17

V

Vocabulary strategies, 206, *206*
assigning, 207–208
concept definition map, 208, *208*
4-square chart, *207*, 208
Frayer model, 209, *209*
purpose, 206–207
semantic feature analysis, 209–210, *210*
visual and verbal word association, 210–211, *210*
word sorts, 211, *211*
See also Literacy strategies
Vygotsky, L. S., 4

W

Wandersee, J. H., 18
Water. *See* Safe drinking water exercise
Websites
for AIM materials, 152, 269
AIM rubrics, 273
for Material Safety Data Sheets, 118
National Association of Biology Teachers (NABT), 135
National Science Teachers Association (NSTA), 135
See also Information resources
Why Science (Trefil), 128

Z

Zygotes, 33, 34